GRANTS AND FUNDING

FIGHTING FRAUD WITH QUI TAM AND THE FALSE CLAIMS ACT

GRANTS AND FUNDING

Additional books in this series can be found on Nova's website at:

https://www.novapublishers.com/catalog/index.php?cPath=23_29&seriesp=Grants+and+Funding

Additional e-books in this series can be found on Nova's website at:

https://www.novapublishers.com/catalog/index.php?cPath=23_29&seriespe=Grants+and+Funding

GRANTS AND FUNDING

FIGHTING FRAUD WITH QUI TAM AND THE FALSE CLAIMS ACT

IAN M. ORTIZ
EDITOR

Nova Science Publishers, Inc.
New York

LIBRARY OF CONGRESS CATALOGING-IN-PUBLICATION DATA

Fighting fraud with Qui Tam and the False Claims Act / editor, Ian M. Ortiz.
p. cm.
Includes bibliographical references and index.
ISBN 978-1-61668-221-7 (hardcover)
1. Public contracts--United States. 2. United States--Claims. 3. Fraud--United States. 4. Government purchasing--Law and legislation--United States. 5. Popular actions--United States. 6. Whistle blowing--Law and legislation--United States. I. Ortiz, Ian M. II. United States. False Claims Amendments Act of 1986.
KF849.F54 2010
346.7302'3--dc22

2010012212

Published by Nova Science Publishers, Inc. ✢ New York

CONTENTS

PREFACE

The False Claims Act (FCA) is one of the government's primary weapons to fight fraud against the government. The Act, as amended in 1986, provides for penalties and triple damages for anyone who knowingly submits or causes the submission of false or fraudulent claims to the United States for government funds or property. Under the FCA's qui tam provisions, a person with evidence of fraud, also known as a whistle blower or relator, is authorized to file a case in federal court and sue, on behalf of the government, persons engaged in the fraud and to share in any money the government may recover. This book examines testimony given before Senate Judiciary Committee hearing on "The False Claims Act Correction Act" and discusses other related federal statutes. This book consists of public documents which have been located, gathered, combined, reformatted, and enhanced with a subject index, selectively edited and bound to provide easy access.

Chapter 1 - The False Claims Act (FCA) is one of the government's primary weapons to fight fraud against the government. The Act, as amended in 1986, provides for penalties and triple damages for anyone who knowingly submits or causes the submission of false or fraudulent claims to the United States for government funds or property. Under the FCA's qui tam provisions, a person with evidence of fraud, also known as a whistle blower or relator, is authorized to file a case in federal court and sue, on behalf of the government, persons engaged in the fraud and to share in any money the government may recover. The Department of Justice (DOJ) has the responsibility to decide on behalf of the government whether to join the whistle blower in prosecuting these cases. From fiscal years 1987 through 2005, settlements and judgments for the federal government in FCA cases have exceeded $15 billion, of which $9.6 billion, or 64 percent, was for cases filed by whistle blowers under FCA's qui tam provisions. The whistle blowers share of the qui tam settlements and judgments was over $1.6 billion during this period.

Chapter 3 – These remarks were delivered as Statement of Michael Hertz, before the Committee on the Judiciary of the United States Senate, dated February 27, 2008.

Chapter 4 - These remarks were delivered as Statement of Tina Marie Gonter, before the Committee on the Judiciary of the United States Senate, dated February 27, 2008.

Chapter 5 - These remarks were delivered as Written Statement of John T. Boese, U.S. Chamber of Commerce and the U.S. Chamber Institute for Legal Reform, before the Committee on the Judiciary of the United States Senate, dated February 27, 2008.

Chapter 6 - These remarks were delivered as Statement of John E. Clarke, before the Committee on the Judiciary of the United States Senate, dated February 27, 2008.

Chapter 7 - These remarks were delivered as Written Statement of Pamela H. Bucy, Bainbridge Professor of Law University of Alabama School of Law, before the Committee on the Judiciary of the United States Senate, dated February 27, 2008.

Chapter 2 - This chapter is edited and excerpted testimony by Senator Patrick Leahy before the Committee on the Judiciary of the United States Senate on February 27, 2008.

Chapter 3 - This chapter is edited and excerpted testimony by Michael Hertz before the Committee on the Judiciary of the United States Senate on February 27, 2008.

Chapter 4 - This chapter is edited and excerpted testimony Tina Marie Gonter before the Committee on the Judiciary of the United States Senate on February 27, 2008.

Chapter 5 - This chapter is edited and excerpted written testimony by John T. Boese before the Committee on the Judiciary of the United States Senate on February 27, 2008.

Chapter 6 - This chapter is edited and excerpted testimony by John E. Clarke before the Committee on the Judiciary of the United States Senate on February 27, 2008.

Chapter 7 - This chapter is edited and excerpted written testimony by Pamela H. Bucy before the Committee on the Judiciary of the United States Senate on February 27, 2008.

Chapter 8 - The False Claims Act (FCA), an important tool for combating fraud against the U.S. government, generally provides that a person who knowingly submits, or causes to be submitted, a false or fraudulent claim for payment to the U.S. government may be subject to civil penalties and damages. Recently, the Supreme Court examined the scope of the FCA in *Allison Engine v. United States ex rel. Sanders,* in which a former employee of a subcontractor brought an action against other subcontractors who had allegedly submitted a false claim to the prime contractor on a U.S. defense contract. The Court struck down the FCA claim against the subcontractors, holding that a demonstration that a false claim was paid for with government funds, without more, does not establish liability under 31 U.S.C. §§ 3729(a)(2) and (a)(3). Under these sections, the Court found that a plaintiff must prove that the defendant intended to defraud the government (and not just a recipient of government funds) when it submitted or agreed to make use of the false claim. Given that the FCA is frequently invoked in the health care context, it has been questioned how this decision could affect these cases. This report provides an overview of the FCA and the *Allison Engine* decision, analyzes how this decision could affect certain FCA health care claims, and discusses proposed legislation that would amend the False Claims Act (*i.e.,* the False Claims Act Clarification Act of 2009 (S. 458), the False Claims Act Correction Act of 2009 (H.R. 1788), and the Fraud Enforcement and Recovery Act of 2009 (S. 386)), which could limit the application of the *Allison Engine* decision.

Chapter 9 - Qui tam enlists the public in the recovery of civil penalties and forfeitures. It rewards with a portion of the recovered proceeds those who sue in the government's name. A creature of antiquity, once common, today qui tam lives on in federal law only in the False Claims Act and in two minor examples found in patent and Indian protection laws.

The False Claims Act, expanded by the Fraud Enforcement and Recovery Act of 2009, P.L. 111- 21 (S. 386), 123 Stat. 1617 (2009), now proscribes: (1) presenting a false claim; (2) making or using a false record or statement material to a false claim; (3) possessing property or money of the U.S. and delivering less than all of it; (4) delivering a certified receipt with intent to defraud the U.S.; (5) buying public property from a federal officer or employee, who may not lawfully sell it; (6) using a false record or statement material to an obligation to pay or transmit money or property to the U.S., or concealing or improperly avoiding or decreasing an obligation to pay or transmit money or property to the U.S.; (7) conspiring to commit any such offense. Additional liability may also flow from any retaliatory action taken against whistleblowers under the False Claims Act. Offenders may be sued for triple damages, costs, expenses, and attorneys fees in a civil action brought either by the United States or by a relator (whistleblower or other private party) in the name of the United States.

If the government initiates the suit, others may not join. If the government has not brought suit, a relator may do so, but must give the government notice and afford it 60 days to decide whether to take over the litigation. If the government declines to intervene, a prevailing relator's share of any recovery is capped at 30%; if the government intervenes, the caps are lower and depend upon the circumstances. Relators in patent and Indian protection qui tam cases are entitled to half of the recovery.

Federal qui tam statutes have survived two types of constitutional challenges—those based on defendants' rights in criminal cases and those based on the doctrine of separation of powers. The courts have found the rights required in criminal cases inapplicable, because qui tam actions are civil matters. They have generally rejected standing arguments, because relators stand in the shoes of the United States in whose name qui tam actions are brought. They have rejected appointments clause arguments, because relators hold no appointed office. They have rejected take care clause arguments, because the residue of governmental control over qui tam actions is considered constitutionally sufficient.

This report is available in an abridged version, as CRS Report R40786, *Qui Tam: An Abbreviated Look at the False Claims Act and Related Federal Statutes*, by Charles Doyle, stripped of the footnotes, quotations, appendix, and most of the citations found here.

In: Fighting Fraud with Qui Tam and the False Claims Act ISBN: 978-1-61668-221-7
Editor: Ian M. Ortiz

Chapter 1

INFORMATION ON FALSE CLAIMS ACT LITIGATION

United States Government Accountability Office

January 31, 2006
The Honorable F. James Sensenbrenner, Jr.
Chairman, Committee on the Judiciary
House of Representatives

The Honorable Chris Cannon
Chairman, Subcommittee on Commercial and Administrative Law
Committee on the Judiciary
House of Representatives
The Honorable Charles E. Grassley
United States Senate

Subject: *Information on False Claims Act Litigation*

The False Claims Act (FCA) is one of the government's primary weapons to fight fraud against the government. The Act, as amended in 1986, provides for penalties and triple damages for anyone who knowingly submits or causes the submission of false or fraudulent claims to the United States for government funds or property.[1] Under the FCA's qui tam provisions, a person with evidence of fraud, also known as a whistle blower or relator, is authorized to file a case in federal court and sue, on behalf of the government, persons engaged in the fraud and to share in any money the government may recover. The Department of Justice (DOJ) has the responsibility to decide on behalf of the government whether to join the whistle blower in prosecuting these cases. From fiscal years 1987 through 2005, settlements and judgments for the federal government in FCA cases have exceeded $15 billion, of which $9.6 billion, or 64 percent, was for cases filed by whistle blowers under FCA's qui tam provisions.[2] The whistle blowers share of the qui tam settlements and judgments was over $1.6 billion during this period.

With regard to your request to provide information on FCA litigation, this report addresses the following questions:

What statutory guidance and DOJ policies exist regarding the relationship between the government and relators in prosecuting qui tam cases?

What is known about DOJ's qui tam caseload based on the data it collects?

To determine what statutory guidance and DOJ policies exist, we reviewed applicable laws, regulations, and DOJ policies regarding the relationship between the government and relators in prosecuting qui tam cases. We interviewed DOJ and other federal officials and private practice attorneys involved in qui tam litigation. To provide information on DOJ's qui tam caseload, we obtained DOJ's qui tam database on closed unsealed qui tam cases for fiscal years 1987 through 2005 and conducted computerized analyses of certain data fields. To assess the reliability of the data, we discussed the data collection methods for ensuring data quality with responsible officials and reviewed the data for reasonableness. We found the data we used for our analyses were sufficiently reliable for the purposes of this report.

In December 2005, we discussed with your offices the results of our work. This document conveys the information provided during those discussions (see enclosure).

We performed our work from April 2005 through January 2006 in accordance with generally accepted government auditing standards.

RESULTS

The briefing slides in the enclosure address our two objectives. In summary, we found the following:

Under the FCA, the federal government has primary responsibility for prosecuting a qui tam case and it is at the DOJ's discretion to involve the relator on a case-bycase basis. DOJ officials told us that their policy is broad and encourages DOJ attorneys to recognize the benefits of a cooperative relationship with relators and to exercise their professional judgment in dealing with them. DOJ does not collect data that document the extent of the relator's participation in the prosecution of a qui tam case, nor is it required to do so.

DOJ's Civil Division received 8,869 FCA cases from fiscal years 1987 through 2005.[3] During this period, the number of qui tam FCA cases generally increased as a proportion of total FCA cases. Agencies under the Departments of Health and Human Services and Defense were named more frequently than other agencies as allegedly defrauded in qui tam cases DOJ received. The 2,490 closed, unsealed qui tam cases that GAO analyzed were filed in 92 U.S. district courts. Health care and procurement fraud cases constituted about 79 percent of all qui tam cases. DOJ pursued health care fraud cases (33 percent or 363 of the total 1,117 health care cases) and procurement fraud cases (29 percent or 237 of the total 819 procurement cases) more than other types of fraud cases.[4] Cases in which DOJ intervened took a median of 38 months to conclude and ranged from 4 months to 187 months. The median FCA recovery in a qui tam case was $784,597, of which the median relator share was $123,885.[5] Recoveries and relator's share amounts in health care fraud cases were larger than in other types of fraud. Recoveries and relator share amounts were greater in cases where DOJ intervened than in cases where DOJ declined to intervene.

AGENCY COMMENTS AND OUR EVALUATION

We requested comments on a draft of this letter from the Departments of Justice, Health and Human Services, and Defense. The Department of Justice provided technical comments, which we incorporated into this letter. The Departments of Health and Human Services and Defense had no comments.

As agreed with your offices, unless you publicly announce its contents earlier, we plan no further distribution of this report until 30 days after the date of this letter. At that time, we will provide copies of this report to the Attorney General and other interested parties. We will also provide copies to others on request. In addition, the letter will be available at no charge on the GAO Web site at http://www.gao.gov.

If you or your staff have any questions or need additional information, please contact me at (202) 512-8777, ekstrandl@gao.gov. Major contributors to this letter were John Hansen, Assistant Director, Nancy Kawahara, Christine Davis, John G. Smale, Jr., George H. Quinn, Jr., and Dorian Dunbar.

Laurie E. Ekstrand
Director, Homeland Security and Justice
Enclosure

INFORMATION ON FALSE CLAIMS ACT LITIGATION BRIEFING FOR CONGRESSIONAL REQUESTERS DECEMBER 15, 2005

INTRODUCTION

Since Congress amended the False Claims Act (FCA)[6] in 1986, the government has won recoveries of over $15 billion from fiscal years 1987 through 2005.

Of the $15 billion, 64 percent, or $9.6 billion, was for recoveries associated with cases filed by whistle blowers under FCA's qui tam provisions.[7] Whistle blowers were entitled to a share of these qui tam recoveries, which totaled over $1.6 billion during this period.

The Department of Justice (DOJ) has the responsibility to decide on behalf of the government whether to join the whistle blower in prosecuting these cases.

DEFINITIONS

Term	Definition
False Claims Act	The FCA is a civil antifraud statute, providing that any person who knowingly submits or causes the submission of false claims for government funds or property is liable for damages and penalties.
Qui tam	Qui tam is an abbreviation for a Latin phrase dating back to 13th century England, meaning a person who sues for the king as well as for himself. Under the FCA, a qui tam case is filed by a private person on behalf of the federal government. The government can also pursue FCA claims through federal agency investigations and referrals without a relator.
Relator	A person who files a civil case for a violation of the FCA. Relators are also known as whistle blowers.
Case under seal	Under the FCA, a relator files a qui tam case under court seal, and the case is not publicly disclosed. Until the court lifts the seal in whole or in part, no records relating to the case may be disclosed, except to DOJ.
DOJ intervenes in a qui tam case	DOJ represents the government and is a named party in every qui tam case. When DOJ decides to intervene in a case, it takes primary respo-nsibility for prosecuting the case.
DOJ declines to intervene in a qui tam case	When DOJ declines to intervene in the case, the relator has the right to pursue the case without the government. However, DOJ can decide to intervene in the case upon showing of good cause, and any settlements in the case are made with the consent of the government.
Qui tam recoveries	The funds the government is entitled to recover as a result of qui tam case settlements or court judgments. These funds may or may not have been co-llected by the government. A DOJ official told us that while most of these funds arise from FCA allegations in the qui tam complaint, some are attributable to government initiated claims under the FCA and other statutory and common law claims, such as breach of contract, bribery, or confl-ict of interest, and that the relator is not entitled to a share of these funds. The official also told us that precise amounts attributable to each claim may not be distinguished in the case of a lump-sum settlement or judgment.
Relator share of qui tam recoveries	If the qui tam case is successful, the relator is entitled to a share of the recoveries.

OBJECTIVES

What statutory guidance and DOJ policies exist regarding the relationship between the government and relator in prosecuting qui tam cases?

What is known about DOJ's qui tam caseload based on the data it collects?

Scope and Methodology

To determine what statutory and DOJ guidance exist regarding the relationship between the relator and the government, we

- reviewed applicable laws, regulations, and DOJ policies and
- interviewed DOJ and other federal officials and private attorneys involved in qui tam cases.

To provide information on DOJ's qui tam caseload, we

- obtained DOJ's qui tam database on closed unsealed qui tam cases for fiscal years 1987 through 2005 and conducted computerized analyses of certain data fields.

Data Reliability

To assess the reliability of the data, we

- discussed the data collection methods with responsible agency staff,
- reviewed the data and information for reasonableness, and
- obtained related documentation where available.

We found that the DOJ qui tam database we used for our analyses was sufficiently reliable for the purposes of this report.

Results in Brief–FCA and DOJ Guidance on the Government-Relator Relationship

- Under the FCA, the federal government has primary responsibility for prosecuting a qui tam case and it is at DOJ's discretion to involve the relator on a case-by-case basis.
- DOJ officials told us that their policy is broad and encourages DOJ attorneys to recognize the benefits of a cooperative relationship with relators and to exercise their professional judgment in dealing with them.
- DOJ does not collect data that document the extent of the relator's participation in the prosecution of a qui tam case, nor is it required to do so.

Results in Brief–Information on Qui tam Cases

- Of the total 8,869 FCA cases[8] DOJ's Civil Division received from fiscal years 1987 through 2005, the number of qui tam FCA cases generally increased as a proportion of total FCA cases.

The Departments of Health and Human Services (HHS) and Defense (DOD) agencies were named more frequently than other agencies as allegedly defrauded in qui tam cases DOJ received.

The 2,490 closed, unsealed qui tam cases that GAO analyzed were filed in 92 U.S. district courts; the Central District of California (Los Angeles) was the busiest, with 10 percent of all cases filed.

Health care and procurement fraud cases constituted about 79 percent of all qui tam cases.

DOJ pursued[9] health care fraud cases (33 percent or 363 of the total 1,117 health care cases) and procurement fraud cases (29 percent or 237 of the total 819 procurement cases) more than other types of fraud cases.

Cases in which DOJ intervened took a median of 38 months to conclude and ranged from 4 months to 187 months.

The median FCA recovery in a qui tam case was $784,597. Of that amount, the median relator share was $123,885.[10]

Recoveries and relator's share amounts in health care fraud cases were larger than in other types of fraud.

Recoveries and relator share amounts were greater in cases where DOJ intervened than in cases where DOJ declined to intervene.

BACKGROUND- QUI TAM PROVISIONS OF THE FALSE CLAIMS ACT

Anyone who knowingly submits or causes the submission of false claims to the government is liable for damages up to three times the erroneous payment, plus civil penalties.

A private individual with knowledge of false claims—called the relator—may bring a suit on the government's behalf— called a qui tam case.

The relator's incentive to sue is the potential to share in the recoveries if the case is successful.

BACKGROUND- QUI TAM PROCEDURES UNDER THE FCA

The relator can file a qui tam complaint under seal in any U.S. district court where any defendant can be found, resides, or transacts business, or in any U.S. district court where the fraud occurred, with a copy of the complaint served on the Attorney General and the appropriate U.S. Attorney.

The complaint remains under seal for 60 days (or longer for good cause shown) while DOJ and/or other federal agency fraud units investigate the allegations and DOJ decides whether to intervene and take over the case.

Qui tam litigation is handled either by DOJ's Civil Division or the United States Attorneys, sometimes on a joint basis. Generally, U.S. Attorneys handle investigations of FCA claims under $5 million, including referrals from federal agencies and qui tam cases. The Civil Division tracks qui tam cases litigated by the United States Attorneys for statistical reporting purposes.[11]

Background-Government Intervention or Declination in a Qui Tam Case

DOJ officials told us that after investigating the allegations and considering the input of relevant government officials, DOJ makes a decision to

- Intervene and take over primary responsibility for prosecuting the case. DOJ may intervene and decide to take over some but not all of the relator's claims.
- Decline to intervene. The relator has the right to continue as a party, but the government retains the right to intervene upon a showing of good cause.
- Settle the case before intervening. Whether or not DOJ intervenes, the government may settle the case over the relator's objections if the court determines that the proposed settlement is fair, adequate, and reasonable.

Background-Relator's Share in Qui Tam Recoveries

In general, the relator in a successful qui tam suit is entitled to a share of the recovery:

- between 25 and 30 percent if the government declines to intervene.
- between 15 and 25 percent if the government intervenes.

Background-Relator's Share in Qui Tam Recoveries

Several factors may affect the relator's share of the recovery, such as

- how substantially the relator contributed to the case,
- whether the case primarily depended on disclosures from other sources (in which case the relator's share can be no more than 10 percent),
- whether the relator planned and initiated the false claim (in which case the relator's share can be reduced to any amount the court deems appropriate), and
- whether statutory bars preclude the relator from sharing in the recovery because of a criminal conviction or a jurisdictional disqualification in the case.

BACKGROUND–HEALTH CARE FRAUD AND ABUSE CONTROL PROGRAM

The Health Insurance Portability and Accountability Act of 1996, among other things, established a Health Care Fraud and Abuse Control Program (HCFAC) to strengthen ongoing efforts to combat fraud and abuse in health care programs.

Under the HCFAC program, a portion of settlements and judgments resulting from FCA cases involving health care fraud are used to finance part of the antifraud activities in HHS and DOJ.

In fiscal year 2004, HHS and DOJ were allocated over $240 million from HCFAC program funds to devote to their health care fraud enforcement activities.

FCA AND DOJ GUIDANCE ON THE GOVERNMENT-RELATOR RELATIONSHIP

FCA Gives Government Discretion in Its Relationship with Relator

If the government intervenes, the FCA gives the government primary responsibility for prosecuting a qui tam case.

The FCA does not specify the degree to which the government must cooperate with the relator.

DOJ attorneys use their discretion in deciding how much the relator and relator's counsel may assist in the case.

DOJ POLICY IS BROAD REGARDING THE GOVERNMENT-RELATOR RELATIONSHIP

DOJ officials told us that their policy is broad and encourages DOJ attorneys to recognize the benefits of a cooperative relationship with relators and to exercise their professional judgment in dealing with them.

Many factors could affect the government-relator relationship, such as

the amount of information the relator possesses about the potential fraud,

the degree of experience possessed by the relator's counsel,

the existence of a criminal investigation and other issues involving sensitivity of data, such as privacy or national security, and

interpersonal dynamics between the relator and defendant.

DOJ Data Documenting the Relationship between the Government and the Relator

DOJ does not collect data that document the extent of the relator's participation in the prosecution of a qui tam case, nor is it required to do so.

Information on DOJ's Qui Tam Caseload for Fiscal Years 1987 through 2005

The Number of New Qui Tam Cases Generally Increased

Of the total 8,869 new FCA cases[1] DOJ's Civil Division received from fiscal years 1987 through 2005, the number of qui tam cases generally increased as a proportion of the total FCA cases.

New FCA Cases, Fiscal Years 1987 through 2005

Fiscal year	Qui tam	Non-qui tam[2]	Total
1987	66	361	427
1988	60	246	306
1989	95	236	331
1990	82	256	338
1991	90	243	333
1992	119	357	476
1993	132	329	461
1994	222	291	513
1995	277	236	513
1996	363	187	550
1997	533	185	718
1998	470	119	589
1999	481	141	622
2000	367	96	463
2001	309	88	397
2002	320	63	383
2003	334	93	427
2004	415	113	528
2005	394	100	494
Total	**5,129**	**3,740**	**8,869**

Source: DOJ's Civil Division Fraud Statistics which include open cases and qui tam cases under seal.

[1]Represents newly received FCA referrals and investigations initiated by the government and newly filed qui tam cases initiated by a relator.

[2]FCA investigative matters initiated by the government without a relator. According to a DOJ official, these data do not include non-qui tam cases generally under $5 million which were initiated and pursued by the U.S. Attorneys. The official also told us that the Civil Division does not maintain data on these cases.

HHS and DOD Agencies More Frequently Named as Allegedly Defrauded

HHS and DOD agencies were more frequently named than other agencies as allegedly defrauded in qui tam cases DOJ received. HHS agencies were named 54 percent of the time and DOD agencies were named 29 percent of the time of the total 5,129 qui tam cases DOJ received from fiscal year 1987 through 2005.

Number of Qui Tam Cases Listed by Allegedly Defrauded Agency, Fiscal Years 1987 through 2005

Fiscal year	HHS	DOD	Other agencies
1987	4	18	12
1988	9	36	20
1989	15	40	46
1990	12	45	33
1991	13	50	38
1992	17	64	57
1993	39	55	66
1994	80	96	105
1995	94	103	134
1996	204	135	163
1997	298	146	366
1998	287	78	168
1999	310	109	153
2000	223	77	165
2001	180	74	134
2002	197	72	122
2003	217	78	136
2004	276	99	180
2005	270	97	184
Total	**2,745**	**1,472**	**2,282**

Note: More than one federal agency could be named in each qui tam case.
Source: DOJ's Civil Division Fraud Statistics, which includes open cases and qui tam cases under seal.

Qui Tam Cases Filed in U.S. District Courts

The 2,490 closed, unsealed qui tam cases GAO analyzed were filed in 92 U.S. district courts. The Central District of California (Los Angeles) was the busiest, with 10 percent of all cases filed.

Qui Tam Cases Filed in U.S. District Courts, Fiscal Years 1987 through 2005

U.S. District Court (location)	Number	Percent
C.D. California (Los Angeles, Calif.)	258	10.36
M.D. Florida (Tampa, Fla.)	130	5.22
E.D. California (Sacramento, Calif.)	78	3.13
N.D. California (San Francisco, Calif.)	77	3.09
E.D. Virginia (Alexandria, Va.)	75	3.01
D. District of Columbia (Washington, D.C.)	74	2.97
D. Maryland (Baltimore, Md.)	74	2.97
E.D. Pennsylvania (Philadelphia, Pa.)	72	2.89
S.D. Florida (Miami, Fla.)	65	2.61
N.D. Illinois (Chicago, Ill.)	64	2.57
S.D. California (San Diego, Calif.)	60	2.41
S.D. Ohio (Dayton, Ohio)	59	2.37
W.D. Texas (San Antonio, Tex.)	58	2.33
D. New Jersey (Newark, N.J.)	56	2.25
S.D. New York (New York City, N.Y.)	55	2.21
N.D. Texas (Dallas, Tex.)	53	2.13
D. Massachusetts (Boston, Mass.)	52	2.09
Remaining 75 district courts	1,130	45.38
Total	**2,490**	**100.00**

Table legend:
C.D. = Central district
M.D. = Middle district
E.D. = Eastern district
D. = Statewide district
S.D. = Southern district
W.D. = Western district
N.D. = Northern district
Source: GAO analysis of DOJ's Civil Division data on closed, unsealed qui tam cases.

MOST CASES INVOLVE HEALTH CARE AND PROCUREMENT FRAUD

Health care and procurement fraud cases constitute about 79 percent of all qui tam cases.

Health care fraud cases were pursued in part by DOJ and HHS staff funded by the HCFAC program.

Types of Fraud Alleged in Qui Tam Cases, Fiscal Years 1987 through 2005

Type of fraud alleged	Number	Percent
Health care	1,145	45.98
Procurement	818	32.85
Miscellaneous[1]	212	8.51
Grant program	109	4.38
Subsidy program	76	3.06
Housing	40	1.61
Student loan	23	0.94
Welfare program	7	0.28
Scientific	7	0.28
Other bribery	6	0.24
Non-housing loan	6	0.24
Highway	5	0.20
Veterans benefits	4	0.16
Overseas bribery	1	0.04
Missing/miscoded	31	1.23
Total	**2,490**	**100.00**

Source: GAO analysis of DOJ's Civil Division data on closed, unsealed qui tam cases.

[1] A DOJ official told us that the miscellaneous fraud category includes cases where the complaint is vague or does not fit into other case types.

DOJ PURSUED HEALTH CARE AND PROCUREMENT CASES MORE OFTEN THAN OTHERS

DOJ pursued health care fraud cases (33 percent or 363 of total 1,117 health care cases) and procurement fraud cases (29 percent or 237 of total 819 procurement cases) more than other types of fraud cases.

Percent of Qui Tam Cases Pursued by DOJ Listed by Type of Fraud Alleged, Fiscal Years 1987 through 2005

Type of fraud alleged	DOJ intervened[1]	Settled by DOJ before intervening	Total cases pursued by DOJ[2]	DOJ declined	Percent pursued by DOJ
Health care	338	25	363	754	32.50
Procurement	207	30	237	582	28.94
Miscellaneous[3]	20	7	27	167	13.92
Grant program	12	0	12	94	11.32
All other types	16	9	25	173	12.63
Total	**593**	**71**	**664**	**1,770**	**27.28**

Note: Does not include 132 cases that were dismissed prior to DOJ's decision to intervene in the case.

Source: GAO analysis of DOJ's Civil Division data on closed, unsealed qui tam cases.

[1] Includes cases where DOJ decided to intervene in some but not all of the relator's claims.

[2] The sum of DOJ intervened cases and cases settled by DOJ before intervention or declination.

[3] A DOJ official told us that the miscellaneous fraud category includes cases where the complaint is vague or does not fit into other case types.

TIME TO CONCLUDE QUI TAM CASES IN WHICH DOJ INTERVENED

Cases in which DOJ intervened took a median of 38 months to conclude and ranged from 4 months to 187 months.[1]

Source: GAO analysis of DOJ's Civil Division data on closed, unsealed qui tam cases.

[1] Includes cases where DOJ decided to intervene in some but not all of the relator's claims. Time period measured between date the complaint was filed to the date the case was concluded by settlement, judgment, or dismissal.

QUI TAM RECOVERIES

Mean: $10,028,482, Median: $784,597

Qui Tam Recoveries, Fiscal Years 1987 through 2005

Settlement and judgment amounts[1]	Number
under $50,000	77
$50,000 to $100,000	54
$100,001 to $500,000	187
$500,001 to $1,000,000	87
$1,000,001 to $5,000,000	182
$5,000,001 to $10,000,000	57
$10,000,001 to $50,000,000	63
$50,000,001 to $100,000,000	15
$100,000,001 to $1,000,000,000	18
Total	**740**

Source: GAO analysis of DOJ's Civil Division data on closed, unsealed qui tam cases.

[1] According to a DOJ official, a portion of these qui tam settlement and judgment amounts could include amounts attributable to government initiated claims under the FCA and other statutory or common law claims, such as breach of contract, bribery, or conflict of interest. The official also told us that precise amounts attributable to each claim may not be distinguished in the case of a lump-sum settlement or judgment.

RELATOR SHARE OF QUI TAM RECOVERIES

Mean: $1,700,153, Median: $123,885

Total Relator Share Amounts of Qui Tam Recoveries, Fiscal Years 1987 through 2005

Relator share of settlement or judgment amounts[1]	Number
0	36
$1 to $10,000	65
$10,001 to $50,000	153
$50,001 to $100,000	82
$100,001 to $500,000	200
$500,001 to $1,000,000	71
$1,000,001 to $5,000,000	87
$5,000,001 to $10,000,000	19
$10,000,001 to $50,000,000	23
$50,000,001 to $100,000,000	4
Total	**740**

Source: GAO analysis of DOJ's Civil Division data on closed, unsealed qui tam cases.

[1] Includes relators whose qui tam case resulted in a settlement or judgment, but the relators received zero or a reduced share of the government's recovery. A DOJ official told us that these cases involved instances where the relator's entitlement to a full statutory share was jurisdictionally barred or in question and that this information is reflected in DOJ case files.

QUI TAM RECOVERIES BY TYPE OF FRAUD ALLEGED

Recoveries for health care fraud cases were larger than in other types of fraud cases.

Qui Tam Recoveries by Type of Fraud Alleged, Fiscal Years 1987 through 2005

Type of fraud alleged	Number	Range	Median	Total recoveries[1]
Health care	385	0-$568,036,761	$1,000,000	$5,021,511,529
Procurement	267	0-$150,500,000	$750,000	$1,641,340,667
Miscellaneous[2]	34	$1,681-$428,507,273	$437,500	$626,741,660
Grant program	21	$5,000–$21,899,856	$200,000	$39,425,601
Housing	13	$2,000-$3,768,100	$78,000	$12,064,091
Subsidy program	5	$50,000-$16,000,000	$362,595	$21,067,595
All other categories	15	$30,000-$27,013,869	$166,885	$58,925,376

Source: GAO analysis of DOJ's Civil Division data on closed, unsealed qui tam cases.

[1]According to a DOJ official, a portion of these qui tam settlement and judgment amounts could include amounts attributable to government initiated claims under the FCA and other statutory or common law claims, such as breach of contract, bribery, or conflict of interest. The official also told us that precise amounts attributable to each claim may not be distinguished in the case of a lump-sum settlement or judgment.

[2]A DOJ official told us that the miscellaneous fraud category includes cases where the complaint is vague or does not fit into other case types.

RELATOR SHARE OF QUI TAM RECOVERIES BY TYPE OF FRAUD ALLEGED

Relator share amounts for health care fraud cases were larger than other types of fraud cases.

Relator Share Amounts by Type of Fraud Alleged, Fiscal Years 1987 through 2005

Type of fraud alleged	Number	Range	Median	Total relator share amounts
Health care	385	0-$96,566,249	$150,000	$841,733,865
Procurement	267	0-$22,575,000	$129,500	$291,101,670
Miscellaneous[1]	34	0-$67,014,530	$75,000	$101,234,736
Grant program	21	0-$5,474,964	$52,500	$9,352,614
Housing	13	0-$300,000	$12,269	$1,209,497
Subsidy program	5	$8,750-$3,056,000	$39,885	$3,351,635
All other types	15	0-$4,052,080	$50,066	$10,128,846

Source: GAO analysis of DOJ's Civil Division data on closed, unsealed qui tam cases.

[1]A DOJ official told us that the miscellaneous fraud category includes cases where the complaint is vague or does not fit into other case types.

QUI TAM RECOVERIES BY DOJ CASE INTERVENTION

Qui tam recoveries from cases where DOJ intervened were greater than in cases where DOJ declined to intervene.

Qui Tam Recoveries by DOJ Case Intervention, Fiscal Years 1987 through 2005

	Number	Range	Median	Total recoveries[1]
DOJ intervened[2] in the case	538	0-$568,036,761	$1,200,000	$6,731,633,038
Cases settled by DOJ before declination or intervention	71	$20,000-$88,707,098	$475,000	$388,454,479
DOJ declined–relator proceeded with case without government	151	$1,681 - $85,697,444	$100,000	$327,599,476

Source: GAO analysis of DOJ's Civil Division data on closed, unsealed qui tam cases.

[1] According to a DOJ official, a portion of these qui tam settlement and judgment amounts could include amounts attributable to government initiated claims under the FCA and other statutory or common law claims, such as breach of contract, bribery, or conflict of interest. The official also told us that precise amounts attributable to each claim may not be distinguished in the case of a lump-sum settlement or judgment.

[2] Includes cases where DOJ intervened in some but not all of the relator's claims.

Relator Share of Qui Tam Recoveries by DOJ Case Intervention

Relator share amounts were greater in cases where DOJ intervened than in cases where DOJ declined to intervene.

Relator Share of Qui Tam Recoveries by DOJ Case Intervention, Fiscal Years 1987 through 2005

	Number	Range	Median	Total relator share amounts[1]
DOJ intervened[2] in the case	538	0-$96,566,249	$175,754	$1,122,171,513
Cases settled by DOJ before intervention or declination	71	0-$9,050,000	$81,000	$54,478,813
DOJ declined—relator proceeded with case without government	151	0-$24,640,000	$22,400	$85,868,226

Source: GAO analysis of DOJ's Civil Division data on closed, unsealed qui tam cases.

[1] Includes relators whose qui tam case resulted in a settlement or judgment, but the relators received zero or a reduced share of the government's recovery. A DOJ official told us that these cases involved instances where the relator's entitlement to a full statutory share was jurisdictionally barred or in question and that this information is reflected in DOJ case files.

[2] Includes cases where DOJ intervened in some but not all of the relator's claims.

GAO's Mission

The Government Accountability Office, the audit, evaluation and investigative arm of Congress, exists to support Congress in meeting its constitutional responsibilities and to help improve the performance and accountability of the federal government for the American people. GAO examines the use of public funds; evaluates federal programs and policies; and provides analyses, recommendations, and other assistance to help Congress make informed oversight, policy, and funding decisions. GAO's commitment to good government is reflected in its core values of accountability, integrity, and reliability.

Obtaining Copies of GAO Reports and Testimony

The fastest and easiest way to obtain copies of GAO documents at no cost is through GAO's Web site (www.gao.gov). Each weekday, GAO posts newly released reports, testimony, and correspondence on its Web site. To have GAO e-mail you a list of newly posted products every afternoon, go to www.gao.gov and select "Subscribe to Updates."

End Notes

[1] The False Claims Act, as amended, is codified at 31 U.S.C. §§ 3729-33.

[2] Represents funds the government is entitled to recover as a result of qui tam case settlements or court judgments. These funds may or may not have been collected by the government. A DOJ official told us that while most of these funds arise from FCA allegations in the qui tam complaint, some funds are attributable to government initiated claims under the FCA and other statutory and common law claims, such as breach of contract, bribery, or conflict of interest, and that the relator is not entitled to a share of these funds. The official also told us that precise amounts attributable to each claim may not be distinguished in the case of a lump-sum settlement or judgment.

[3] Represents newly received FCA referrals and investigations initiated by the government and newly filed qui tam cases initiated by a relator. These include open cases and cases under seal. According to a DOJ official, this does not include non-qui tam cases under $5 million handled by the United States Attorney's offices. The official also told us that the Civil Division does not maintain data on these cases.

[4] Includes DOJ intervened cases and cases settled by DOJ before declination or intervention.

[5] Includes relators whose qui tam case resulted in a settlement or judgment, but the relators received zero or a reduced share of the government's recovery. A DOJ official told us that these cases involved instances where the relator's entitlement to a full statutory share was jurisdictionally barred or in question and that this information is reflected in DOJ case files.

[6] The False Claims Act, as amended, is codified at 31 U.S.C. §§ 3729-33.

[7] Represents funds the government is entitled to recover as a result of qui tam case settlements or court judgments. These funds may or may not have been collected by the government. A DOJ official told us that while most of these funds arise from FCA allegations in the qui tam complaint, some funds are attributable to government initiated claims under the FCA and other statutory and common law claims, such as breach of contract, bribery, or conflict of interest, and that the relator is not entitled to a share of these funds. The official also told us that precise amounts attributable to each claim may not be distinguished in the case of a lump-sum settlement or judgment.

[8] Represents newly received FCA referrals and investigations initiated by the government and newly filed qui tam cases initiated by the relator. These include open cases and cases under seal. According to a DOJ official, these cases do not include non-qui tam cases under $5 million handled by the United States Attorneys' Offices. The official told us that the Civil Division does not maintain data on these cases.

[9] Includes DOJ intervened cases and cases settled by DOJ before declination or intervention.

[10] Includes cases in which DOJ intervened and cases settled by DOJ before declination or intervention. [5]Includes relators whose qui tam case resulted in a settlement or judgment, but the relators received zero or a reduced share of the government's recovery. A DOJ official told us that these cases involved instances where the relator's entitlement to a full statutory share was jurisdictionally barred or in question and that this information is reflected in DOJ case files.

[11] According to a DOJ official, the Civil Division does not track non-qui tam cases generally under $5 million which were initiated and pursued by the U.S. Attorneys' Offices.

In: Fighting Fraud with Qui Tam and the False Claims Act
Editor: Ian M. Ortiz
ISBN: 978-1-61668-221-7

Chapter 2

HEARING ON "THE FALSE CLAIMS ACT CORRECTIONS ACT OF 2007: STRENGTHENING THE GOVERNMENT'S MOST EFFECTIVE TOOL AGAINST FRAUD FOR THE 21ST CENTURY"

Patrick Leahy

Nearly a century and half ago, President Abraham Lincoln pushed through the False Claims Act in order to combat rampant fraud and war profiteering during the Civil War. It is fitting that we hold this hearing on legislation to strengthen "Lincoln's Law" the same month we celebrate President Lincoln's birth.

Today, again in the midst of war and facing reports of billions lost to fraud and waste in Iraq and Afghanistan, we are considering important new improvements to the False Claims Act – not only to punish and deter those who seek to defraud our nation, but also to recover billions in taxpayer dollars stolen from the public trust.

In recent years, the False Claims Act has become the government's most effective tool against fraud. Since 1986, it has been used to recover more than $20 billion lost to fraud, about half of that coming in just the past five years. It has been used to punish contractors selling defective body armor to our police, to recover hundreds of millions from oil and gas companies bilking the government on valuable leases on federal land, to thwart major technology corporations from colluding in bids for government contracts, and to uncover massive fraud by insurance companies illegally shifting their losses from Hurricane Katrina to the Federal Government.

Perhaps the Act's greatest success has been to expose complex schemes that have defrauded billions from federal health care programs. Just this month, the drug company Merck agreed to pay a $650 million false claims settlement for illegally overcharging Medicaid for Vioxx, Zocor, and other drugs. This settlement was among the largest ever under the False Claims Act, and part of more than five billion dollars recovered in health care cases just this decade.

More than 600 false claims cases are still pending against health care and drug companies, and 150 of those involve overcharging the government for pharmaceuticals. It seems clear that future false claims settlements will soon dwarf what we have seen so far.

But these recent successes do not tell the full story, as the False Claims Act has yet to fulfill its true potential for combating fraud. In 1986, Senator Grassley led the effort to reinvigorate the False Claims Act by amending the law to encourage citizens to report fraud against the government. Since then, citizen whistleblowers have become the greatest source for uncovering complex frauds against the government, and their cases now account for about 70 percent of all the money recovered under the False Claims Act. Yet, opponents of the False Claims Act, those who defend the major defense contractors and big drug companies, have worked hard to undermine the original intent of these amendments, and a series of recent court decisions have placed new, technical impediments on false claims cases. These court decisions threaten to weaken the law, and undo the successes of recent years.

Today, we consider bipartisan legislation – the False Claims Act Corrections Act of 2007 – that will correct these judicial interpretation problems and strengthen the False Claims Act for the 21st Century. In doing so, I want to recognize the longstanding leadership of my friend Senator Chuck Grassley, who recently introduced this bill in order to restore the original intent of his 1986 amendments. Senator Grassley has worked tirelessly over the years in defense of the False Claims Act, and I am proud to join with him, as well as Senators Durbin, Specter, and Whitehouse, in support of this bill. I look forward to working with all these Senators and the Committee to make the False Claims Act even more effective, and to provide important, new protections for the citizen whistleblowers, who are so vital to uncovering these frauds.

At our hearing today, we will ask important questions of the Justice Department, about its failure to dedicate sufficient lawyers and investigators to pursue these fraud cases. The Justice Department has a backlog of more than 1,000 false claims cases, which at its current pace would take nearly 10 years to resolve, even if no new cases were brought. When one considers that a recent study found that for every dollar spent enforcing the law in health care cases, the government recovered 15 dollars on behalf of the American taxpayer, there's no excuse for failing to pursue these cases aggressively.

In light of the politicization of the Bush Justice Department, many wonder whether it has resisted pursuing certain false claims cases for political reasons – most notably those involving contracting fraud related to the war in Iraq and Afghanistan. Over the past five years, the Justice Department has participated in more than 600 false claims settlements nationwide and recovered more than $10 billion. Yet, during that same time, the Justice Department participated in only five cases involving contracting fraud in Iraq and Afghanistan and has recovered a mere $16 million – that's less than two tenths of one percent of the overall total. Since 2002, our government has spent nearly $500 billion on the wars in Iraq and Afghanistan, much of it on government contracting, and billions of taxpayers' dollars have been lost to fraud, waste, and abuse. The False Claims Act was designed to attack such rampant war profiteering, and it is just as necessary today, as it was during the Civil War. Iraq Study Group Chairman Lee Hamilton said in testimony to this Committee that nothing undermines our efforts in Iraq more than abuse and fraud in the reconstruction of the country. I share these concerns with Chairman Hamilton and others who have recognized the tremendous harm this conduct causes. Yet, this administration has apparently decided that pursuing unscrupulous defense contractors would be embarrassing and aggressively pursuing these frauds is not their priority.

This morning we will hear from a courageous citizen whistleblower, who will tell us how she used the False Claims Act not only to hold one of our nations' largest defense contractors to account, but also to keep the Justice Department honest. Tina Gonter was a quality engineer was working for a submarine parts supplier in Ohio when she discovered the valves produced at her plant were faulty and could lead to catastrophic failure for our nation's submarine fleet. She reported the problem to her superiors, but they did nothing. After contacting a lawyer, she reported her observations to criminal investigators, she agreed to volunteer as an undercover informant, and wore a secret tape recorder gathering evidence against her bosses. After the criminal investigation was complete, she filed a False Claims Act case, but even after her immediate bosses went to jail, the Justice Department refused to join her case against the defense contractors who also knew about and benefited from the fraud, and she pursued the case alone, until a judge scolded the Justice Department for not taking action and they joined in the settlement at the last minute.

Ms. Gonter is a testament to the courage of citizen whistleblowers. She risked her job and was retaliated against but she took on the powerful, moneyed defense contractors anyway. These whistleblowers should be recognized as "citizen soldiers," as President Lincoln called them when the False Claims Act was first passed so many years ago. They keep government contractors honest and are responsible for returning billions to the American taxpayers. Her story demonstrates how the False Claims Act works for all Americans, and why new protections for citizen whistleblowers in the bill we consider today are necessary to encourage others to come forward and tell their stories.

I expect that some may suggest that citizens should not be allowed to bring these cases against their employers, or that this law creates unnecessary incentives for lawsuits against defense contractors and drug companies. But no one can deny that these citizen whistleblowers are now the single, most important source for uncovering fraud against the government, and their cases have returned tens of billions to the American taxpayers, money that the government would never have recovered without them.

I hope all Senators will join us to honor the legacy of Lincoln's Law and take action now to strengthen and improve the False Claims Act for the next century.

In: Fighting Fraud with Qui Tam and the False Claims Act ISBN: 978-1-61668-221-7
Editor: Ian M. Ortiz

Chapter 3

FALSE CLAIMS ACT HEARING

Michael Hertz

Mr. Chairman, Ranking Member Specter, Members of the Committee: Thank you for inviting me to testify regarding our efforts under the False Claims Act, and to present the views of the Department of Justice on S. 2041, The False Claims Corrections Act of 2007. I appreciate having this opportunity to review with you the Department's experience with qui tam actions, or whistleblower suits, since the 1986 amendments, and the success of the False Claims Act generally in meeting the goal we all share: preventing and redressing fraud against the Government.

The Department of Justice is committed to the vigorous enforcement of the laws against those who perpetrate fraud to obtain money from the Government. The False Claims Act has been a very important civil statutory weapon against fraud. Since the Act was amended and liberalized in 1986, over $20 billion has been recovered on behalf of taxpayers by the Civil Division working closely with the Offices of the United States Attorneys. The recoveries in the period before the amendments, as compared with the period after 1986, are illustrative of the overall effectiveness of the Act. In Fiscal Year 1986, the year prior to the amendments of the False Claims Act, the Department recovered $54 million under the Act1. Since then, we have seen a steady increase in recoveries, culminating in settlements and judgments of more than $5 billion in just the past two years.

This remarkable accomplishment has been with the assistance of the qui tam provisions, which have augmented our resources to address fraud in connection with Government contracts and programs and which we continue vigorously to support. As this Committee well knows, the False Claims Act Amendments in 1986 substantially changed the qui tam provisions to encourage more citizens to report fraud, and to increase the Government's ability to recover its losses. Since the qui tam provisions of the False Claims Act were amended, there have been more than 5800 suits filed with the Department through Fiscal Year 2007. Indeed, of the $20 billion recovered under the FCA since 1986, $12.6 billion has been the result of qui tam actions.

We have encouraged the Department's litigators to make every effort to work cooperatively with relators to maximize the Government's recovery. The Department and its client agencies have dedicated enormous resources to the investigation and prosecution of these cases. We have advanced or supported legal arguments in courts throughout the nation, and at every level, that both vigorously enforce the liability provisions of the False Claims Act and advocate the rights of relators.

Several facts about the Department's experience with the qui tam provisions of the False Claims Act are noteworthy. First, the Act has been widely used to allege fraud in a broad range of agency programs and contracts. More than half of these cases, 3117 of the 5800 filed since the 1986 amendments, focus on fraud against government health care programs such as Medicare and Medicaid. These health care fraud cases also are the largest source of dollars recovered in False Claims Act qui tam cases, representing $9.1 billion, or more than 72 percent of the total $12.6 billion in qui tam recoveries. Qui tam cases alleging fraud against the Department of Defense constitute about 20 percent of the qui tam cases filed under the Act since 1986, and about 13 percent of the qui tam recoveries (a total of $1.6 billion).

While these two areas are predominant among various fraud schemes addressed by the Act since 1986, there are no government programs that are immune from possible fraud, as reflected by our caseload. Cases brought by the Department under the Act, including those initiated by whistleblowers, have recovered significant funds on behalf of the Department of Interior, the General Services Administration, the Department of Housing and Urban Development, the Department of Agriculture, the Department of Education, the Department of State, the Department of Energy, NASA, and more recently, the Department of Homeland Security, to name but a few. The following results from this past year illustrate the variety that exists in our pending case matters:

Just this month, Merck & Company paid more than $650 million to resolve allegations that it failed to remit legally-required rebates to Medicaid and other government health care programs and paid illegal remuneration to health care providers to induce them to prescribe the company's products.

Bristol-Myers Squibb Company (BMS) and its generic division, Apothecon, paid over $515 million to resolve a broad array of allegations involving illegal drug pricing and marketing activities.

A judgment was obtained against Amerigroup Illinois, Inc. for $334 million that included $172 million for allegations under the False Claims Act relating to the federal share of Medicaid. A court determined that Amerigroup fraudulently skewed enrollment in its Medicaid HMO program by discouraging pregnant women and other potentially costly patients from joining.

Medco Health Solutions, Inc. paid $155 million to settle allegations that Medco submitted false claims in connection with the mail order prescription drug benefit offered under the Federal Employee Health Benefits Program. The government alleged that Medco cancelled prescriptions it could not fill timely to avoid late penalties, shorted pills, and billed for pharmacy services it didn't provide. The government also alleged that Medco solicited kickbacks from pharmaceutical manufacturers to favor their drugs on Medco's formulary, and paid kickbacks to health plans to obtain business.

Oracle Corporation, in a record fraud settlement involving the General Services Administration (GSA), paid $98.5 million to resolve allegations that PeopleSoft Inc., which was acquired by Oracle in 2005, violated the False Claims Act when it provided GSA with pricing disclosures for its software and related maintenance services that were not complete, accurate and current.

Burlington Resources, Inc., a subsidiary of ConocoPhillips, the third largest integrated energy company in the United States, paid $97.5 million to settle claims that Burlington underpaid royalties owed on natural gas produced under federal and Indian leases.

Harbert International, Inc., Bill Harbert International Construction, Inc., Bilhar International Establishment f/k/a Harbert International Establishment, a Liechtenstein company, and Harbert Corporation were found liable after a seven-week trial and ordered to pay $90 million. The defendants were found liable under the False Claims Act for conspiracy to rig bids on contracts to construct wastewater treatment facilities in Cairo, Egypt. These contracts were financed by the U.S. Agency for International Development.

Maximus, Inc. paid $42.65 million to settle allegations in connection with false claims it submitted to the District of Columbia's Medicaid program. The District of Columbia Child and Family Services Agency (CFSA) hired Maximus to assist it in submitting claims to Medicaid for targeted case management services provided by the District to children in its foster care program. The United States alleged that Maximus caused CFSA to submit claims for every child in the foster care program whether or not targeted case management services had been provided to the child. Maximus also entered into a deferred prosecution agreement with the U.S. Attorney's Office.

Mellon Bank, N.A., paid $34.6 million to resolve allegations that the bank violated the False Claims Act when in April, 2001, several of its employees hid and then destroyed approximately 77,000 individual income tax returns, together with tax payment checks, instead of processing the returns and checks as required by its Lockbox Depositary Agreement with the Internal Revenue Service (IRS).

Last week, the 7th Circuit affirmed a $64 million judgment against Peter Rogan, the CEO of an Illinois hospital, for paying doctors to refer patients to the hospital. After a bench trial, the district court found that Rogan had violated various prohibitions on the payment of compensation for referrals to federal health care programs.

Whistleblowers played an important role in many of these cases, and the 1986 qui tam amendments to the Act that strengthened whistleblower provisions have allowed us to recover losses to the federal fisc that we might not have otherwise been able to identify. Moreover, the qui tam provisions have had a more subtle and unquantifiable impact in our fight against fraud. In the wake of well-publicized recoveries attributable to qui tam cases, those who might otherwise submit false claims to the federal government are more aware than ever of the "watchdog" effect of the qui tam statute. We have no doubt that the Act has had the salutary effect of deterring fraudulent conduct.

As I indicated at the outset of my remarks, the Department continues to actively support the qui tam provisions of the Act by dedicating the resources necessary to investigate allegations to the fullest extent, by litigating the meritorious cases vigorously, and by ensuring that settlements reflect both the gravity of the violations and the loss to the Treasury. In addition to the efforts of relators, who often come forward at the risk of personal hardship, we believe that the success of the Act's qui tam provisions are in large part due to the efforts of the government attorneys, agents, auditors and other personnel charged with responsibilities under the statute, as the statistics bear out. We have now approximately 75 full-time attorneys in the Civil Division responsible for False Claims Act cases, as well as scores of Assistant United States Attorneys throughout the country. This is a highly professional, skilled and dedicated group of lawyers who are fully committed to the task at hand and who have elected to intervene in approximately one in four of the qui tam suits filed since 1986. At the conclusion of those cases, and as required by the False Claims Act, the Department has paid awards to qui tam relators of $2 billion since 1986. In Fiscal Year 2007 alone, the Department paid relator awards of more than $177 million. And although the Department has declined to intervene in 75 to 80 percent of the qui tams that have been filed, only 2.6 percent of total recoveries since 1986 under the Act, or $520 million, has been recovered in those cases where we have declined or otherwise not participated. This latter statistic reveals that the Department has been appropriately judicious in its review of qui tam matters and has been highly successful in intervening in those cases that have true merit. However, even in those cases in which we decline to intervene, the Department is often called upon to expend considerable resources by briefing legal issues at the request of the relator or the court, producing documents and witnesses from throughout the government, and otherwise ensuring that the False Claims Act is properly applied by relators and interpreted by courts.

We have reviewed carefully S. 2041. While the Administration is sympathetic to some of the proposed amendments, it cannot support the bill in its current form. Among our concerns are the proposals narrowing the public disclosure bar to permit those with no first hand knowledge beyond that available in the public domain to serve as relators, and permitting government employees to serve as relators in certain circumstances, which is unsound public policy as all government employees have an obligation to report fraud. Moreover, many provisions of S. 2041 deal with issues that have not yet been fully resolved by the courts. The False Claims Act and its qui tam provisions have proven to be an extremely effective weapon in the Government's fight against fraud and we see no pressing need for major amendments at this time.

CONCLUSION

Mr. Chairman, Ranking Member Specter, Members of the Committee: Let me restate my appreciation, and that of my colleagues in the Department of Justice, for this opportunity to comment on the success of the False Claims Act since enactment of the 1986 amendments, as well as our overall views on S. 2041. We appreciate the efforts that have been made by you and your staffs to further improve the False Claims Act. I reiterate the offer, contained in the views letter, to work with the Committee and its staff to find the best approach for furthering our common goal of fighting fraud against the public fisc.

I look forward to your questions. Thank you.

1 This figure does not account for inflation.

In: Fighting Fraud with Qui Tam and the False Claims Act
Editor: Ian M. Ortiz
ISBN: 978-1-61668-221-7

Chapter 4

FALSE CLAIMS ACT HEARING

Tina Marie Gonter

Good morning, Mr. Chairman and Members of the Committee. My name is Tina Gonter. I am what many people call a whistleblower. I used to be uncomfortable with that term, but now I understand that it means someone who has no choice but to do the right thing when others are willing to turn a blind eye. In my case, what dozens of others were willing to let slide was the safety of the sailors aboard the submarine fleet of the United States Navy. The False Claims Act allowed me to report terrible misconduct by a subcontractor which had gone on for years. Much of this misconduct was known to the prime contractors. As a result of my case, two senior executives of a defense contractor went to federal prison, their company was, we hope, rehabilitated, and the Navy had the opportunity to assess the extent to which it was harmed by delivery and installation of thousands of potentially-nonconforming submarine valves.

Despite overwhelming evidence that Navy prime contractors General Dynamics and Northrop Grumman knew what was going on at Hunt, the government did not intervene in our case against them. Because the False Claims Act allows *qui tarn* relators to go forward on their own when the government decides not to intervene, we were able to carry our case forward to resolution. If this right did not exist, our case would have disappeared. We would have gotten almost nothing for reporting this massive fraud against the taxpayers and spending four years of our lives helping the government investigate the extent of the fraud.

Also, if the False Claims Act did not permit cases against subcontractors, then Hunt Valve would have been immune for its massive fraud against the taxpayers.

I am here today to ask that you make sure that those who know of danger to American troops or American citizens be able to come forward with confidence that the False Claims Act lives up to its full potential by ensuring that relators can carry on cases against government contractors even when the government decides not to participate; by ensuring that subcontractors and suppliers who cheat the taxpayers not be able to hide behind the skirts of prime contractors; and by ensuring that the False Claims Act's protection of those who are retaliated against for doing the right thing is as strong as possible.

Background

After the *U.S.S. Thresher (SSN 593)* and all 129 men aboard were lost in 8,400 feet of water on April 10, 1963, because a pipe joint failed, the Navy imposed the strictest quality requirements in history on suppliers who choose to make parts for submarines. This program is called "Level One/SUBSAFE," and requires cradle-tograve documentation on all major systems. The point of the system is that if a valve or other part has a problem, documents exist which allow the Navy to trace that problem back to its source and figure out what other parts are affected and what submarines may be impacted.

My husband, Bill, and I worked for many years as civilian employees of the Department of Defense, until 1996. We were assigned to the Quality Assurance Department of Norfolk Navy Shipyard. My title was Nuclear Mechanical Systems Inspector. I learned all about Level One/SUBSAFE because it was my job to ensure that its strict standards were met. I completed a four-year quality assurance apprenticeship with the Department of the Navy. I held Level 2 certifications in Radiographic Inspection, Material Certification, Visual Inspection, Magnetic Particle Inspection, Liquid Penetrant Inspection, and Precision Measurement Devices. I was trained and/or certified in ISO 9000, Supplier Source Inspections, QC Marking and Material Verifications, Receipt Inspection, Level 1 Material Handling, Storage, Inspection and Certification, Valve Repair Inspection, Hydrostatic Testing, Welding Procedures and Joint Design.

While at the Shipyard, my responsibilities included verifying that the paperwork relating to valves and other components to be installed on Navy submarines was in order. Once a valve is assembled, many critical surfaces and components are not accessible, and the certifications and inspection reports which are completed by the manufacturer are the only available evidence of what lies beneath the surface.

In 1996, Bill, a Vietnam combat veteran of the United States Navy, and I decided to move to Rogers, Ohio, where he had grown up. He had inherited some land from his father and we planned to build our dream house. Our plans for an early retirement were dashed when I was diagnosed with cancer. My treatment wiped out our savings. Once I recovered, we both looked for jobs.

In mid-1999, Bill got a job at Hunt Valve Company in Salem, Ohio, close to Youngstown. Hunt made valves for nuclear submarines and the uranium enrichment process. These are not valves like on a kitchen sink: Some of them are six feet across, weigh several thousand pounds and cost tens of thousands of dollars. Others are smaller, but all the valves, no matter what size, are to be manufactured to precise standards, and inspected to be sure that those precise standards are met.

Bill and I knew about Hunt from our work at the Navy Shipyard and believed that it was a reputable company.[1] Bill's job involved reviewing paperwork and on their face, Hunt's paperwork seemed to be in order.

The Truth about Hunt

A few months later, I got a job at Hunt. My title was Military Quality Assurance Manager. Supposedly, my job was to help make sure that Hunt's production of critical submarine valves complied with the Navy's strict quality and manufacturing requirements. I was excited to be back in the submarine quality-assurance business.

Within just a few clays, I began to suspect that Hunt was committing fraud. Its personnel routinely falsified certified paperwork, skipped inspections, and cheated on production. They used the wrong materials and did not supervise their subcontractors. Once I started trying to get my arms around the scope of the problem, I learned that these things had been going on for more than a decade without anyone doing anything about it, much less telling the Navy about these systemic problems. Hunt was devoted to creating paperwork which looked great but had little to do with the valves it shipped.

Hunt was a Disaster Waiting to Happen

As a former civilian Navy Inspector, I was shocked at the extreme level of violations I saw. I was even more shocked that dozens of people—including employees from General Dynamics who were actually on-site at Hunt most days—not only knew about these problems, but had watched it happen for years. But nobody did anything about it, and bogus valves just kept shipping out. I made my concerns known to management, who ignored me—they knew full well what they were doing. When I attempted to order that things were done correctly, my instructions were ignored. I knew that the men and women aboard our nuclear submarines and ships were exposed to the risk that a Hunt valve would fail at sea. I began taking copies of documents home because I was afraid that evidence was being changed on a daily basis to hide the problems which I saw before my eyes.

2001: Blowing the Whistle

Because I had heard about the False Claims Act, I contacted Rick Morgan, a lawyer who had experience with the False Claims Act and with quality systems. At first, he did not believe that things could possibly be as bad as I said. He and his partner Jennifer Verkamp, spent more than a month working with me to understand why I was so concerned about what was going on at Hunt. Then Rick set up a meeting with agents of the Defense Criminal Investigative Service.

My husband and I met with DCIS Agents Jay Strauch and Mike Hampp in early March 2001. That meeting, which was the first of too many to count, started after work and lasted until late that night. Believing I had only one opportunity to convince the government of the problems, I poured out my story to the agents, who expressed concerns that if my allegations could be proved, the impact to the Department of Defense was serious. Prior to the meeting, my lawyers had helped me organize the documents I had copied and make notes of what was happening and the agents seemed convinced that there were serious issues with Hunt Valve. The agents explained that a case like this, their ability to prove the allegations would be greatly improved if I would agree to wear a tape recorder and record conversations with Hunt Valve and General Dynamics employees. Although I was fearful of wearing a recorder, I knew I had to do it. They had brought what they called "consensual monitoring" equipment with them, and I left the meeting with a miniature tape recorder and body microphone. I was "enrolled as a confidential source" for the Department of Defense in a criminal investigation of Hunt Valve Company and its customers.

For the next several months, I wore the recorder under my clothes every work day. Before I went to work in the morning, I had to make sure that the recorder was securely strapped under my clothes so that it could not be seen, and had to make sure that it operated properly. I spent each day trying to do my best to make sure that defective valves did not ship out of Hunt while also engaging my co-workers and others in conversations about the fraud that they were committing. If there was a lot going on, I would have to go into the restroom and change the tape in order to get all that was said. We made copies of documents showing the use of bad parts or procedures, or skipped or falsified inspections, when we could, and carried them under our clothes or in files to hide them in a box so that the agents could find them later. Every night, I had to catalog the day's tapes, make notes about what topics were discussed, and talk to my lawyers and the investigators about what had happened that day. Even so I knew that there was much more fraud at Hunt than I could ever document. I was sometimes physically ill from the stress and fear of these activities, and of course my husband was worried sick about me and the future of our family. I recorded hundreds of hours of conversation which filled almost 8,000 transcript pages.

In April 2001, my husband and I filed a *qui tarn* case under the False Claims Act. From the beginning, we put enormous resources into our case. The government did not have the resources to transcribe all the tapes, and my lawyers helped with that; in addition, Mary Jones, their paralegal, and I each listened to every tape and compared it to the transcripts. This took thousands of hours. My lawyers were able to dedicate so much effort to our case because they not only believed in our case, but knew that if we won our False Claims Act case, with or without the government, the defendants would have to pay my legal fees.

Bill and I feared constantly for our jobs and our personal safety. We were always looking over our shoulders and I worried every day that someone would figure out that I was taping. I had a recurrence of cancer, and major surgery. I knew that chemotherapy would make me sick, and so I skipped those treatments and went to work earlier than my doctors recommended because I knew how important the government's investigation was, and that without my tapes that investigation would not proceed.

It is impossible to exaggerate how bad things were at Hunt. For example, Hunt's janitor routinely did inspections of valves and valve parts—something which was never documented but which my tapes proved to be true. When the Quality Manager used fingernail polish to trick a General Dynamics inspector, his bragging about it was recorded for all time. And when welders admitted that they cut corners all the time, the tapes backed up my observations.

Although what was going on at Hunt made me sick, I was even more troubled by the response of General Dynamics and Northrop Grumman, which were the prime government contractors. General Dynamics had an employee named Harry Arnold who worked onsite at Hunt Valve. Mr. Arnold and I talked frequently about how bad things were. He told me that he never had any confidence in Hunt's ability to produce valves which met the Navy's requirements. Another time, he told me he had "lost all confidence" in Hunt. I recorded many statements by Mr. Arnold, and many conversations between him and Hunt management. Here are just a couple of examples.

In March, Hunt was ready to ship a valve which was not inspected. I required an inspection, which showed that the valve was seriously cracked. Mr. Arnold talked to his managers at General Dynamics and told Hunt that while the valve would be rejected, Hunt would not be required to provide a report showing why it had not been tested and what would be done, which is called "cause and corrective action." Mr. Arnold said his boss, Mr. Smelings, said to tell Hunt management he was giving them an "Easter present."

One day, Mr. Arnold said to me, "I don't know how you're ever gonna straighten this mess out, I just don't even know where to begin." When I asked him if he had any suggestions, Mr. Arnold replied "Yeah, stick of dynamite, blow this freaking place up."

Hunt's Non-Destructive Testing Inspector routinely signed NDT reports falsely certifying that testing was done when it was not, or when he did not know that it had been; routinely performed nondestructive testing without following contractually- required procedures; and routinely permitted uncertified personnel to perform nondestructive testing after which he would certify that the testing had been conducted by certified personnel.

In August, Hunt became fed up with my constant efforts to get its personnel to do their jobs and fired me. I was told that I was fired because it cost Hunt so much to fix the problems I found that it could not afford my $64,000 salary. But I believe that I was fired because Hunt knew that I was unwilling to allow it to cut corners on Level One submarine hardware and insisted that Hunt follow the Navy's requirements. Laughably, I was told that there was an "extensive cut" that "affected my job," but I was the only person fired.

On September 17, 2001, the Defense Department, with the help of the Nuclear Regulatory Commission, the Naval Criminal Investigative Service, and the Department of Energy, swarmed Hunt Valve with a search warrant and more than 40 federal agents. They took all of Hunt's records—well over a million pages worth. They copied all the computer data and hard drives in the plant. They also found and recovered our box of "hot documents," which corroborated much of the fraud at Hunt.

After the raid, Hunt management held meetings where they said that Hunt did nothing wrong and the government was on a witch hunt. The president of the company had the gall to compare the "attack" on Hunt to the destruction of the World Trade Centers just a week earlier. Hourly workers made threats to "take care of whoever did this."

Bill was still working for the company, but we decided he had to leave because we feared for his safety—and mine. When he was at work, I carried a pistol from room to room in our house. Unknown cars were coming partway up our rural driveway and we felt like we were in danger.

Bill resigned from Hunt. Our family income went from $106,000 a year to zero. We sold our property, in which we had heavily invested, at a huge loss so that we would have money to live on.

2002-2005: SUPPORTING THE GOVERNMENT

In order to help the agents make sense of the huge volume of records they seized, we moved to Columbus, where we had no family or friends. Because our *qui tam* case was under seal, we couldn't tell anyone—not even our friends and family—what we were doing. Our lawyers became like family as I spent the next two years working almost full-time going through those files with the help of my lawyers and their staff, and answering question after question about what the documents showed. The government did not have enough people assigned to the case to review the files. For many months, the civil part of the Justice Department did not want us involved in the file review, even though we had moved to Columbus to perform that review, because they were worried that we would try to take credit for claims we didn't already know about. The Defense Department investigators and the criminal prosecutor on the case, Assistant United States Attorney Richard Blake, insisted that our work was necessary to their criminal prosecution. For many months, that was the only way we could get access to Hunt's records, even though the government had no personnel who could review the records.

After we exhausted the money from selling our house, Bill got a quality- assurance job with the Defense Logistic Agency. I continued working on the investigation. Our income was well below half what it would have been if, like everybody else, we had decided to just keep our mouths shut about what was going on at Hunt Valve Company.

Our review of the documents seized from Hunt, which we performed in tandem with John Carruthers and Bob Hardin of the Defense Contract Audit Agency ("DCAA"), showed—among many other things—that more than half of Hunt's certifications were demonstrably falsified; that Hunt welding personnel were improperly and illegally qualified; and that material was not properly documented or maintained.

We also met with many Navy engineers and scientists. One such meeting, which took place in September of 2002, was attended by 17 government employees, including experts in welding, quality assurance, engineering, and submarine valves. They questioned us for two full days. I believe they shared our concern with the gravity of the situation at Hunt, because shortly afterward they sent a huge audit team of Navy and civilian experts to survey conditions at Hunt. We were not surprised to learn that the auditors found that things were no better a year after the search warrant was executed than while we were there, because we believed that Hunt's people simply did not know how to do it right, and the shipbuilders never showed them.

We were shocked to learn that the Navy allowed Northrop Grumman and General Dynamics to conduct an inspection of some Hunt valves which had been delivered. This was very concerning to us, because I knew from my conversations with Harry Arnold and other people from the prime contractors that those two companies—the same companies accused of inspecting, buying and installing valves which they knew, or at a minimum should have known, were bogus—were a huge part of the problem. I could not for the life of me understand why an independent company was not tasked with testing the valves. When I expressed my wonderment at this, however, my concerns were dismissed even as Bill and I were thanked for our service.

In any event, the contractors looked at 331 valves, and identified 495 physical defects—an average of 1.5 defects per valve. Since the Level 1/SUBSAFE watchwords are "ZERO

DEFECTS," we thought this was significant. Moreover, early in the investigation, the Navy actually concluded that *all* of Hunt Valve's paperwork was fraudulent and decreed that it had to be completely ignored—meaning that the taxpayers and the Navy were cheated every time they got a Hunt valve.

At the same time the Navy was investigating, we also spent many days meeting with investigators fur the Department of Energy and the Nuclear Regulatory Commission regarding Hunt's fraudulent sale of uranium hexafluoride ("$UF_{6;}$") containment valves. Public exposure to UF_6 is the primary health and safety hazard for consideration at gaseous diffusion plants. Hunt made and sold tens of thousands of those valves without using proper procedures or properly-trained personnel.[2] A number of Hunt's valves failed tests conducted by the NRC.

2005-06: Going it Alone

Because Bill and I blew the whistle, Hunt Quality Manager Wayne Aldrich pled guilty to fraud and went to federal prison for almost three years.[3] My boss, Hunt Vice President Larry Kelly, went to prison for two years.[4] I do not believe that these convictions ever could have been obtained without our whistleblowing and, just as octant, without our continued gathering and assessing of evidence from 2001-2004. These two are convicted felons and they can never work on another government contract for the rest of their lives.

Hunt Valve was sold and is under new management. We pray that it is doing a better job and hope that its customers, who continue to be Northrop Grumman and General Dynamics, are doing their job of ensuring that Hunt supplies conforming valves. The Navy, we were told, has revamped the way it buys and inspects hardware for its ships. The agents in charge of the case, for whom I have profound respect, have told me that they believe this to be one of the most important cases of their careers. The DoD, NRC, NCIS and Department of Energy agents, by the way, received an award from the President's Council on Integrity and Efficiency for their work on this case. That award said:

> This award recognizes the members of the Hunt Valve Investigative Team for outstanding performance and sustained distinguished performance for their efforts to protect United States military personnel and the nation's nuclear programs in the investigation of large scale, complex corporate fraud by a U.S. Government contractor.

Agents Strauch and Hampp, who spearheaded the government's effort, received a separate award from the DoD Inspector General.

Much was done, but much more could have been done. The Justice Department never sought subpoenas from General Dynamics or Northrop Grumman, and the government never, so far as we know, investigated how much those prime contractors knew about Hunt's misconduct—or how many other subcontractors were using subcontracts with these companies to defraud the Navy and deliver bogus submarine hardware.

We also found evidence that Hunt was forced by General Dynamics to use a company called All Stainless to cheat on General Dynamics's minority subcontractor promises to the Navy by having All Stainless act as a "distributor" of Hunt Valves, even though all it did was shuffle paperwork and get paid a kickback by Hunt. Under this arrangement, General Dynamics required Hunt to pay as much as 3% of its price to All Stainless for doing nothing, and of course this additional expense got passed through to the taxpayers. To our knowledge, nothing was done to recover the money paid by the government on this and similar arrangements.

In early 2005, our case was still under seal. The judge assigned to it, Honorable Dan Aaron Polster in Cleveland, became frustrated with the duration of the seal and ordered the government to make its intervention decision.

The government decided to intervene against Hunt Valve. In fact, Hunt Valve *begged* the government to intervene, to protect Hunt from our lawsuit. Hunt had delivered an estimated 40,000 suspect valves with bogus paperwork to the shipbuilders and the Navy. 15,000 of those valves were required to meet Level 1/SUBSAFE standards. Hunt also had delivered thousands of improperly-inspected and, in some cases, obviously-defective valves for containment of hazardous nuclear byproducts. There is no way to know how many of those valves include bad workmanship, incorrect materials, or would have failed proper inspection. We estimated the loss to the government in the tens of millions of dollars. The government's investigation alone cost at least $4.2 million.

The government settled with Hunt for $666,000 paid over several years. Bill and I shared 15% of this amount with our lawyers. Hunt is still making small payments. While we could have objected to the settlement, the government represented to us that it was more important for Hunt to keep making valves than for the government to be paid for its losses.

Although we had rooms full of evidence, the Justice Department decided not to intervene in our case against General Dynamics and Northrop Grumman. This decision was never explained to us. However, much later, we were present when the judge was told that the Navy believed that if it recovered money from General Dynamics and Northrop Grumman, they would just acid the money to a future contract bid and the Navy would end up paying them back.

Because the *qui tarn* provisions of the False Claims Act allow whistleblowers, to go forward on their own, we were able to proceed, and after much anxious soul- searching and much analysis by our lawyers, we decided that we had to carry our case forward. Our lawyers served our 116-page Amended Complaint on the defendants. The shipyards were represented by Mr. Boese's firm and other huge Washington law firms. They filed massive motions to dismiss, contending that we *still* did not have enough evidence, because we did not have the bills that the shipyards submitted to the Navy for the submarines. The shipyards also tried to convince the Judge that the government had concluded that our case against them was worthless because it did not intervene. However, Judge Polster "invited" the Justice Department and the Navy to participate in settlement discussions, and they debunked the defendants' statements.

In the fall of 2005, we settled our case with the shipyards for $12.6 million. Most of the money went to the Navy, of course, but my husband and I shared 29% of the money (before taxes, of course) with our lawyers. We bought a small house in Jacksonville to be close to our daughter and are getting on with our lives as best we can. Neither of us can ever work in our chosen field, using the skills we learned over decades as nuclear quality-assurance specialists, because our history as whistleblowers is but a Google search away.

If the Justice Department's decision not to intervene against General Dynamics and the other defendants had ended my case, my husband and I would have gotten virtually nothing for the loss of our jobs and the many years we spent helping the government investigate Hunt

Valve and the corporate felons who worked for it. Instead, because we and our lawyers were able to forge ahead, we were able to put our lives back together.

Several of the Amendments now under consideration are relevant to my case. We had access to the claims submitted to General Dynamics and Northrop Grumman by Hunt Valve, but not the claims they submitted to the Navy. Some would say that we could not make our case without them. I hope you make it crystal clear that we could—that is, that subcontractors who cheat the government are no different than prime contractors who cheat the government. Perhaps, if Civil Investigative Demands had been easier to obtain and use, the Justice Department would have sought information from the shipyards. Hunt hid its misconduct for many years, and clarifying the statute of limitations is important. We suspected that Hunt's customers encouraged Hunt to fire me. I don't know whether this is true, but it is important to clarify that anyone who retaliates against a whistleblower be held to answer—not just "employers." And there should be no question that when somebody like me reviews documents to help the government, that is not a "public disclosure" under the Act.

Without the False Claims Act, I would not have been able to force the government to focus on the fraud at Hunt Valve Company. I am eternally grateful to the United States Congress for making that possible. Maybe I would have tried to get someone to pay attention, but I don't think they would have believed me. More likely, I would have left the company, and lain awake at night worrying that my inaction would cost sailors' lives. Perhaps more important, without the strong *qui tarn* provisions in the False Claims Act, the shipyards would have suffered no consequences for what they did.

A Navy website about the Level 1/SUBSAFE Program says: "The bitterness of poor quality lingers long after the sweetness of meeting a schedule is forgotten." In fact, however, the government contractors in this case wasted untold millions of federal dollars because they were more concerned with their schedules—and the incentives they got for meeting those schedules—than with taking the time and expending the effort to require Hunt Valve Company to do the job for which it was paid millions of federal taxpayer dollars. From this whistleblower's chair, it looks like a pretty sweet deal for them.

There are other Tina Gonters out there. Senators, anyone who says there are not also other Hunt Valve Companies out there is kidding herself—and not reading the news. I have read this Committee's report from 1986 and while my experience shows that you accomplished much of what you set out to achieve, work remains to be done.

Thank you for allowing me to tell you my story. It is a profound honor to appear before you in support of the False Claims Act Amendments. I urge you in the strongest possible terms to do everything you can to help others like me to do the right thing. Do not doubt that in addition to the billions of dollars recovered under the False Claims Act, lives hang in the balance.

End Notes

[1] According to a DoD press release regarding the conviction of one of Hunt's senior executives:

> Hunt Valve is a major supplier of valves and valve parts to the U.S. Navy. These valves are used in Level I/SUBSAFE and non-Level I applications. Hunt Valve also marketed valves under the brand names of Union Flonetics, WAECO Valves, Morland Valves and PJ Valves. From 1993 to 2003, Hunt Valve sold approximately 40,000 valves to the Navy or prime contractors of which approximately 15,000 were Level 1/SUBSAFE.

Hunt Valve supplied valves directly to the Navy and to prime contractors of the Department of Defense. The company also sold spare valves and valve parts directly to the government through the Naval Inventory Control Point (NAVICP), Mechanicsburg, PA and the Defense Supply Center Columbus (DSCC), Columbus, OH. These valves are used on five Navy programs including Seawolf class submarines, Virginia class submarines, AEGIS class Arleigh Burke guided missile destroyers, nuclear-powered aircraft carriers and the amphibious transport dock. Hunt Valve also supplied valves to the Department of Energy and the United States Enrichment Corporation, a certificate of the Nuclear Regulatory Commission. These valves are used on containers that store and transport uranium hexafluoride (UF6) and depleted uranium hexafluoride (DUF6).

[2] As stated in the Criminal Information against Hunt Quality Manager Wayne Aldrich,

Hunt Valve supplied valves to the United States Enrichment Corporation ("USEC") and DOE through USEC, for use on containers that transport and are part of the processing and storage of uranium hexafluoride (UF6) and depleted uranium hexafluoride ("DUF6") at various sites, including the Paducah Gaseous Diffusion Plant, Paducah, Kentucky; the Portsmouth Gaseous Diffusion Plant, Portsmouth, Ohio; and, the East Tennessee Technology Park ("K-25"), Oak Ridge, Tennessee.

[3] According to the government's press release,

Aldrich worked for Hunt Valve from April 1980 until he resigned in May 2001. Aldrich was the Quality Assurance Manager from April 1992 until he resigned. The investigation disclosed that from approximately April 1992 to May 2001, Aldrich and other co-conspirators altered and created false documentation and delivered or caused the delivery of valves that failed to conform to physical and contractual requirements mandated by the U.S. Government. Aldrich used scanners, computers and facsimile machines to alter vendor certifications by changing revision dates, adding signatures and adding or changing test results; falsified Hunt Valve certifications indicating non-destructive testing (NDT) was performed when he knew it had not been; permitted non-certified personnel to perform NDT inspections; and manufactured or repaired valves using unapproved and improper techniques and procedures. As a result of Aldrich's actions a sample of the valves supplied by Hunt Valve were tested by the U.S. Navy and their shipbuilders at a cost of over $4 million.

[4] In the plea agreement which Kelly filed with the U.S. District Court he admits that he:

Aided in the falsification and delivery to the United States Navy and the U.S. Department of Energy of certification packets for valves that did not meet requirements for traceability of component parts to their origin; and

Aided in the submission of falsified certifications when he learned that a subordinate employee had altered the original documents by adding information to the certifications and faxing the certifications from one Hunt Valve fax machine to another in the same building to make the documents appear "fuzzy."

In: Fighting Fraud with Qui Tam and the False Claims Act
Editor: Ian M. Ortiz
ISBN: 978-1-61668-221-7

Chapter 5

WRITTEN STATEMENT OF THE CHAMBER OF COMMERCE AND THE U.S. CHAMBER INSTITUTE FOR LEGAL REFORM IN OPPOSITION TO S.2041, THE FALSE CLAIMS ACT

John T. Boese

I appreciate the opportunity to submit my views on behalf of the U.S. Chamber of Commerce and the U.S. Chamber Institute for Legal Reform in opposition to S. 2041. For the last 25 years, I have had the privilege of representing a wide variety of defendants in False Claims Act cases. My clients have included large and small companies in healthcare, oil and gas, technology and defense, as well as colleges and universities, municipal airports, churches, individuals, and local government agencies — precisely the diverse group that this proposed legislation threatens to affect most dramatically. In addition to my practice, I have also taught and studied the False Claims Act for many years. My two-volume treatise, *Civil False Claims and Qui Tam Actions*, was originally published in 1993 and is now in its Third Edition. It was the first treatise on the False Claims Act and *qui tam* enforcement and remains the leading authority cited by academics and practitioners as well as by Federal district and appellate courts on this topic.

The Chamber fully supports the Department of Justice's efforts to remedy fraud on the Government and does not countenance or support those who defraud the Federal Treasury. The Chamber recognizes the importance of an appropriate use of the False Claims Act in those efforts. The Chamber opposes S. 2041, however, because it will not assist the DOJ in its fraud- fighting efforts, it will not increase the monies returned to the Treasury, and it will not encourage more whistleblowers to bring new allegations of real fraud to the attention of the Government.

We oppose this bill because it would:

greatly expand the scope of the Act to private contract disputes which do not affect the Treasury;

cost the Treasury far more than it might gain by rewarding those who bring no new allegations of fraud to the attention of the Government;
allow Government employees to abuse Government information for personal profit;
create an administrative nightmare for any person, company, or institution that pays or receives Federal money;
disassociate the whistleblower protection provisions of the Act from any activities regarding *qui tam* enforcement; and
encourage private counsel access to information obtained under a Civil Investigative Demand to supplement *qui tam* complaints that do not state a claim under the Act.

In short, the amendments in S. 2041 would increase the possibility that False Claims Act enforcement will be abused by *qui tam* relators' counsel, particularly in the 80% of *qui tam* cases in which the DOJ declines to intervene because the cases are meritless.

The concerns being expressed by the Chamber on behalf of the business community are supported by more distant experience with *qui tam* enforcement. In fact, another country's experience with a very broad *qui tam* enforcement system provides an excellent preview of things to come if the proposed amendments are enacted. That history is described in a scholarly study published in 2000 by Professor Randy Beck, who traced the decline and ultimate repeal, in 1951, of England's *qui tam* laws. *See* J. Randy Beck, *The False Claims Act and the English Eradication of Qui Tam Legislation*, 78 N.C. L. Rev. 539 (2000). Professor Beck describes a country plagued by malicious and harassing *qui tam* prosecution and reports that public sentiment turned against *qui tam* enforcement in England because of "the obnoxious practices of common informers," who were widely perceived to be practicing a "form of legalized blackmail." *Id.* at 603-04. As Professor Beck notes:

> A further defect in the system of *qui tam* enforcement related to selection of targets for prosecution. Ideally, a public prosecutor exercises discretion in choosing prosecution targets in order to avoid applying a statute in ways that undermine the public interest. A *qui tam* statute eliminates any incentive for a benevolent exercise of prosecutorial discretion. The common informer has little reason to consider broader issues of public policy raised by a particular prosecution, and in fact has a strong financial incentive not to take such considerations into account. The result is that informers pursue litigation that disinterested prosecutors would consider contrary to the public good.

Id. at 583 (internal citations omitted). Adoption of the amendments in S. 2041 will likewise undermine public support for the goals of the False Claims Act in this country.

I. The Amendments Will Expand *Qui Tam* Enforcement, Which Has Been Abused by the Plaintiffs' Bar

Before I address the amendments themselves, I believe it is important to address five (5) common misconceptions about the False Claims Act ("FCA" or "the Act"), and particularly *qui tam* enforcement in FCA cases declined by the DOJ.[1] This, after all, is the focus of the vast majority of these amendments, and this discussion should inform the Committee's view of the amendments that benefit those *qui tam* relators and their lawyers.

Some background information on FCA litigation will also help the Committee better understand why the proposed legislation poses a grave threat to the economic viability of many businesses, non-profit groups, and local governmental entities. It is against this background that the Committee should exercise great caution before expanding a statute that threatens such severe consequences for so many.

A. *Qui Tam* Enforcement Does Not Result in Large Recoveries

There is a common misconception, perpetuated by the plaintiffs' bar, that these particular amendments are necessary for private attorneys to combat major fraud by the big corporate interests who outgun DOJ attorneys. The opposite is true: Of the $20 billion recovered under the False Claims Act since the 1986 Amendments, only 1.4% was recovered in *qui tam* cases in which the DOJ did not intervene.[2] These amendments, designed only to expand this type of litigation with such a low track record for success, benefit only *qui tam* relators and their attorneys, not the U.S. taxpayer.

The fact is, the FCA works best when the Government investigates, intervenes, and determines whether or not a case has merit and, if so, prosecutes the case. These declined cases[3] are, by and large, meritless, and are focused on questionable cases or small businesses and institutions which can ill afford to defend themselves. They involve violations of regulations without loss to the Treasury and are contrary to public policy and common sense.

B. *Qui Tam* Enforcement Does Not Target Only Large American Businesses

A second common misconception, perpetrated by the plaintiffs' bar that profits from these cases, is that whistleblowers need the amendments so they can pursue big corporate frauds. While some *qui tam* cases are filed against large companies, the majority of defendants in *qui tam* cases are small businesses, local governments, and non-profit institutions. A sample from just the last few years includes:

Arkansas
Game and Fish Commission

California
Santa Clara County Office of Education
Old Baldy Council of Boy Scouts of America

Georgia
Augusta-Richmond County
Providence Missionary Baptist Church of Atlanta

North Carolina
Easter Seals UPC

Ohio
Cuyahoga Falls General Hospital

Pennsylvania
Mercy Hospital of Pittsburgh
Tyrone Hospital
Lavender Hill Herb Farm

Tennessee
St. Jude's Children's Research Hospital

Illinois
Village of River Forest
Board of Education of Chicago
Pekin Memorial Hospital

Michigan
Oakland Livingston Legal Aid

Missouri
City of St. Louis

New York
State Division of Housing and Community Renewal
Erie County Medical Center

Memphis Baptist Hospital
Valley Milk Products, LLC

Texas
Dallas-Forth Worth Int'l Airport Board
Hudson Independent School District
Ector County Hospital

Vermont
City of South Burlington

Virginia
George Mason University

Washington
Housing Authority of Seattle

These non-profit institutions and public entities cannot, in many cases, afford to defend themselves against the treble damages and oppressive penalties assessed under the FCA, but they must divert valuable resources to do so because failing to do so would expose them to the very real risk of bankruptcy.

C. Innocent Companies and Institutions Are Adversely Affected by *Qui Tam* Enforcement of the FCA

A third common misconception is that *qui tam* enforcement only targets those who clearly defraud the Government. In fact, the opposite is true, and these meritless cases cost the American public dearly. As shown above, *qui tam* cases are filed every day against almost every type of institution in America. In 80% of those cases, the Government investigates and then declines to intervene, yet the *qui tam* relator and lawyer proceed with hopes of a big payoff. Those declined cases bring in only 1.4% of all FCA recoveries, yet they must be vigorously defended because the onerous treble damages and penalties will bankrupt most institutions. And they cost a fortune to defend.

I have two examples for the Committee from my own experience:

Example 1: A municipal airport was sued by a former environmental compliance officer under the FCA for applying for FAA grants and allegedly falsely certifying compliance with environmental regulations. The DOJ did not intervene. The court denied most pretrial motions, and the case went to trial. The jury entered a verdict against the *qui tam* relator and in favor of the airport, and the Fifth Circuit recently affirmed.

Cost of that trial and appeal to the airport: approximately $5 million.

Example 2: A non-profit hospital was sued by its former head nurse alleging violations of Medicare regulations. The DOJ did not intervene. Preliminary motions were denied, and the case went to full discovery. A month before trial, the court ruled in favor of the hospital on a summary judgment motion. No appeal was taken.

Cost to defend the hospital without a trial or appeal: approximately $1.7 million.

While some large defense contractors can try to pass on a portion of these defense costs to the Government, most small businesses and grantees have no ability to do so. They must simply absorb those costs as a "cost of doing business" with the U.S. Government. For many businesses, *qui tam* enforcement makes that cost too high.

D. Many *Qui Tam* Cases Are Inconsistent with Government Policy and the Public Interest

Most FCA cases brought by *qui tam* relators without DOJ intervention do not involve claims for services that were never rendered or products that were defective or never delivered. Instead, they more commonly involve allegations that, in the course of manufacturing a product or providing a service, a defendant falsely represented, or certified, that it was complying with various laws, regulations, and contract terms. *Qui tam* relators allege that such certifications are a basis for liability even if the Government is accurately billed for the correct amount.

The increasing tendency of *qui tam* relators to bootstrap regulatory violations onto the FCA is cause for great concern to the business community because most operate in highly regulated environments. Most of those laws and regulations — though perhaps important — have little or no direct bearing on the project or service being funded or the Government's purposes for funding that project. In a typical contract or grant, for example, the recipient must certify that it is and will remain in compliance with more than 50 specified laws, regulations, executive orders, and other Federal requirements.

But imagine the daunting task of conducting business in an environment where such certifications become whistleblower-driven compliance traps, which can cost hundreds of millions of dollars and have the very real capacity to cripple organizations that are often among the most important employers in a community.

Medicare cost report certifications are good examples: the preparer must certify that he or she is "familiar with the laws and regulations regarding the provision of health care services and that the services identified in [the] cost report were provided in compliance with such laws and regulations." *United States ex rel. Thompson v. Columbia/HCA*, 20 F. Supp. 2d 1017, 1041 (S.D. Tex. 1998). The Federal "laws and regulations regarding the provision of health care services" occupy, according to one reliable estimate, "more than 130,000 pages of rules and regulations for all Government healthcare programs, over 100,000 of which are related to Medicare." *Rx for the Health Care System*, WALL ST. J. at A1 8 (Oct. 8, 1998) (quoting Robert R. Waller, M.D., president and CEO of the Mayo Foundation). This staggeringly broad certification has been the basis for dozens of *qui tam* suits.

Congress has wisely refrained from creating a private enforcement mechanism for most of these laws and regulations, but the FCA is already widely used by private plaintiffs to litigate alleged regulatory and statutory violations indirectly. When such cases involve little or no economic harm to the Federal Treasury (where, for example, an otherwise perfectly fine product was delivered and a well-performed service was actually rendered), the high per-claim penalties available under the FCA mean that penalties can quickly accrue to the point where they far exceed any actual out-of-pocket loss experienced by the Government.[4] It is safe to say that most legislators and regulators would not and did not impose such draconian sanctions for the underlying regulatory or statutory violations: The public outcry over such a regime would be deafening. Yet, the Act allows *qui tam* relators, for their own profit, to sue for just such extraordinary sanctions.

E. Extravagantly Excessive Bounties Encourage Frivolous *Qui Tam* Litigation

Under existing law, *qui tam* relators can receive up to 30% of an FCA settlement or judgment. Large settlements paid in recent years have produced extravagantly large relator share payments. Two relators received a $95 million payment in connection with a settlement paid by TAP Pharmaceuticals in 2001.[5] Another relator recently received a $62 million bounty in connection with a settlement paid by Merck.[6] But if the relators would, as is likely, have been very satisfied with $20 million each, then the Government overpaid the two TAP relators by a total of $55 million and the Merck relator received $42 million more than necessary, resulting in an economically inefficient misallocation of $97 million that should have been paid to the U.S. Treasury.

This analysis is relevant to the Senate's consideration of the proposed amendments because it reveals how the lottery-like aspect of the existing system encourages frivolous litigation that comes at significant direct and indirect cost to consumers, businesses and taxpayers. Although most relators get much less than the amounts listed above, the hope of a Lotto payoff encourages individuals to take a chance on a *qui tam* suit. If nothing else, claiming whistleblower status often allows problematic employees to extract some sort of payment from their former employers. The proposed amendments would increase the economic inefficiencies and abuses in the existing system and could have particularly catastrophic effects on American businesses in the current difficult economic environment.

II. The Committee Should Reject the New Definition of "Government Money or Property" to Cover Private Contract and Tort Disputes With No Loss to the Federal Treasury

A. Summary

Section 2 of S. 2041 would define "Government money or property" to include any money the Government possesses, handles, or processes in any way, regardless of whether the Government has a property interest in those funds as a matter of law. It would dramatically re-define historical concepts of property and would allow the FCA to be used in disputes over money or property held by a bankruptcy trustee or Federal employee donations made to private charities participating in the Combined Federal Campaign. It constitutes a gross overreaction to issues raised in a very small number of cases that are better addressed through already existing remedies. The proposed amendment would divorce the FCA from the protection of the Federal Treasury and would "federalize" routine private contract disputes between private parties simply because one of the parties receives some Federal funds. In many ways, this effort to dramatically re-characterize "Government money or property" would trivialize the Act and subject the statute to public ridicule and to constitutional challenges that have a high probability of success.

B. Current Law

1. The FCA currently requires a call upon the public fisc

Under current law, the False Claims Act reaches any "claim," which includes "any request or demand which is made to a contractor, grantee, or other recipient if the United States Government provides any portion of the money or property which is requested or demanded, or if the Government will reimburse such contractor, grantee, or other recipient for any portion of the money or property which is requested or demanded." 31 U.S.C. § 3729(c).

For FCA liability to arise under current law, there must be an actual call upon the public fisc. *See, e.g., Harrison v. Westinghouse Savannah River Co.*, 176 F.3d 776, 785 (4th Cir. 1999). The First Circuit held, in *United States v. Rivera*, 55 F.3d 703, 710 (1st Cir. 1995), that the FCA attaches liability not to the underlying fraudulent activity or to the Government's wrongful payment, but to the "claim for payment." Courts must examine whether a false claim or statement actually has "the practical purpose and effect" of causing the Government to pay when it otherwise would not have done so. *Id.* at 710. Similarly, in *United States ex rel. Hutchins v. Wilentz, Goldman and Spitzer*, 253 F.3d 176, 183-84 (3d Cir. 2001), the Third Circuit emphasized that the ultimate payer or reimburser of the claim must be the United States Government.

2. Courts have properly concluded that wages paid to federal employees are not federal funds once they vest in the employee, even if the federal government processes those funds

Under current law, alleged schemes targeting funds that belong to Federal employees are not actionable under the FCA. The proposed amendments, however, would change that, despite the lack of any justifiable Federal interest in such cases.

One relator already tried to pursue a *qui tam* case under this theory, suing the United Way for allegedly misrepresenting its eligibility to participate in the Combined Federal Campaign ("CFC"). The relator claimed that because Federal employees are paid from the U.S. Treasury, "[t]his is a fraud perpetrated on recipients of federal funds to gain access to a portion of those funds." *United States ex rel. Bustamante v. United Way/Crusade of Mercy, Inc.*, No. 98C5551, 2000 WL 690250, at *4 (N.D. Ill. May 25, 2000). Under current law, the court easily rejected this expansive theory of liability, holding that although the federal government, as the employer, is responsible for deducting the designated contribution from an employee's paycheck, this does not convert the employee's personally paid charitable contribution into federal money. . . . [I]t would indeed be an illogical result if any time a federal employee spent her federal wages, she was considered to be expending federal funds and therefore protected from fraud by the FCA.

Id. at *5. *See also Sakote v. District of Columbia*, 56 Fed. Appx. 519 (D.C. Cir. 2003). However, as is explained below, this "illogical result" is exactly what S. 2041 would produce.

C. Analysis of the Proposed Amendment

S. 2041 proposes to define "Government money or property" as "money or property belonging to the United States Government; money or property the United States Government provides, has provided or will reimburse to a contractor, grantee, agent or other recipient to be spent or used on the Government's behalf or to advance Government programs; or money or property belonging to any 'administrative beneficiary.'" S. 2041, § 2(1)(b)(2).

An "administrative beneficiary" is further defined in a proposed new definition as any "natural person or entity, including any governmental or quasi-governmental entity, on whose behalf the United States Government, alone or with others, collects, possesses, transmits, administers, manages, or acts as custodian of money or property." *Id.* § (2)(1)(b)(4).

1. The proposed legislation would disassociate fca liability from the act of submitting claims to the federal government

By changing the definition of Government funds, the amendment alters the definition of "claim" — removing from the liability assessment the critical element of Government approval or denial of payment — and thus eliminates that which is the "*sine qua non* of liability under the FCA: the submission of the false claim to the Government." *See, e.g., United States ex rel. Karvelas v. Melrose-Wakefield Hosp.*, 360 F.3d 220, 225 (1st Cir. 2004); *United States ex rel. Clausen v. Lab. Corp. of Am., Inc.*, 290 F.3d 1301, 1311 (11th Cir. 2002). By allowing FCA liability to extend to transactions between individuals based on some loose "association" with the Government rather than on the relatively well-defined act involved in an affirmative decision — *by the Government* — to pay or not to pay claims, the bill would change the statute's fundamental concern from preventing fraud against the Government to something completely different. It would apply the Act's lower intent threshold, punitive damages, and mandatory penalties to non-governmental transactions that are now covered by the higher intent standards that states require for proving common law fraud. Changing the law so drastically represents a fundamental policy change that should not occur because of a poorly conceived or unintended response to a few cases that resulted in rulings adverse to *qui tam* relators. They are not "corrections" to the law, but rather drastic changes to both common law and the FCA.

2. The proposed amendments would federalize disputes between private parties

The primary flaw in the proposed language re-defining "Government money or property" is the breadth of subsections (b) and (c). Viewed literally and broadly, a disputed claim to a Federal employee or retiree or Social Security beneficiary — who is arguably paid with Federal funds "to advance Government programs" — would be swept under the False Claims Act. This would include claims by roofers, contractors, or landscapers who work at the private homes of Government employees, grantors, or contractors. Although the drafters clearly tried to avoid a broad result by inserting language purportedly limiting the application of the FCA to "money to be spent or used on Government programs," that effort is undone by the language that follows — a virtually limitless category of sums spent "to advance Government programs." Clearly, wages paid to Federal employees and benefits paid to Social Security beneficiaries advance Government interests and would thus lead to the absurd scenarios described above.

Relators will also inevitably assert that the allegations easily rejected in *Bustamante* are a valid basis for liability under this theory. In the unlikely event that they fail under the legislation's new definition of what qualifies as Government money or property, S. 2041 provides a generous second chance: FCA plaintiffs would also argue that the Federal Government transmits and administers money on behalf of Federal employees and CFC charities as "administrative beneficiaries." The 2007 list of CFC charities contains the names of 2,053 organizations, including the Tibet Fund, the Desmund Tutu Peace Foundation, and Bikes Not Bombs, Inc. Even if one assumes that an outright fraud has been committed against one of these organizations, it is difficult to understand how relatively small donations made with the personal funds of Federal employees justify the application of the civil FCA in such circumstances, particularly when the costs of such litigation described above are considered.

3. The proposed legislation intrudes on rights traditionally reserved to the states

Section 2 of S. 2041 would transform disputes traditionally addressed through state tort, contract, or fraud law into — literally — a Federal case. This raises significant federalism concerns because it shifts functions traditionally reserved to the states to individual whistleblowers and DOJ. S. 2041 creates a Federal fraud statute for private frauds, which is both unprecedented and, we hope, unintended.

This would have a particularly adverse effect on the cost of commercial products. Under this amendment, an allegedly defective product would, if purchased by a Federal employee (or Social Security recipient or any person or entity receiving Federal funds), be subject to the treble damages and penalty provisions of the Act. The cost of such litigation would cause the price for those products to skyrocket, even though such disputes have traditionally been resolved under state tort law.

4. The proposed legislation is a gross overreaction to a small number of cases involving unusual facts

The sponsors of this amendment explained that it is intended to overrule *United States ex rel. DRC, Inc. v. Custer Battles, LLC*, 376 F. Supp. 2d 617 (E.D. Va. 2005), which is now on appeal to the U.S. Court of Appeals for the Fourth Circuit. That decision, which is still on appeal, concerned allegedly false claims to the Coalition Provisional Authority ("CPA") in Iraq, an international entity that ceased to exist in 2004.[7] This is one case out of thousands brought under the FCA since 1986. Even if published reports of other sealed cases involving allegedly false claims to the CPA are true, amending the False Claims Act so drastically to allow it to apply to a small category of cases that are so unique — and incapable of repetition — is simply unnecessary and threatens the viability of American businesses.

5. The proposed legislation would be vulnerable to constitutional challenges that are very likely to be successful

This provision, if enacted, will face vigorous constitutional challenge. The Supreme Court has held in a series of decisions that FCA damages and penalties that exceed a reasonable multiple of the actual loss to the Government are unconstitutional under both the Due Process and Excessive Fines Clauses. *United States v. Halper*, 490 U.S. 435 (1989); *Hudson v. United States*, 522 U.S. 93 (1997) (stating that "[t]he Due Process and Equal Protection Clauses already protect individuals from sanctions which are downright irrational [and] [t]he Eighth Amendment protects against excessive civil fines"); *see also United States v. Mackby*, 261 F.3d 821, 831 (9th Cir. 2001) (ruling that because FCA damages and penalties have a punitive purpose, they both must be analyzed under the Eighth Amendment to determine whether they are unconstitutionally excessive). By definition, the Government suffers no economic loss when non-Government funds are at stake. There is, therefore, serious question as to whether such a provision, if passed, would survive a constitutional challenge.

Even more fundamentally, the question for the Senate is whether it wishes to impose on an even broader sector of the American economy the type of litigation described in the Introduction — where the False Claims Act is wielded as a sledgehammer in litigations involving an almost endless universe of organizations, entities, and beneficiaries whose transactions would potentially fall within the reach of the FCA under the sweeping definitions found in Section 2 of this proposed legislation.

III. The Committee Should Reject the Amendment Allowing Nonwhistleblowers to Bring *Qui Tam* Cases by Eliminating the "Public Disclosure/Original Source" Defense

A. Summary

Section 4 of S. 2041 effectively eliminates a core tenet of *qui tam* enforcement — encouraging whistleblowers to come forward with new allegations of fraud against the Government. The Government pays up to 30% of all recoveries to a *qui tam* plaintiff because that person is a true whistleblower who exposes a fraud that has escaped the attention of the Federal Government. Section 4 of S. 2041 abandons that sensible approach and instead allows relators to turn public information into a winning lottery ticket for no other reason than the relators were the first to file a *qui tam* case and thus entitled to their share of the Government's recovery, even though they brought no new fraud allegations to the attention of the Government.

One of the most effective bars to meritless and parasitic lawsuits under the False Claims Act has been and continues to be the "public disclosure" bar that Congress included as part of the 1986 Amendments. The public disclosure bar allows defendants to seek dismissal if the relator's case is based on publicly disclosed information and the *qui tam* relator is not an "original source" to the Government.[8] This jurisdictional defense was the result of Congress' legitimate efforts in 1986 to strike a balance between the twin goals of preventing such "parasitic exploitation" of public information while still encouraging legitimate "whistleblowers" to give the Government important substantive information about fraud. The provisions of S. 2041 turn that delicate balance on its head, creating ample prospects for opportunistic relators to recycle stale information as they file parasitic suits that do little to enhance the Government's fraud investigation. Indeed, the bill would allow recovery in so-called "whistleblower" cases by those who are not whistleblowers at all.

In the end, the proposed elimination of the public disclosure/original source defense in *qui tam* cases will not increase the recovery of money lost to the U.S. Treasury from fraud. Instead, this provision will simply enrich the plaintiffs' bar and increase the costs of *qui tam* litigation to innocent American companies and institutions. By effectively eliminating the "public disclosure/original source" defense, these amendments will force American businesses and institutions to defend themselves against *qui tam* relators who do not bring any new fraud allegations to the attention of the Government.

B. Current Law

The purpose, of course, of the *qui tam* provisions of the False Claims Act is to "enhance the Government's ability to recover losses sustained as a result of fraud against the Government." S. Rep. No. 99-345, at 1 (1986), *reprinted in* 1986 U.S.C.A.A.N. 5266, 5266.

Qui tam enforcement accomplishes this goal by encouraging "private individuals who are aware of fraud being perpetrated against the Government to bring such information forward" in exchange for a percentage of the Government's ultimate recovery. H.R. Rep. No. 99-660, at 22 (1986). In other words, the *qui tam* enforcement mechanism essentially allows the Government to "purchase" from private citizens the information they may have about fraud on the U.S. Treasury. *United States ex rel. Russell v. Epic Healthcare Mgmt. Group*, 193 F.3d 304, 309 (5th Cir. 1999).

The effectiveness of *qui tam* enforcement, however, also makes it susceptible to abuse by opportunistic bounty hunters masquerading as whistleblowers. Creating a statutory scheme that weeds out the former and encourages the latter has proved to be a tricky task. Thus, there should be no surprise that "[t]he history of the FCA *qui tam* provisions demonstrates repeated congressional efforts to walk a fine line between encouraging whistle-blowing and discouraging opportunistic behavior." *United States ex rel. Springfield Terminal Railway Co. v. Quinn*, 14 F.3d 645, 651 (D.C. Cir. 1994).

In 1986, after over 100 years of living with two different extremes — one that allowed parasitic *qui tam* relators to cut and paste allegations from the Government's own pleadings and another that disallowed *qui tam* suits where the Government had knowledge of the information even if the relator was the Government's source[9] — Congress forged a more balanced approach to screening for proper *qui tam* relators when it enacted the "public disclosure/original source" provision codified in 31 U.S.C. § 3730(e)(4). This provision states in full:

> (4) (A) No court shall have jurisdiction over an action under this section based upon the public disclosure of allegations or transactions in a criminal, civil, or administrative hearing, in a congressional, administrative, or Government Accounting Office report, hearing, audit, or

> investigation, or from the news media, unless the action is brought by the Attorney General or the person bringing the action is an original source of the information.
>
> (B) For purposes of this paragraph, "original source" means an individual who has direct and independent knowledge of the information on which the allegations are based and has voluntarily provided the information to the Government before filing an action under this section which is based on the information.

31 U.S.C. § 3730(e)(4). Although not without its own ambiguities and interpretive challenges, Section 3730(e)(4) deprives courts of jurisdiction over claims that are based upon publicly disclosed allegations and transactions unless the relator is an "original source."

Lower courts have long understood Section 3730(e)(4)'s public disclosure provision to be a "quick trigger" test that, if necessary, will lead to the more nuanced original source analysis to determine whether the particular *qui tam* relator in a given case is a true whistleblower. *See United States ex rel. Fine v. MK-Ferguson Co.*, 99 F.3d 1538, 1545 (10th Cir. 1996); *United States ex rel. Hagood v. Sonoma Co. Water Agency*, 81 F.3d 1465, 1476 n.18 (9th Cir. 1996); *Cooper v. Blue Cross & Blue Shield of Fla., Inc.*, 19 F.3d 562, 568 n.10 (11th Cir. 1994) (per curiam). The "original source" analysis is designed "to bar parasitic suits through which a plaintiff seeks a reward even though he has contributed nothing significant to the exposure of fraud," *United States ex rel. Devlin v. State of California*, 84 F.3d 358, 362 (9th Cir. 1996), and the original source provisions are structured "to encourage individuals who are either close observers or involved in the fraudulent activity to come forward" and to avoid "windfalls for people with secondhand knowledge," *United States ex rel. Kinney v. Stoltz*, 327 F.3d 671, 674 (8th Cir. 2003). Taken together, this scheme is designed to obtain "the golden mean between adequate incentives for whistle-blowing insiders with genuinely valuable information and discouragement of opportunistic plaintiffs who have no significant information to contribute of their own." *United States ex rel. Fine v. Sandia Corp.*, 70 F.3d 568, 571 (10th Cir. 1995) (internal quotation marks and citation omitted).

C. Analysis of the Proposed Amendment

S. 2041 entirely dismantles the balance to *qui tam* enforcement that Congress achieved with the 1986 Amendments — amendments that allowed true whistleblowers to proceed with their actions while at the same time allowing defendants the opportunity, early in the litigation, to fend off truly parasitic *qui tam* suits. This bill abandons that sensible approach and, instead, effectively returns the FCA to the infamous pre-1943 days of "parasitic exploitation of the public coffers," where copying information from the Government's own criminal indictment could serve as a basis for a successful *qui tam* suit. *Springfield Terminal Railway*, 14 F.3d at 649 (citing *Marcus v. Hess*, 317 U.S. 537 (1943)). This bill also discards over 20 years of developed case law, culminating in the Supreme Court's recent decision in *Rockwell International Corp. v. United States*, 127 S. Ct. 1397 (U.S. 2007), that has brought the current public disclosure/original source provisions into sharper focus.

The proposed bill hits American companies and institutions with a triple whammy: (1) it neutralizes the meaning of "public disclosure," (2) it strips defendants of their standing to challenge relators who fail to meet the jurisdictional bar, and (3) it eliminates the requirement that the relator be an original source and instead substitutes a new threshold (whether the relator provides any "essential element of liability") that is so low almost any competent attorney could draft a complaint to satisfy it. This wholesale abandonment of the public disclosure/original source provisions of the current FCA is unwarranted and will revolutionize *qui tam* enforcement, but not in a good way.

1. The definition of "public disclosure" is far too narrow

S. 2041 redefines the term "public disclosure" to mean "the public disclosure of allegations or transactions in a Federal criminal, civil, or administrative hearing, in a congressional, Federal administrative, or Government Accountability Office report, hearing, audit or investigation, or from the news media." S. 2041, § 4(b). It goes further, though, to narrow the definition even more by limiting public disclosures to include "only disclosures made on the public record or that have otherwise been disseminated broadly to the general public." *Id.*

Thus, under the proposed bill, public information does *not* include information from state and local proceedings, hearings, administrative reports, audits, or investigations, regardless of whether the Federal Government already has that information or has access to it. Moreover, by redefining "public disclosure" to mean only those disclosures made on the public record or disseminated broadly to the general public, opportunistic relators will be permitted to scavenge suits from otherwise public information that does not meet this new "public record" or "disseminated broadly to the general public" standard. Indeed, the very term "disseminated broadly to the general public" defies clear definition — does that mean it has to be in the *New York Times*, or will the Scranton *Times-Tribune* suffice?

The bottom line effect of this amendment will be to encourage more *qui tam* cases based on public information by relators who add nothing to the Government's knowledge or fraud fighting efforts. This means that anyone in Juneau, Alaska, with Internet access, a PACER account, and enough patience to monitor pleadings filed in the U.S. District Court for the Southern District of Florida could cobble together a *qui tam* complaint from criminal indictments filed against any federal contractor in Miami, never mind whether the purported whistleblower has ever *witnessed* any fraudulent activity by the defendants, ever *met* the alleged perpetrators, or even *visited* Miami.

2. The elimination of the defendant's ability to dismiss parasitic cases is unwarranted

S. 2041 also strips a defendant of its standing to challenge the jurisdiction of a *qui tam* relator who brings a case based on publicly available information. A defendant's ability to make this kind of challenge, however, has been a mainstay of the False Claims Act since 1943. This jurisdictional defense has allowed defendants to bring to an early end those parasitic cases that should never have been brought in the first place. This bill, instead, provides that only the United States may challenge the status of a *qui tam* relator, thus providing defendants no defense or remedy whatsoever when they face *qui tam* suits based on public information where the Government has declined to intervene in the case. *See* S. 2041, § 4.

Under the proposed bill, a defendant would have no standing at all to challenge the jurisdiction of a *qui tam* relator who derived every aspect of every element of every claim against it from publicly available, broadly disseminated information found in the news media and openly discussed in Federal hearings. Even the Government would lack the power to challenge a relator who had gathered his key information about the fraud from public sources rather than from his own substantive knowledge and who has built a case on information the Government already has.

Putting aside these more fundamental flaws in the bill, there still is no reason to deprive defendants of the ability to seek dismissal of parasitic *qui tam* suits. Stripping defendants of their standing to challenge the jurisdiction of relators who have filed frivolous claims effectively eliminates the jurisdictional bar altogether. The Government has consistently demonstrated that it lacks the resources and the willingness to challenge a relator's satisfaction of the jurisdictional bar and usually does so only on those few occasions when a dispute occurs concerning a relator's claim to a settlement. The Government, instead, has relied on the resources of defendants to challenge parasitic lawsuits.

By placing the burden solely on the DOJ, S. 2041 places yet another burden on the limited resources of the DOJ. The Government already must investigate every *qui tam* lawsuit to determine whether to intervene in the case (*see* 31 U.S.C. § 3730(b)). With this bill all but eliminating the requirement that *qui tam* relators be true whistleblowers, a dramatic proliferation in the filing of *qui tam* suits is sure to follow, and the DOJ will have to investigate each and every one of these suits. The DOJ does not have the resources, and likely will not have the inclination, to seek dismissal of even those cases that qualify for dismissal under the otherwise stringent public disclosure provisions of S. 2041.

3. The grounds for dismissal are too narrow

Moreover, even in the rare circumstance where the Government might seek dismissal of a parasitic *qui tam* action, S. 2041 erects such a high threshold for obtaining such a dismissal that there would be very few motions, if any, that could succeed. The bill allows dismissal of only those cases where "the allegations relating to *all essential* elements of liability" are based "*exclusively* on the public disclosure." S. 2041, § 4 (emphasis added). Meeting *that* burden will be, quite literally, impossible, especially at an early stage of the litigation. This hurdle, such as it is, could be overcome by a relator basing just part of any one of the allegations that comprise the elements of a False Claims Act violation — *including* a general allegation that the defendant acted with the requisite "knowledge" (either actual knowledge, deliberate ignorance, or reckless disregard), *see* 31 U.S.C. § 3729(b) — on anything other than the public disclosure. Rather than shifting the law to give relators the benefit of this low threshold, the focus should remain, as the law does now, on examining the relator's knowledge of the substance of the alleged fraud.

This "all essential elements" test is also misguided. More importantly, it is difficult to understand why a *qui tam* lawsuit should go forward simply because at least some of the relator's allegations were derived from one source that, for one reason or another, does not qualify as a "public disclosure," when those same allegations and transactions were described in detail in a GAO report (for example) published the year before. There is little reason for the Government to pay a bounty to a relator who was savvy enough not to base his entire *qui tam* complaint on the contents of the GAO report (either out of ignorance of the report or by design) when the purpose of paying that bounty in the first place is to encourage whistleblowers to inform the Government of fraud.

4. The "source" of the public information should be irrelevant

Finally, although Section 4 of S. 2041 appears to include a provision meant to be an analog to the current "original source" requirement, this provision only allows a court to *reduce* a *qui tam* relator's bounty at the end of a case. Specifically, this provision allows a court to reduce the share of the proceeds for *qui tam* relators who derive their knowledge "primarily from specific information relating to the allegations or transactions" that the Government publicly disclosed or privately disclosed to the relators "in the course of its investigation." S. 2041, § 4.

Two features of this provision render it almost a nullity. First, a court must find that the relator not only derived some of his knowledge from a public disclosure — the court must find that the relator derived his knowledge "*primarily* from *specific* information relating to the allegations or transactions" in the public disclosure. (Emphasis added.) These limitations all but ensure that the only relators who will get caught by this provision are those who literally cut and paste their complaints from public disclosures obtained from the Government. Second, for the very few relators who may qualify for a reduction under this new provision, the reality is that even 5% or 10% of a multi-million dollar judgment is better than nothing. The low risk that a court, at the end of the case, *might* reduce a parasitic *qui tam* relator's share is simply too remote and, in any event, too insignificant to discourage such relators. And, perhaps more importantly, this provision would do absolutely nothing to discourage the attorneys of parasitic *qui tam* relators — S. 2041 does nothing to change the current provision in 31 U.S.C. § 3730(d)(4) that awards attorneys' fees and costs to successful *qui tam* relators.

5. The amendment further erodes the constitutionality of qui tam enforcement

The Chamber has taken the consistent position that *qui tam* enforcement of the False Claims Act is unconstitutional under Article II of the U.S. Constitution, as it violates the Separation of Powers doctrine. *See Morrison v. Olson*, 487 U.S. 654 (1988) (the "degree of control exercised by the executive branch over a suit on behalf of the United States is determinative of the separation of powers issue"). We submit that, through the *qui tam* enforcement provisions, Congress has improperly delegated prosecutorial functions to private persons, whereas the Constitution vests the power to execute the laws exclusively in the executive branch. U.S. Const. art. II, § 3. *Qui tam* enforcement also violates the Due Process Clause because the provisions authorize representation of the United States by parties whose financial interests in the cases they prosecute unavoidably conflict with the duty of a government representative to seek a just and fair result. *Cf. Young v. United States ex rel. Vuitton et Fils S.A.*, 481 U.S. 787, 811-13 (1987) (holding that counsel for a party that is the beneficiary of a court order may not be appointed as a prosecutor in a contempt action alleging a violation of that order). The provisions of S. 2041 that eliminate the original source/public disclosure requirements only heighten the constitutional concerns that courts will consider in the future.

The False Claims Act has had a jurisdictional public disclosure bar since 1943. By redefining what constitutes a "public disclosure" and by eliminating altogether the "original source" provisions of the current law, S. 2041 renders this jurisdictional bar a dead letter. Rather than rewarding *qui tam* relators who come forward with knowledge about fraud on the Federal Treasury, S. 2041 opens the door to a wave of parasitic lawsuits by the relators' bar while at the same time slamming shut the one procedure by which such suits can be exposed. Section 4 of S. 2041 should not be adopted.

IV. THE COMMITTEE SHOULD REJECT THE AMENDMENT ENCOURAGING FEDERAL EMPLOYEES TO ABUSE THEIR GOVERNMENT POSITIONS BY FILING *QUI TAM* SUITS

A. Summary

The Senate should not, under any circumstances, pass Section 3 of S. 2041, which allows former and current Government employees to enrich themselves by filing *qui tam* cases based on information gained as Government employees. This is bad public policy. Such suits destroy any respect and deference given to Government employees who interact with the American public and who demand and receive the most confidential and sensitive information on individual citizens, companies, and institutions. Allowing Government employees to misappropriate that information to enrich themselves is the best way to degrade and undermine Government functions.

Courts have long recognized, and the DOJ consistently agrees, that this is bad public policy. The proposal to "clarify" existing law by explicitly allowing Government employees to act as relators is an open invitation to suits by Government accountants, auditors, investigators, attorneys, and technical staff, creating clear conflicts of interest, perpetuating perverse incentives, undermining the credibility of Federal employees, and advancing the personal financial interest of Government employees and their lawyers — all at the public's expense. The proposed "safeguards" set forth is S. 2014 to avoid abuse are unworkable and restrictive, to the point that any protections they offer are illusory. The American public will understand only one thing: They are being sued by a Government employee using Government information for personal gain. That is toxic.

Instead of barring *qui tam* suits by Government employees, this bill for the first time explicitly allows such suits. The proposed legislation strips defendants of their standing to challenge suits by Government employee relators, instead granting this right only to the Government and then making it practically impossible for the Government to prevail on such a motion.

Under this flawed scheme, the Government would only have 60 days to move to dismiss a Government employee relator, even where the relator's action is derived from an "open and active fraud investigation by the Government" and then only if "*all* the necessary and material allegations" were derived from that investigation. S. 2041, § 3 (emphasis added). The other ground for the DOJ to seek dismissal is if the relator failed to first notify his agency's Inspector General, the Attorney General, and his supervisor before filing. Based on these requirements, only the most egregious cases of interference with a Government investigation — where the *qui tam* allegations were derived directly from an active Government investigation that had elicited a high degree of specific information — would subject a *qui tam* suit to dismissal. Under the great number of other circumstances, the Government lacks the ability to challenge a Government employee's attempt to use Government information gained on the job to enrich herself and destroy the Government's relationship with the American people.

The "protections" in the proposed amendment are woefully inadequate to avoid the harm that will come by allowing Government employees to use Government information to enrich themselves. Instead of protecting those who are regulated by the Government and expect Government employees to act in good faith, the amendment practically encourages auditors, investigators, and regulators to file such suits.

B. Current Law

1. Pre-1986 law

Prior to the 1986 Amendments, Government employees could not file *qui tam* suits because of a jurisdictional prohibition in the law. In 1943, in response to the filing of parasitic *qui tam* actions based upon publicly disclosed indictments and hearings, Congress amended the False Claims Act to prohibit suits based upon information already possessed by the Government. *See, e.g., Pettis ex rel. United States v. Morrison-Knudsen Co.*, 577 F.2d 668, 671 (9th Cir. 1978). This 1943 amendment effectively barred Government employees from filing *qui tam* actions by prohibiting actions "based upon evidence or information in the possession of the United States, or any agency, officer, or employee thereof, at the time such suit was brought." 31 U.S.C. § 232(C) (1976).

Recognizing that this provision unduly restricted *qui tam* enforcement by true whistleblowers, Congress eliminated this provision in 1986 and replaced it with the "public disclosure/original source" limitation found in the current law, 31 U.S.C. § 3730(e)(4). The legislative history to the 1986 Amendments contains no indication that Congress intended — for the first time — to allow Government employees to bring *qui tam* cases, for their own financial benefit, based on information learned on the job. In fact Congress never intended to allow Government employees to bring *qui tam* actions by abusing their positions.

2. The law after the 1986 amendments

While there was no indication in 1986 that Congress intended to change prior law with regard to *qui tam* suits by Government employees, the result of the change in statutory language had an unintended result. Despite vigorous and consistent opposition by the Government since 1986, most courts have reluctantly allowed *qui tam* suits by Government employees to proceed. Although many judges have severely criticized this result (see below), most courts have held that the current language of Section 3730(e)(4) left them no choice. For this reason, challenges to Government *qui tam* relators then shifted to other defenses. Importantly, current law gives both defendants and the Government latitude to challenge the right of Government employees to bring *qui tam* cases.

Where a *qui tam* action is based upon publicly disclosed allegations, the relator must be an "original source" of that information. 31 U.S.C. § 3730(e)(4); *United States ex rel. Fine v. Chevron, U.S.A., Inc.*, 72 F.3d 740, 741 (9th Cir. 1995). To qualify as an "original source," the relator must *voluntarily* provide the information forming the basis of the claim to the Government prior to filing the suit. *Chevron*, 72 F.3d at741. Where a Government employee provides the information underlying his claims as part of his job responsibilities, courts have held that such a disclosure is not made "voluntarily" within the meaning of the False Claims Act and the relator therefore is not an original source. *Id.*

The Ninth Circuit in *Chevron* premised its decision on this logic. There, the putative relator was an auditor within the Office of Inspector General of the Department of Energy. *Id.* His job required him to supervise audits that other employees had conducted and to edit audit reports that others had written; as many as 97% of the audit reports from the Western Region Audit Office came from employees under his supervision. *Id.* As the court wrote, "he was a salaried Government employee, compelled to disclose fraud by the very terms of his employment. He no more voluntarily provided information to the Government than we, as Federal judges, voluntary hear arguments and draft dispositions." *Id.* at 743 -44.

In finding that a Government employee was ineligible to act as a relator, the First Circuit, in *United States ex rel. LeBlanc v. Raytheon Co.*, 913 F.2d 17 (1st Cir. 1990), based its decision on different reasoning, but reached the same result. There, the court said that the Government employee's knowledge could not qualify as "independent" since his employment was conditioned on the duty to uncover fraud, rendering the "fruits of his effort" the property of his employer.

Existing law, however, by no means provides an absolute jurisdictional bar to Government employees acting as relators under many circumstances. The rationale for the dismissal of the Government employee relators in the cases referenced above only occurred because the allegations had been "publicly disclosed." Without such disclosure, the case proceeds. In *United States ex rel. Williams v. NEC Corp.*, 931 F.2d 1493 (11th Cir. 1991), for example, an Air Force attorney discovered suspected bid rigging on Federal contracts in Japan. He reported the allegations to his superiors and then filed a *qui tam* suit. Because the allegations had not been made public and the Air Force attorney/relator complied with the procedural requirements of the FCA, the Eleventh Circuit ruled that he was a proper *qui tam* plaintiff. Mr. Williams therefore became eligible for as much as $30 million, or 30% of the settlement.

As the *Williams* case demonstrates, courts have reluctantly allowed some Government employees to bring *qui tam* cases under very limited circumstances despite DOJ's efforts. Even these limited circumstances, however, have been criticized by judges and commentators as improper.

C. Analysis of the Proposed Amendment

1. Sound public policy requires rejection of this amendment

No matter how they arrive at their conclusion, courts generally tend toward the same result: Government employees should not be permitted to receive a financial windfall for merely doing their jobs. *See United States ex rel. Biddle v. Board of Trustees of Leland Stanford, Jr. Univ.*, 147 F.3d 821, 829 (9th Cir. 1998). According to one editorial discussion of certain Government employee suits, "the conflict of interest here is as clear as it would be if judges were empowered to set fines and keep a percentage of everything they collect." *Qui Tam Scam*, WASH. POST, Dec. 26, 1991, at A22.

Citing a brief by the Government, the *Chevron* court offered a persuasive and comprehensive statement on the relator status of Government employees, and the perverse incentives that unfettered relator status creates:

> To spend work time looking for personally remunerative cases . . . rather than doing their assigned work; to conceal information about fraud from superiors and government prosecutors so that they can capitalize on it for personal gain; to race the government to the courthouse to file ongoing audit and investigatory matters as *qui tam* actions before those cases have been sufficiently developed by the government to justify a lawsuit, this prematurely tipping off the target, undermining the likely effectiveness of the case, and diverting unnecessarily up to 30% of the government's recovery to the government employee; and to use the substantial powers of the federal government conferred upon public investigators . . . to advance their personal financial interests . . . . Public confidence in the integrity and impartiality of Government audits and investigations will necessarily decrease.

Chevron, 72 F.3d at 745, citing Amicus Brief of the United States in Support of Defendants- Appellees' Petitions for Rehearing and Suggestions for Rehearing En Banc at 8-9 (footnotes omitted).

The concurring opinion of Judge Trott in the *Chevron* case acknowledged this policy consideration and argued that Government employees should therefore be prohibited from bringing a *qui tam* suit. The judge's examples are devastating:

> Permitting auditors to sue literally would destroy the government's anti-fraud and anti-waste programs. The "perverse incentives" outlined by the government and adopted by the majority exceed worrisome. Imagine, for example, an employee of the IRS bringing a *qui tam* lawsuit against a company that the employee had just audited on behalf of the government. Shades of the days leading up to the French Revolution of 1789 when taxes were collected by a private concern called the "Ferme Generale," or "Tax Farm." The first to be guillotined in the Place de la Revolution during the incarnadine Reign of Terror were the hated private tax collectors who made a profit by collecting more from the public than the amount needed by the government. One day, *Inspector* Fine uses the awesome power of the federal government to investigate you; the next, *Mr.* Fine uses the information he pries loose from you with that power to augment his bank account. Can anyone say when Inspector Fine wields the coercive tools of the government that he is also not working for himself? Dr. Jekyll one day, Mr. Hyde the next. Such an abuse could only cause the public to distrust government officials even more than the public already does.

Chevron, 72 F.3d at 747-48.

Other Federal law prohibits parties from making, and certain Government employees from receiving, payments that compensate those employees for their Government service. 18 U.S.C. § 209(a). Another provision prescribes criminal and civil penalties for violation of that provision. 18 U.S.C. § 216.

2. The POGO case

A recently-tried case demonstrates the evils of allowing Government employees to profit from *qui tam* cases. That case, *United States v. Project on Government Oversight*, underscores the potential for abuse when they do so. In that case, a senior economist with the Department of the Interior, Robert Berman, was given a $383,600 "public service award" from the Project on Government Oversight ("POGO") after POGO was one of several *qui tam* plaintiffs to secure a *qui tam* settlement stemming from the oil industry's alleged underpayment of royalties to the Government. In fact, that "award" was really a payment to Mr. Berman pursuant to an agreement with POGO to pay him 10% of whatever POGO recovered in its *qui tam* suits. In pursuit of its case, POGO published four investigative reports that contained citations to memoranda written by Mr. Berman. Moreover, around the time that POGO was making its efforts to initiate an action against the oil companies in question, Mr. Berman was himself allegedly participating in proposed rulemaking governing valuation for oil royalties. The United States maintained that, while he was employed at the Department of the Interior, Mr. Berman drafted a memorandum to the director of the agency responsible for managing oil royalties that contained suggestions intended to "ensure that the pending *qui tam* litigation would not be jeopardized."

After the scheme became public, the Government filed suit against both POGO and Mr. Berman, claiming the "public service award" violated 18 U.S.C. § 209(a). On February 11, 2008, the jury found both Mr. Berman and POGO guilty of violating that law. *See generally United States v. Project on Government Oversight,* Civil Action No. 03 -0096 (JDB), Memorandum Opinion 12/3/07 and Verdict Form 2/1/08.

Cases like *Project on Government Oversight* make clear the potential for self-enrichment that the provisions of S. 2041 offer to Government employees. Government employees are in the unique position of interpreting the very rules and regulations that are the basis for allegations that companies violate the False Claims Act. Their interpretation must be above reproach and unaffected by personal conflicts. If Congress is to amend the rules on Government employee relators in any way, it should amend existing law to ensure that Government employees are not presented with conflicts of interest which threaten not only their own integrity but also the integrity of the programs, investigations, and audits with which the public has entrusted them. As currently written, S. 2041 would strip defendants of their standing to challenge relators' jurisdiction to file suit and leave the Government virtually powerless to dismiss many suits by Government employee relators. Such an amendment stands to undermine the very policies that form the foundation of the False Claims Act.

3. The "exceptions" in S. 2014 would allow more government employees to file qui tam cases

Under S. 2041, the DOJ can dismiss a Government employee's *qui tam* case if it is based on an "open and active fraud investigation," but only under the following conditions: (1) the DOJ motion must be filed no more than 60 days after the relator files the case under seal and serves the Government and (2) all necessary and specific material allegations must derive from that open and active investigation. There is no rational basis for these restrictions.

If there is an existing "open and active fraud investigation," why should the Government reward any *qui tam* relator for filing such a suit, much less one who learned of the allegations as a Government employee? Why is DOJ only given 60 days to move to have the relator dismissed? The DOJ may not even be aware of a grand jury or Inspector General investigation within that time period. Why must "all necessary and specific material allegations" derive from that investigation? These restrictions encourage Government auditors and investigators to misappropriate information they receive on the job and file *qui tam* cases to enrich themselves.

S. 2041 also allows a Government employee to bring a *qui tam* case if he or she notifies his or her agency's Inspector General (or the Attorney General) and if, after 12 months, the DOJ has not filed an FCA suit. This allows a Government auditor, investigator, or regulator to bring a *qui tam* action even if the agency and DOJ determine there was no fraud.

One cannot imagine a more outrageous situation: The Federal regulatory agency and the chief enforcement agency conclude that no fraud exists, yet a Government employee, using Government information, can sue a regulated entity and attempt to force a settlement to enrich himself.

Allowing *qui tam* suits by Government employees will destroy whatever trust and confidence exists between the American people and the Government employees who regulate them. If Congress is to amend the False Claims Act, it should amend it to prohibit — without exception — all *qui tam* suits by Government employees based on information gained as a Government employee.

V. The Committee Should Reject the Amendment Creating An Administrative Nightmare for American Businesses and Federal Grantees by Extending the Statute of Limitations and the Tolling Provisions

A. Summary

Two provisions of Section 6 of S. 2041 dramatically lengthen the time period for filing *qui tam* cases. By extending the statute of limitations to 10 years in all cases, regardless of actual Government knowledge of the alleged fraud, S. 2041 allows the Government or a *qui tam* relator to bring a lawsuit long after the documents and witnesses essential to the case have disappeared.

This same proposed amendment also provides that this lengthy limitations period does not even begin to run in a *qui tam* case until that case is unsealed. Today, cases often are not unsealed for at least 2 years after filing, and many are not unsealed for over 5 years, since there are no legal limits on how long a *qui tam* case can remain under seal. Nor is there any requirement in existing law that the Government give notice to a defendant of the pendency of a sealed *qui tam* case.

If amended as proposed, the False Claims Act will have one of the longest statutes of limitations in all Federal law. It will require any individuals, institutions, or companies that receive money from, or pay money to, the Federal Government to retain records and files almost forever. Witnesses who can explain the circumstances of a business relationship, contract term, or claim process will inevitably retire, disappear, or die in the decade or more that transpires between the relevant events and the subsequent litigation. Even when witnesses remain available, memories — especially regarding the kinds of details that can make or break an FCA case — grow increasingly unreliable with each passing year. Access to critical documents in the files of third parties or Government agencies will be unavailable. This will create an administrative nightmare for anyone dealing with the Government and make it extraordinarily difficult to mount a defense to such stale claims.

B. Current Law

The False Claims Act currently requires that that the Government bring an action within 6 years of submission of the alleged false claim, or within three years of the date that the Government learns, or should have learned, that a fraud has been, or might have been, committed. There is also a 10-year cutoff date for all actions, *see* 31 U.S.C. § 3731(b), but this 10-year period applies only when the Government is not aware of the alleged fraud. Where the Government *is* aware of the fraud, however, the limitations period is 6 years. The 10-year repose provision was meant as an ultimate cutoff date to protect defendants from precisely the scenario threatened today — litigation of stale issues from the distant past. The limitations period prescribed under current law forces the Government to act expeditiously when it learns of an alleged fraud so that defendants are aware of the allegations and can retain records, witnesses, and other sources of evidence relevant to the fraud. The proposed legislation turns this system on its head.

Outside the context of False Claims Act cases, civil complaints are not filed under seal and must be served within 120 days of filing, giving a defendant almost immediate notice of the allegations. Fed. R. Civ. P. 4. This is significant because Federal Rule of Civil Procedure 15(c)(2) normally allows an amendment to a pleading to relate back to the date of the original pleading when the claim or defense asserted in the amended pleading arose out of the conduct, transaction, or occurrence set forth in the original pleading. Recent appellate decisions have generally held that the statute of limitations will run despite the fact that a case is under seal; the fact that a case is under seal will not toll the running of the statute.

For example, the Second Circuit recently held that the secrecy of the allegations in *qui tam* complaints filed under seal conflicts with principles of fundamental fairness and common sense. *United States v. Baylor Univ. Med. Ctr.*, 469 F.3d 263 (2d Cir. 2006). Rule 15(c) assumes that a defendant has notice of the allegations once a case has been filed. The *Baylor* court held that a rule that would allow additional allegations to relate back to the date of a *sealed* complaint lacks the necessary notice to defendants of the claims filed against them on the date that the original pleading was filed. The *Baylor* decision rested on the principle of fundamental fairness — that a defendant should not have to defend allegations over 10 years old unless the defendant had been formally notified of those allegations.

The proposed legislation threatens to unravel the balance achieved by the current system, which values notice to defendants and litigation of claims before evidence disappears.

C. Analysis of the Proposed Amendment

The proposed 10-year limitations period is unfair, unworkable, and unprecedented. The proposed amendments in S. 2041 extend the statute of limitations to 10 years in all cases, regardless of Government knowledge of alleged fraud, and overrule the *Baylor* decision by allowing the period a *qui tam* case is under seal to stop the running of the limitations period. *See* S. 2041, § 6.

1. The limitations period unfairly burdens defendants

The 10-year statute of limitations period, coupled with the provision that the statute of limitations is tolled while the case is under seal, would require all organizations that receive money from, or pay money to, the Federal Government — no matter how small, no matter how unsophisticated — to defend themselves for actions that occurred 12, 15 or even 20 years ago, depending on how long a *qui tam* case remains under seal. The amendments would require small businesses, churches, and other similar organizations to keep records for staggering lengths of time. More importantly, witnesses critical to both the interpretation of contracts and regulations, as well as to demonstrating good faith, could be deceased or otherwise unavailable.

The proposed limitations period also poses the risk of subjecting defendants to unfair, seemingly unending delay on the part of the Government. *United States ex rel. Health Outcomes Techs. v. Hallmark Health Sys., Inc.*, 409 F. Supp. 2d 43 (D. Mass. 2006), illustrates the problem. There, the court applied Federal Rule of Civil Procedure 1 5(c)(2) to new allegations that the Government attempted to add as amendments to the original complaint. The court found that the Government's long delay conflicted with the spirit of the False Claims Act. The court wrote, "[a]fter Health Outcomes brought its complaint in 1996, the Government strategically chose not to intervene in the action but rather to stand to one side and pick off defendants *seriatim*. The Government's investigation dragged on incessantly, and with respect to these particular hospital-defendants seven years, until it chose officially to intervene." *Id.* at 50.

In addition to the threat of Government delay, the legislation will provide relators with an opportunity to further delay *qui tam* suits to increase recoveries and force ever higher settlements. Instead of encouraging the Government and *qui tam* relators to bring their cases as quickly as possible, these amendments will encourage more delay because every day brings higher damages and more penalties.

The proposed legislation will subvert existing law on tolling, which is designed to ensure that defendants have notice of the claims against them and can retain documents and other evidence to prepare for litigation.

2. The limitations period is unworkable for the government

In FCA cases, Government documents, as well as the documents of third parties, are almost always critical. Agency documents are particularly critical, since the agency's interpretation of a regulation or contract or grant term is essential to determining whether a particular claim or statement is "false" and to calculating the amount of damages suffered by the Government. By extending the time limitations period to 10, 12 or 15 years, those documents will inevitably become unavailable or irretrievable.

Issues of stale proof will inevitably arise beyond just the context of document retention. The Government and defendants alike will be faced with the unworkable prospect of finding witnesses who are knowledgeable about events that took place years — potentially decades — in the past. Witnesses forget. Witnesses move. Witnesses change their names. Witnesses die. The Government cannot build a case, and parties cannot defend themselves, where witnesses are expected to provide information from the distant past.

3. The limitations period is unprecedented

The proposed limitations period is a complete aberration. A look to other Federal laws with significant damages and civil enforcement mechanisms like those of the False Claims Act is illustrative. Both the Racketeer Influenced and Corrupt Organizations ("RICO") statute, 18 U.S.C. § 1961, and the Clayton Antitrust Act, 15 U.S.C. § 15, like the False Claims Act, contain a private right of action and provide for the recovery of treble damages, costs, and attorneys' fees.

All civil claims under RICO are subject to a 4-year statute of limitations. *Agency Holding Corp. v. Malley-Duff & Assocs., Inc.*, 483 U.S. 143 (1987). The Supreme Court based its decision in *Agency Holding Corp.* on the statute of limitations period found in the civil enforcement provision of the Clayton Antitrust Act, which is also 4 years. *Id.* at 150-56.

The limitations provisions of S. 2041 are drastically out of line with analogous law and are so unreasonably long that they offer few of the protections normally inherent in a statute of limitations.

VI. Expansion of the Whistleblower Retaliation Definition Provision Is Unnecessary

A. Summary

Currently, Section 3730(h) of the FCA provides relief from retaliation by employers against employees who take lawful steps in furtherance of a *qui tam* suit. Section 3730(h) protects employees who have engaged in such protected conduct, but it also protects employers from unfounded claims of retaliation that are not based on protected conduct. S. 2041 invites unfounded claims, however, by eliminating the test for retaliation that requires the employee to take steps in furtherance of FCA allegations that notify the employer about the allegations. S. 2041 substitutes another test that is poorly drafted and ambiguous, under which no clear steps toward initiating FCA claims are apparently required. It also enlarges the pool of individuals who will bring these suits to include those that are not employees and includes protection for undefined actions that are unrelated to FCA claims.

The new standards in the bill are poorly drafted, ambiguous, and overbroad. They remove necessary protections provided under the current law and will open the door to suits that are based on conduct that is unrelated to FCA actions without helping true whistleblowers or the Government.

B. Current Law

Under Section 3730(h), an employee is protected from an employer's retaliation for protected conduct that is defined as:

> lawful acts . . . in furtherance of an action under this section, including investigation for, initiation of, testimony for, or assistance in an action filed or to be filed under this section . . . .

In order to recover under Section 3730(h), employees must show that the following elements are met:

1. that the employee engaged in conduct protected under the statute,
2. that the employer was aware of the protected conduct, and
3. that the employer discriminated against the employee because of her protected conduct.

In applying the FCA's whistleblower protection, courts have looked to the common law and similar statutes for definitions of employer-employee relationships to define the parameters of the protection, but they differ on the correct test that triggers its application. *See, e.g., Neal v. Honeywell*, 33 F.3d 860, 865 (7th Cir. 1994) (whether litigation is a distinct possibility); *United States ex rel. Ramseyer v. Century Healthcare Corp.*, 90 F.3d 1514 (10th Cir. 1996) (if employee's job is to report wrongdoing to supervisors, such reports, without more, would not necessarily meet "in furtherance" test); *Wilkins v. St. Louis Housing Auth.*, 314 F.3d 927, 933 (8th Cir. 2002) (whether reasonable employee would have believed that employer was committing fraud against the Government). No bright line test, such as a requirement that a *qui tam* complaint was filed or that the Government was alerted to the fraud, has developed. Instead, the caselaw in this area establishes the following basic parameters: Where serious allegations of fraud are made by an employee whose job responsibility does not involve investigating fraud in the company, courts are likely to find protected activity, but where the employee's complaints are such that it is the employee's job to disclose such fraud, courts are less likely to find simple complaints protected activity without a distinct possibility of a *qui tam* suit.

C. Analysis of the Proposed Amendment

Section 5 of S. 2041 enlarges the pool of individuals entitled to relief from "any employee" to "any employee, Government contractor, or agent" and removes from the definition of retaliatory acts the requirement that limits them to acts "by . . . [the] employer." It also defines protected acts as those taken in furtherance of "other efforts to stop 1 or more violations of this subchapter" and includes within protected acts those that are taken by a protected individual on behalf of "associated others."

Most employment-related discrimination occurs within the relationship of an employment contract and thus is covered by the current law. Protected conduct that occurs outside of the employment relationship should, if it is important enough to protect, at least be clearly defined. S. 2041 enlarges the members of the protected group to include contractors and agents without carefully defining the group receiving protection or the protected acts, and it removes the requirement that limits retaliatory acts to those taken by employers. The bill's removal of the phrase "by his or her employer" that limits liability to employers is a deceptively simple change and masks the exponential expansion of liability it would allow, including any and all persons that interact with the plaintiff in the workplace, whether in their individual capacities or in their capacities as employers. Without that limit, extending liability to anyone in any of these contexts yields absurd results and claims that have no place in a whistleblower protection statute.

In addition, protecting acts on behalf of "associated others" is entirely open-ended and so vague that it could include acts on behalf of a business acquaintance or a neighbor or acts undertaken at the direction of a *qui tam* attorney. Such conduct does not properly fall within the purposes of a retaliation provision and the False Claims Act and should not be a basis for recoveries under it.

Under the current law, courts generally limit relief under Section 3730(h) to employees who have engaged in conduct that sends a clear signal of serious allegations about fraud against the Government to their employers so that the employer understands that the employee's actions are in furtherance of a whistleblower claim. If the employee's job responsibilities include alerting the employer to fraud within the company, the employee usually must do more than point out the fraud to the employer to produce this understanding. Mere "saber-rattling" is unprotected because it does not provide this notice to th*e employer. Hutchins v. Wilentz, Goldman & Spitzer*, 253 F.3d 176, 193 (3d Cir. 2001); *Yesudian v. Howard Univ.*, 153 F.3d 731, 740 (D.C. Cir. 1998); *Zahodnick v. Int'l Bus. Machs. Corp.*, 135 F.3d 911 (4th Cir. 1997). The importance of establishing a clear standard that incorporates notice to employers was enunciated in *United States ex rel. Luckey v. Baxter Healthcare Corp.*, 183 F.3d 730 (7th Cir. 1999). The court in *Luckey* affirmed the lower court's grant of summary judgment on behalf of defendant, holding that defendant's decision to terminate the relator's employment was permissible because the relator's actions could not be understood as acts in furtherance of a whistleblower claim. The court explained that:

> [i]ntra-corporate debates about optimal testing protocols cannot be equated to knowledge of litigation . . . . An employer is entitled to treat a suggestion for improvement as what it purports to be rather than as a precursor to litigation . . . . [E]mployees who use reports of fraud to better their own position, or who behave like Chicken Little, impose costs on employers without advancing any of the goals of the False Claims Act. Saber-rattling is not protected conduct. Only investigation, testimony, and litigation are protected.

Id. at 733 (quotations and citations omitted).

The bill's ambiguous reference to "other efforts" to stop violations puts the basis for retaliation claims on unsteady ground. It removes the guidance provided under the long history of the current law and opens this provision to use in disputes without requiring a clear relationship to FCA allegations. Specifically, the bill's substitution of acts "in furtherance of other efforts to stop" a violation for the current requirement of acts that are "in furtherance of an action under this section, including investigation for, initiation of, testimony for, or assistance in an action filed or to be filed under this section" removes the key language in Section 3730(h) that ties the protected acts to FCA claims.

At bottom, the ambiguities in this new provision and the potential overbreadth associated with it would allow extension of whistleblower protections to cases where no false claims allegations are involved and where no retaliation by an employer is required. The provision would extend the benefits intended for whistleblowers to others who do not act on the Government's behalf and would subject non-employers to liability for normal interactions in the workplace. The current retaliation provision should remain limited to protect those who truly engage in acts in furtherance of false claims allegations, rather than make other complaints, and the protections for employers and other individuals from unfounded retaliation suits should remain.

VII. The Changes to the Civil Investigative Demand Process Are Unnecessary and Would Encourage Abuse by Relators

A. Summary

The Civil Investigative Demand ("CID") is a tool which authorizes the Attorney General to request information (by way of documents, sworn depositions, interrogatories, and other forms of discovery) as part of the Government's investigation of false claims. The bill would permit the Government to share the information obtained through a CID with any *qui tam* relator if, in the Attorney General's judgment or that of a designee, it is "necessary as part of any false claims act investigation." *See* S. 2041, § 7. It would also allow the Attorney General to share the authority to issue CIDs with a "designee," without defining who that person or persons would be.

Government investigators already have adequate tools to obtain documents under the subpoena power of the Inspectors General and can allow a relator, or any other witness, to review those documents as part of the investigation. The only purpose for this amendment must be to allow non-documentary evidence — particularly depositions — taken under a CID to be shown to a relator's counsel. Its effect, however, is to allow relators expansive discovery prior to unsealing, without regard to the merits of their allegations, whether or not they would meet the stringent pleading requirements of Rule 9(b) without such discovery, even when the Government ultimately decides not to bring the case. These changes give private parties sensitive information on an *ex parte* basis without helping the Government or true whistleblowers.

B. Current Law

Under 31 U.S.C. § 3733(a)(1), the Attorney General may issue a CID when he or she has reason to believe that any person may be in possession, custody, or control of any documentary material or information relevant to a false claims law investigation. Before the commencement of an FCA proceeding, the Attorney General may require the person to produce documentary evidence, answer interrogatories, give oral testimony, or furnish a combination of such evidence.

The Attorney General may not delegate the authority to issue a CID to anyone else, and the information received in response to the CID is allowed to be disclosed to no one other than Government agencies or Congress.

C. Analysis of the Proposed Amendment

Section 7 of S. 2041 allows "the Attorney General, or a designee (for purposes of this section)" to issue a CID, authorizing him or her to share the authority to issue CIDs without defining who the designee would be. In addition, the bill provides that:

> [a]ny information obtained by the Attorney General or a designee of the Attorney General under this section may be shared with any *qui tam* relator if the Attorney General or designee determine it is necessary as part of any false claims act investigation.

Thus, the bill allows the information received in response to a CID to be shared with "any *qui tam* relator" if the Attorney General or designee believes it is "necessary for any false claims act investigation."

The bill represents a complete about-face from existing law, and it threatens to expand abusive *qui tam* suits by allowing relators who are not true whistleblowers. The purpose of CID authority is to allow the Government to get the information it needs in order to determine whether there is sufficient evidence to file an FCA suit. That is the reason that the exercise of this authority is limited to the period prior to the commencement of an FCA proceeding under Section 3730. *See* H.R. Rep. No. 99-660, at. 26 (1986) (citing to similar CID provisions in HartScott-Rodino Anti-Trust Improvements Act of 1976, 15 U.S.C. §§ 1311-1314). In fact, courts have noted that "using the CIDs for a purpose other than to determine if there is sufficient evidence to file" a suit would be improper. *United States v. Witmer,* 835 F. Supp. 208, 219 (M.D. Pa. 1993). *See also United States v. Seitz,* No. MS2-93-063, 1993 WL 501817 (S.D. Ohio Aug. 26, 1993). The purposes of relators are not so limited, however, because they are potential litigants in FCA actions, whether the Government decides to proceed with the suit or not. That difference is a major reason why information gathered by the Government on an *ex parte* basis through CIDs in advance of intervention should not be shared with them and why, instead, relators should gather their information according to the discovery provisions of the Federal Rules.

Despite the critical difference between the Government's purpose and the purposes of relators and their counsel in accessing CID information, the bill makes the information easily accessible to relators when a "designee" determines that it is necessary as part of any FCA investigation. It gives relators expanded access to information that they should already have, since true whistleblowers should have enough information to make *qui tam* allegations without the help of discovery or publicly disclosed information. *See, e.g., United States ex rel. Karvelas v. Melrose-Wakefield Hosp.,* 360 F.3d 220, 231 (1st Cir. 2004); *Yuhasz v. Brush Wellman, Inc.*, 341 F.3d 559, 566 (6th Cir. 2003); *United States ex rel. Clausen v. Lab Corp. of Am., Inc.*, 290 F.3d 1301, 1313 n.24 (11th Cir. 2002).

Moreover, easy access to the information submitted to the Government by CID recipients can be abused by relators who are also business competitors, disgruntled employees, or others for purposes other than helping to uncover fraud against the Government. *See, e.g., United States ex rel. Taylor v. Gabelli,* Civ. No. 03 8762(PAC), 2005 WL 2978921 (S.D.N.Y. Nov. 4, 2005) (*qui tam* suit by competitor relator); *Clausen*, 290 F.3d 1301 (*qui tam* suit by competitor relator). Providing this information to these relators prior to unsealing assists them in cases that the Government declines. These changes are unwarranted, and do not help, true whistleblowers.

This provision is entirely unnecessary. Under current law, the Government is fully empowered to issue a CID in order to gain information that will be useful in its fraud investigations. A *qui tam* relator, on the other hand, is supposed to be a whistleblower who brings new information and new allegations of fraud to the Government and is richly rewarded for that information. Existing law already provides that documents obtained in compliance with an Inspector General subpoena can be shared with relators if it is part of the investigation. *See* Inspector General Act of 1978, 5 U.S.C. app. 3 § 6(a)(4) (2000) (authorizing Inspectors General to serve subpoenas for documentary evidence). Whatever the propriety of that sharing, no court has prohibited it. The only information not obtainable through an IG subpoena that can be obtained through a CID is oral testimony. The bill would allow relators' attorneys to gain access to this information when true whistleblowers do not need it. This does not advance the goal of ferreting out fraud perpetrated against the Treasury. Allowing the Government to share the information gleaned from depositions stands only to strengthen the hand of those who bring cases that the Government declines.

CONCLUSION

I want to urge the Committee to recognize the potential abuse that these amendments will impose not only on large and small American businesses but also on all other institutions that receive Federal funds — the churches, local Government entities, schools and colleges, and other contractors and grantees. When these companies and institutions deal with the Government, they are properly expected to do so honestly and forthrightly. But the Government also promises that it will deal with them fairly. These amendments, if passed, would break that promise.

ATTACHMENT A

John T. Boese, Fried, Frank, Harris, Shriver & Jacobson LLP
1001 Pennsylvania Avenue, N.W., #800
Washington, D.C. 20004-2505
(202) 639-7220
E-Mail: John.Boese@FriedFrank.com

John T. Boese is a partner in the Washington, D.C. office of Fried, Frank, Harris, Shriver & Jacobson LLP. Mr. Boese is a nationally-recognized expert on the civil False Claims Act. For over 25 years, he has represented defendants in numerous fraud investigations and False Claims Act cases brought by *qui tarn* relators or by the Department of Justice. His clients include corporations and institutions in a broad variety of industries. He has represented defense contractors, hospitals, churches, construction companies, insurance companies, pharmaceutical companies, oil & gas companies, major retailers, import/export firms, computer manufacturers, software and computer service providers, universities and airports in False Claims Act litigation.

He is the author of the book, *Civil False Claims and Qui Tam Actions* (Aspen Publishers 3d ed.), a comprehensive, two-volume treatise on the civil False Claims Act and *qui tam* enforcement at both the Federal and state levels. This book, updated biannually, was published originally in 1993, and is now in its Third Edition. The book is commonly cited as authority on this subject by courts at all levels, as well as by practitioners and academics. His other journal publications include: "Why Thompson Is Wrong: Misuse of the False Claims Act to Enforce the Anti-Kickback Act," *Alabama Law Review,* Vol. 51, No. 1, Fall 1999 (John T. Boese, Beth C. McClain); "When Angry Patients Become Angry Prosecutors: Medical Necessity Determinations, Quality of Care and the *Qui Tam* Law," *Saint Louis University Law Journal,* Vol. 43, No. 1, Spring 1999 (John T. Boese); and "Private Enforcement of State Fraud Laws: A Comparative Analysis of State *Qui Tam* Provisions," *Journal of Health and Hospital Law,* Vol. 31, No. 1, Winter 1998 (John T. Boese, Shannon L. Haralson).

Mr. Boese lectures frequently to private and public groups on civil fraud issues. He is the co-chair of the biennial ABA National Institute on the Civil False Claims Act & *Qui Tam* Enforcement, and he moderates the *"Qui Tam* Lawsuits" session at the annual ABA National Institute on Health Care Fraud and Abuse. He was co-chair of the *Qui Tam* Subcommittee of the American Bar Association Section of Criminal Justice from 1998 to 2006, and he is a Vice-Chair of the Debarment and Suspension Committee of the Section on Public Contract Law.

Prior to joining Fried Frank in 1977, Mr. Boese was a trial attorney with the Civil Division of the U.S. Department of Justice, where he was awarded a Special Commendation for Outstanding Service in 1976. He received a Bachelor of Science degree from Washington University in 1969 and graduated, *magna cum laude,* with a Juris Doctor degree from St. Louis University Law School in 1972, where he served as an associate editor of the *St. Louis University Law Journal.* He is admitted to practice before the United States Supreme Court; the United States Courts of Appeals for the Second, Fifth, Seventh, Ninth, Tenth, and Eleventh Circuits; the United States Court of Appeals for the District of Columbia Circuit; the District of Columbia Court of Appeals; and the United States Court of Appeals for the Federal Circuit. He has appeared in more than 50 different Federal district and appellate courts.

He is a member of the American Law Institute.

ATTACHMENT B

Fraud Statistics – Overview October 1, 1986 - September 30, 2007 Civil Division, U.S. Department of Justice

FA'	NEW MATTERS[1]		SETTLEMENTS AND JUDGMENTS[3]					RELATOR SHARE AWARDS'		
			NON QUI TAM[2]	QUI TAM						
	NON QUI TAM	QUI TAM	TOTAL	WHERE U.S. INTERVENED OR THERWISE PURSUED	WHERE U.S. DECLINED	TOTAL	TOTAL QUI TAM AN NON QUI TAM	WHERE U.S. INTERVENED OR OTHERWISE PURSUED	WHERE U.S. DECLINED	TOTAL
1987	340	31	86,479,949	0	0	0	86,479,949	0	0	0
1988	210	43	173,287,663	2,309,354	33,750	2,343,104	175,630,767	88,750	8.437	97,187
1989	221	88	197,202,180	15,111,719	1,681	15,113,400	212,315,580	1,446,770	200	1.446,970
1990	240	75	189,564,367	40,483,367	75,000	40,558,367	230,122,734	6,590,936	20,670	6,611,606
1991	234	84	270,445,467	70,384,431	154,500	70,538,931	340,984,398	10,667,537	18,750	10.686,287
1992	285	113	137,358,206	134,549,447	994,456	135,543,903	272,902,109	24,196,648	259,784	24,456,432
1993	304	138	181,945,576	183,643,787	6,078,000	189,721,787	371,667,363	27,576,235	1,766,902	29,343,137
1994	279	219	706,022,897	379,018,205	2,822,323	381,840,528	1,087,863,425	69,453,350	838,896	70,292,246
1995	232	269	269,989,642	239,024,292	1,635,000	240,659,292	510,648,934	45,162,296	465,800	45.628,096
1996	186	344	247,357,271	124,361,203	13,390,011	137,751,214	385,108,485	22,119,619	3,731,978	25.851,597
1997	187	546	465,568,061	621,919,274	6,021,200	627,940,474	1,093,508,535	65,857,419	1,658,485	67,515,904
1998	118	467	151,435,793	438,834,846	30,248,075	469,082,921	620,518,714	70,264,372	8,486,645	78,751,017
1999	140	493	195,390,485	492,924,785	5,067,503	497,992,288	693,382,773	63,018,064	1,374,487	64,392,551
2000	95	363	367,887,191	1,208,715,188	1,688,957	1,210,404,145	1,578,291,342	183,682,977	375,143	184,058,120
2001	86	311	492,196,974	1,167,531,786	128,587,151	1,296,118,937	1,788,315,911	186,908,812	30,701,881	217.610.693
2002	62	318	119,598,292	1,077,375,794	25,786,140	1,103,161,934	1,222,760,226	160,914,076	4,582.319	165.496.395
2003	92	334	703,003,368	1,512,457,284	5,185,911	1,517,643,195	2,220,646,563	331,873,857	1,382,741	333.256,598
2004	120	431	115,656,023	557,080,136	9,261,879	566,342,015	681,998,038	110,113,220	2,376,128	112,489,348

Table. (Continued)

FA'	NEW MATTERS'		SETTLEMENTS AND JUDGMENTS'					RELATOR SHARE AWARDS'		
			NON QUI TAM'	QUI TAM						
	NON QUI TAM	QUI TAM	TOTAL	WHERE U.S. INTERVENED OR THERWISE PURSUED	WHERE U.S. DECLINED	TOTAL	TOTAL QUI TAM AN NON QUITAM	WHERE U.S. INTERVENED OR OTHERWISE PURSUED	WHERE U.S. DECLINED	TOTAL
2005	107	406	276,914,983	1,148,057,102	7,081,143	1,155,138,245	1,432,053,228	168,409,043	1,911,560	170,320,603
2006	85	384	1,714,824,081	1,482,048,337	22,493,863	1,504,542,200	3,219,366,281	218,392,497	5,598,336	223,990,833
2007	128	356	559,255,115	1,436,468,132	15,370,120	1,451,838,252	2,011,093,367	173,221,033	4,169,498	177,390.53 I
TOTAL	3,751	5,813	7,621,383,590	12,332,298,469	281,976,663	12,614,275,132	20,235,658,722	1,939,957,511	69,728,640	2,009,686,151

NOTES:

1. New Matters" refers to newly received referrals, investigations, and *qui tarn* actions.
2. Non *qui tarn* settlements and judgments do not include matters delegated to United States Attorneys' offices. The Civil Division maintains no data on such matters.
3. Relator share awards are calculated on the portion of the settlement or judgment attributable to the relator's claims, which may be less than the total settlement or judgment. Relator share awards do not include amounts recovered in subsection (h) or other personal claims. See 31 U.S.C. § 3730(h).

Fraud Statistics - Health & Human Services[1] October 1, 1986 - September 30, 2007 Civil Division, U.S. Department of Justice

FY	NEW MATTERS[2]		SETTLEMENTS AND JUDGMENTS[3]			
			NON QUI TAM[3]	QUI TAM		TOTAL QUI TAM AND NON QUI TAM
	NON QUI TAM	QUI TAM	TOTAL	TOTAL	RELATOR SHARE[4]	
1987	12	3	11,361,826	0	0	11,361,826
1988	8	5	2,182,675	355,000	88,750	2,537,675
1989	20	16	350,460	5,099,661	50,000	5,450,121
1990	27	11	10,327,500	903,158	119,474	11,230,658
1991	22	12	8,670,735	5,420,000	861,401	14,090,735
1992	29	15	9,821,640	2,192,478	446,648	12,014,118
1993	22	38	12,523,165	151,760,404	22,946,101	164,283,569
1994	42	76	381,470,015	6,520,815	1,185,597	387,990,830
1995	26	87	96,290,779	85,681,789	14,803,782	181,972,568
1996	20	179	63,059,873	51,576,698	9,374,568	114,636,571
1997	50	274	351,440,027	579,079,581	58,872,855	930,519,608
1998	35	275	40,107,920	258,638,736	47,822,301	298,746,656
1999	28	315	38,000,792	408,128,379	45,492,385	446,129,171
2000	36	210	208,899,015	725,011,203	115,759,246	933,910,218
2001	35	177	433,549,179	900,260,345	147,318,543	1,333,809,524
2002	24	194	74,567,427	960,450,528	153,825,657	1,035,017,955
2003	26	219	536,834,879	1,287,796,031	279,770,601	1,824,630,910
2004	28	275	34,816,447	475,370,142	97,434,278	510,186,589
2005	34	271	204,821,548	911,972,558	122,597,758	1,116,794,106
2006	18	223	1,047,745,714	1,239,957,154	166,506,405	2,287,702,868
2007	22	196	461,582,993	1,084,809,242	153,138,241	1,546,392,235
TOTAL	564	3,071	4,028,424,609	9,140,983,902	1,438,414,591	13,169,408,511

NOTES:

1. The information reported in this table covers matters in which the Department of Health and Human Services is the primary client agency.
2. "New Matters" refers to newly received referrals, investigations, and qui tam actions.
3. Non *qui tam* settlements and judgments do not include matters delegated to United States Attorneys' offices. The Civil Division maintains no data on such matters.
4. Relator share awards are calculated on the portion of the settlement or judgment attributable to the relator's claims, which may be less than the total settlement or judgment Relator share awards do not include amounts recovered in subsection (h) or other personal claims. See 31 U.S.C. § 3730(h).

Fraud Statistics - Department of Defense[1] October 1, 1986 - September 30, 2007 Civil Division, U.S. Department of Justice

FY	NEW MATTERS[2]		SETTLEMENTS AND JUDGMENTS'			
			NON QUI TAM[3]	QUI TAM		
	NON QUI TAM	QUI TAM	TOTAL	TOTAL	RELATOR SHARE[4]	TOTAL QUI TAM AND NON QUI TAM
1987	236	22	27,897,128	0	0	27,897,128
1988	122	28	149,136,213	33,750	8,438	149,169,963
1989	119	32	154,588,297	10,002,058	1,394,770	164,590,355
1990	74	41	117,715,978	21,743,463	3,804,470	139,459,441
1991	78	44	227,813,245	57,327,000	8,636,300	285,140,245
1992	73	61	62,003,695	129,294,456	23,874,784	191,298,151
1993	93	53	83,742,840	29,707,641	4,951,923	113,450,481
1994	62	82	226,083,266	370,666,206	68,163,879	596,749,472
1995	54	87	111,424,866	140,563,237	28,348,711	251,988,103
1996	44	81	78,085,099	61,833,653	12,522,473	139,918,752
1997	46	82	33,723,347	36,528,913	6,392,620	70,252,260
1998	29	62	71,063,139	150,180,185	20,511,801	221,243,324
1999	33	70	30,522,711	15,859,646	2,863,936	46,382,357
2000	10	46	53,007,693	96,287,825	15,812,059	149,295,518
2001	10	42	17,715,878	116,188,794	25,067,682	133,904,672
2002	16	44	15,017,365	19,407,658	2,957,196	34,425,023
2003	10	36	107,337,000	205,124,468	48,640,795	312,461,468
2004	16	50	10,098,491	17,684,000	3,031,610	27,782,491
2005	16	49	19,049,935	102,234,052	21,649,855	121,283,987
2006	13	74	586,430.385	48,809,599	10,488,996	635,239,984
2007	22	66	16,400,000	32,035,609	1,681,419	48,435,609
TOTAL	1,176	1,152	2,198,856,571	1,661,512,213	310,803,717	3,860,368,784

NOTES:

1. The information reported in this table covers matters in which the Department of Defense is the primary client agency.
2. "New Matters" refers to newly received referrals, investigations, and qui tam actions.
3. Non *qui tam* settlements and judgments do not include matters delegated to United States Attorneys' offices. The Civil Division maintains no data on such matters.
4. Relator share awards are calculated on the portion of the settlement or judgment attributable to the relator's claims, which may be less than the total settlement or judgment. Relator share awards do not include amounts recovered in subsection (h) or other personal claims. See 31 U.S.C. § 3730(h).

Fraud Statistics - Other (Non-HHS, Non-DOD)[1] October 1, 1986 - September 30, 2007
Civil Division, U.S. Department of Justice

FY	NEW MATTERS[2]		SETTLEMENTS AND JUDGMENTS[3]			
			NON QUI TAM[3]	QUI TAM		
	NON QUI TAM	QUI TAM	TOTAL	TOTAL	RELATOR SHARE[4]	TOTAL QUI TAM AND NON QUI TAM
1987	92	6	47,220,995	0	0	47,220,995
1988	80	10	21,968,775	1,954,354	0	23,923,129
1989	82	40	42,263,423	11,681	2,200	42,275,104
1990	139	23	61,520,889	17,911,746	2,687,662	79,432,635
1991	134	28	33,961,487	7,791,931	1,188,586	41,753,418
1992	183	37	65,532,871	4,056,969	135,000	69,589,840
1993	189	47	85,679,571	8,253,742	1,445,113	93,933,313
1994	175	61	98,469,616	4,653,507	942,770	103,123,123
1995	152	95	62,273,997	14,414,266	2,475,603	76,688,263
1996	122	84	106,212,299	24,340,863	3,954,557	130,553,162
1997	91	190	80,404,687	12,331,980	2,250,430	92,736,667
1998	54	130	40,264,734	60,264,000	10,416,915	100,528,734
1999	79	108	126,866,982	74,004,263	16,036,231	200,871,245
2000	49	107	105,980,489	389,105,117	52,486,815	495,085,606
2001	41	92	40,931,918	279,669,798	45,224,468	320,601,716
2002	22	80	30,013,500	123,303,748	8,713,542	153,317,248
2003	56	79	58,831,489	24,722,697	4,845,202	83,554,186
2004	76	106	70,741,084	73,287,873	12,023,461	144,028,957
2005	57	86	53,043,500	140,931,636	26,072,989	193,975,136
2006	54	87	80,647,982	215,775,447	46,995,431	296,423,429
2007	84	94	81,272,122	334,993,400	22,570,872	416,265,522
TOTAL	**2,011**	**1,590**	**1,394,102,410**	**1,811,779,018**	**260,467,847**	**3,205,881,428**

NOTES:

I. The information reported in this table covers matters in which the primary client agency is neither the Department of Health and Human Services nor the Department of Defense.

2. "New Matters" refers to newly received referrals, investigations, and qui tam actions.

3. Non *qui tam* settlements and judgments do not include matters delegated to United States Attorneys' offices. The Civil Division maintains no data on such matters.

4. Relator share awards are calculated on the portion of the settlement or judgment attributable to the relator's claims, which may be less than the total settlement or judgment. Relator share awards do not include amounts recovered in subsection (h) or other personal claims. See 31 U.S.C. § 3730(h).

Fraud Statistics *Qui tam* Intervention Decisions & Case Status as of September 30, 2007
Civil Division, U.S. Department of Justice

	ACTIVE	SETTLEMENT OR JUDGMENT	DISMISSED	UNCLEAR	TOTAL
U.S. Intervened	93	947	52	2	1,094
U.S. Declined	363	212	3,170	7	3,752
Under Investigation					967
					5,813

End Notes

[1] Under the Act, a *qui tam* case must be filed under seal to give the Government the opportunity to investigate the allegations. After that investigation, DOJ can either intervene, in which case it has primary responsibility for the litigation, or decline to intervene, in which case the *qui tam* relator can proceed alone. 31 U.S.C. §§ 3730(b)(4) & (c). Historically, the DOJ intervenes in approximately 20% of *qui tam* cases. Department of Justice, Fraud Statistics for 2007-Overview (2007) (hereinafter "DOJ Statistics"), *available at* http://www.ffhsj.com/practice_groups. A copy of the DOJ Statistics is appended hereto as Attachment B.

[2] DOJ Statistics at pp. 2 & 6.

[3] When the Justice Department chooses not to exercise its statutory right to intervene in and take over *qui tam* FCA cases, such cases are commonly referred to as "declined" cases.

[4] This draconian and excessive penalty is compounded dramatically when plaintiffs argue that all claims made during the period of alleged non-compliance were "false" and that the measure of damages is not the Government's economic loss (which is often zero), but rather three times the total amount received from the Government during that period. *See, e.g., United States ex rel. Harrison v. Westinghouse Savannah River Co.*, 352 F.3d 908 (4th Cir. 2003); *Ab-Tech Constr., Inc. v. United States*, 31 Fed. Cl. 429, 430-33 (Fed. Cir. 1994). Although both of these courts rejected this approach to calculating damages, many of the FCA settlements involving the pharmaceutical industry involved drugs that were actually prescribed and provided, but the Government and relators asserted that the corresponding payment claims were "tainted" by kickbacks. Plaintiffs typically argue that the damages in "tainted" claims cases are measured by the total sum paid by the Government for a claim it allegedly would have refused to pay, if it had known of the alleged legal violation.

[5] *See* "TAP Pharmaceuticals and Others Charged With Health Care Crimes: Company Agrees to Pay $875 Million to Settle Charges," DOJ Press Release # 513 (Oct. 31, 2001), *available at* http://www.usdoj.gov/ opa/pr /2001/October/513civ.htm. What is extremely telling about subsequent developments in this case is that the 11 individual defendants indicted by the Justice Department who fought these charges at trial were *acquitted* by a jury of all of the charges against them. Because of the overwhelming failure of proof in this case (the defendants did not put on a defense because the case in chief was so inadequate), the court set aside the guilty plea that had been entered by one defendant before the case went to trial.

[6] *See* "Merck to Pay More Than $650 Million to Resolve Claims of Fraudulent Price Reporting and Kickbacks,"DOJ Press Release # 08-094 (Feb. 7, 2008), http://www.usdoj.gov/opa/pr/2008/February

[7] That case held that two categories of funds at issue were Government funds within the meaning of the FCA: deposits in U.S. banks that once belonged to the Government of Iraq, but were seized by the United States during the first Gulf War, and funds and moveable property seized by Coalition forces on the ground in Iraq. *Custer Battles*, 376 F. Supp. 2d at 626, 645-46. Claims for one category of funds, however, were not "claims" within the meaning of the FCA because they had always been Iraqi funds: money from the Development Fund for Iraq, which originated primarily from sales of Iraqi oil under the United Nations Oil for Food program. *Id.* at *87.

[8] Importantly, this "public disclosure/original source" bar does not apply to the Government, only to *qui tam* relators, and is normally relevant only in *qui tam* cases in which the DOJ investigates and declines to prosecute. Unless the relator claims enormous attorneys' fees, the issue rarely arises in cases in which the DOJ intervenes because the case proceeds regardless of the status of the relator.

[9] The first example is the infamous case of *United States ex rel. Marcus v. Hess*, 317 U.S. 537 (1943), in which an enterprising *qui tam* relator made a direct copy of a criminal indictment, incorporated those allegations in a civil action under the False Claims Act and requested half of any subsequent civil judgment. *Id.* at 545. He ultimately prevailed, and, in response, Congress quickly amended the False Claims Act in 1943 to bar *qui tam* actions "based on evidence or information the Government had when the action was brought." Act of Dec. 23, 1943, Pub. L. No. 78-2 13, ch. 377, 57 Stat. 608.

The second example is from the equally infamous *United States ex rel. State of Wisconsin v. Dean,* 729 F.2d 1100 (7th Cir. 1984), in which the court refused to allow Wisconsin to act as a *qui tam* relator in a Medicaid fraud action (even though the investigation had been conducted solely by the State of Wisconsin and the Federal Government learned of the fraud only because Wisconsin had reported it) because, the court held, the FCA barred *qui tam* actions "whenever the government has knowledge of the 'essential information upon which the suit is predicated' before the suit is filed, even when the plaintiff is the source of that knowledge." *Id.* at 1103.

The *Marcus* case was largely responsible for the 1943 Amendments to the FCA; the *Dean* case was a key motivator for the 1986 Amendments. For a complete discussion of the history and policy behind the 1943 and 1986 Amendments, *see* John T. Boese, *Civil False Claims and Qui Tam Actions*, 3d ed. ch. 4.02.

In: Fighting Fraud with Qui Tam and the False Claims Act ISBN: 978-1-61668-221-7
Editor: Ian M. Ortiz

Chapter 6

TESTIMONY OF JOHN E. CLARK BEFORE THE SENATE JUDICIARY COMMITTEE HEARING ON "THE FALSE CLAIMS ACT CORRECTION ACT (S.2041): STRENGTHENING THE GOVERNMENT'S MOST EFFECTIVE TOOL AGAINST FRAUD IN THE 21ST CENTURY"

John E. Clark

As a long-time False Claims Act practitioner, I submit this testimony in support of Senate Bill 2041, the False Claims Act Correction Act of 2007 ("S. 2041").[1] I am a member of the qui tam bar, the unofficial term for the attorneys who specialize in representing private parties who bring cases under the federal False Claims Act ("FCA") on behalf of the United States. For more than 15 years, my practice has consisted almost exclusively of qui tam cases.

I have been a member of legal teams representing qui tam plaintiffs whose claims have resulted in recoveries exceeding half a billion dollars ($500,000,000) for the United States. The cases have involved both health care fraud and defense contracting fraud, the two primary areas of fraud against the government today. Many of the defendants have been publicly traded companies, including such familiar names as HealthSouth Corporation, SmithKline Beecham Clinical Laboratories, Science Applications International Corporation, and prescription drug manufacturers Bayer, Aventis, Bristol Myers Squibb, and GlaxoSmithKline. I have also represented qui tam plaintiffs in cases brought under the Texas Medicaid Fraud Prevention Act, which is patterned after the federal FCA, that have resulted in recoveries of approximately $70 million for Texas and the United States to date.

My whistleblower clients have included physicians and other health care professionals; corporate executives; clerical and administrative personnel; non-executive salaried employees; hourly skilled workers; a competitor of a corporate health care provider; and, an 83-year-old physical therapy patient (a veteran of World War II, Korea, and Vietnam) who saw and understood that Medicare was being systematically cheated by a major corporate health care provider.

The clients who were employees of the entities sued have all had one thing in common: before seeking the assistance of a qui tam attorney, each had tried, without success, to get his or her employer to cease its unlawful conduct. Even the physical therapy patient tried first, without success, to get the corporate provider to change its conduct voluntarily.

Currently, I practice law at Goode Casseb Jones Riklin Choate & Watson, a San Antonio, Texas law firm that I helped found in 1991. I also serve on the Board of Directors of Taxpayers Against Fraud (TAF), the non-profit public interest organization dedicated to combating fraud against the Federal Government through the promotion and use of the Federal FCA and its qui tam provisions.

My views on S. 2041 are informed by my previous government service as well as by my current career representing qui tam plaintiffs. From 1969 to 1977, as a litigation attorney in the Justice Department's Criminal Division, as an Assistant U.S. Attorney, and finally as the United States Attorney for the sprawling Western District of Texas, I handled and oversaw a wide variety of civil and criminal litigation for the United States. I served as U.S. Attorney for the Western District of Texas from 1975 to 1977. In addition, I served as a Justice on the Texas Fourth Court of Appeals, the state counterpart to the federal circuit courts, in 1981-1982.

S. 2041 is important to remedy and deter fraud on U.S. government programs. The Bill's proposed amendments to the FCA – many of which are clarifications of the existing statute – are needed to correct a number of decisions by courts that have misconstrued the statute and limited its effectiveness. A number of unfortunate, judicial rulings inhibit the law from operating as Congress intended when it enacted the law in 1863 to combat fraud in Civil War defense contracts. Other rulings hinder the law from working as Congress intended when it amended the law in 1986 to put in place sufficient incentives to encourage private citizens to come forward. In my testimony, I will address my reasons for supporting each of the key provisions of S. 2041 and I will discuss two other areas that are badly in need of legislative correction:

The permissible uses of Civil Investigative Demand material in FCA proceedings need to be clarified so that Department of Justice attorneys will use this tool when appropriate; and,

The procedural provisions need to be clarified to confirm that qui tam plaintiffs need not plead the specifics of billing documentation to survive a motion to dismiss.

I. Provisions in the Current Bill

A. Fixing the "Public Disclosure" Jurisdictional Bar

Perhaps the most critical aspect of this bill is its amendment of the so-called "public disclosure bar" – a provision that has been misinterpreted by too many courts. The case law has veered so far off the course Congress intended that it has seriously handicapped the fight against fraud. After setting out the legislative history of this provision and summarizing the state of the case law, I will offer examples from my own experience that demonstrate the need for legislative action.

1. Summary of Legislative History

Congress amended the FCA to add the public disclosure bar in 1986. This provision deprives a court of jurisdiction over any qui tam action "based upon" the "public disclosure" of "allegations or transactions" in the news media, or in an administrative, congressional or judicial report, audit or proceeding, unless the qui tam plaintiff is an "original source" of the information and has disclosed it to the government before filing suit.

When Congress added the "public disclosure bar" to the FCA in 1986, it deliberately removed another jurisdictional bar, colloquially referred to as the "government knowledge bar." The government knowledge bar, which was added to the statute in 1943, had deprived courts of jurisdiction over qui tam actions "based on evidence or information the Government had when the action was brought." Congress had added the "government knowledge bar" to the statute in 1943 to address concerns about "opportunistic" or "parasitic" relators who brought no information of any value to the Government, but merely lifted public materials, such as an indictment, into their complaints.

In practice, however, the "government knowledge bar" had not worked as intended. It was far too sweeping, disqualifying meritorious and non-meritorious actions alike, and potential whistleblowers were unwilling to put their careers on the line when facing the risk that their cases would be barred if information about the apparent false claims lay dormant somewhere in the government's vast files. As a result, the government knowledge bar deterred qui tam filings, and the qui tam cause of action fell into virtual disuse for over forty years. (In eight years of service as a federal prosecutor, from 1969 to 1977, I never heard of the FCA.) Meanwhile, defense procurement fraud ran rampant, and was inadequately redressed by the government.

By 1986, Congress had determined to eliminate the so-called "government knowledge bar" in light of its stated concern about cases in which "the Government knew of the information that was the basis of the qui tam suit, but in which the Government took no action." See H.R. REP. NO. 660, 99th Cong., 2d Sess. 22-23 (1986). Congress wished to "encourage more private enforcement suits" and consequently amended the statute to eliminate the government knowledge bar in 1986. S. REP. NO. 345, 99th Cong., 2d Sess. 23-24 (1986), reprinted in 1986 U.S. Code Cong. & Admin. News 5266, 5288-89. Congress remained concerned, however, about "parasitic" or "opportunistic" relators such as those filing complaints simply copied from a government indictment.

To address the continued concern about the opportunistic relator, Congress' 1986 amendments created a jurisdictional bar that was intended to strike a balance between "encouraging people to come forward with information and . . . preventing parasitic lawsuits."[2] As well stated by the Court of Appeals for the District of Columbia: Seeking the golden mean between adequate incentives for whistle-blowing insiders with genuinely valuable information and discouragement of opportunistic plaintiffs who have no significant information to contribute of their own, Congress has frequently altered its course in drafting and amending the qui tam provisions since initial passage of the FCA over a century ago.[3]

The result of Congress' 1986 effort to find the right balance between providing adequate incentives for relators with inside information and discouraging those that add nothing to the government's efforts was the current "public disclosure bar." This bar precludes a qui tam plaintiff's action if his complaint is "based upon" publicly disclosed allegations or transactions, unless the plaintiff is an "original source of the information." The jurisdictional bar no longer focuses on whether the government is on notice of the fraud. Importantly,

Senator Grassley, who sponsored these amendments, explained that the new jurisdictional bar would apply only to actions based "solely" on public disclosures. Cong. Record, S. 11244 (August 11, 1986)

2. State of the Case Law

Although it was intended to benefit the government, the "public disclosure bar" unfortunately has evolved into little more than a cudgel for defendants seeking to escape judgment for their misdeeds. The Department of Justice rarely invokes the clause. Defendants, however, can be counted on to assert it on even the flimsiest pretext, and all too many courts seem eager to seize upon it as if indulging a presumption that whistleblower claims are not favored and should be discouraged. Armed with the best defense counsel in the country and virtually unlimited financial resources for litigation, large defense contractors and health care providers have brought hundreds of jurisdictional challenges to qui tam cases under the public disclosure provision. They have exploited what some courts have characterized as ambiguities in the provision, arguing that "based upon" means "similar to" and that "public" disclosures include even those disclosures made in private settings. These challenges have led to case law that, in effect, has restored aspects of the "government also have depleted the financial resources of whistle- blowers, wasted precious judicial resources, and led to a confounding array of conflicting interpretations of the terms "based upon" and "public disclosure."

To give the Senate Judiciary Committee a sense of the scope of the problem, I point out the following:

The United States Code Annotated currently reports nearly 200 published and unpublished rulings in 103 separate cases on questions relating to the proper interpretation of the "public disclosure" bar and its "original source" exception.

In a case that reached the Supreme Court last year, Rockwell International, Inc. successfully used the public disclosure bar to deny an award to a whistle- blower over the strong objections of the United States.[4]

Most of the Courts of Appeals that have looked at the issue have agreed with defendants that the term "based upon" should be interpreted to mean "similar to" rather than "derived from."[5] In doing so, they have determined that the proper inquiry is whether the information in the public domain is sufficient to put the government "on notice" of the alleged misconduct, in effect restoring - - as the first part of the "public disclosure" jurisdictional analysis - - the "government knowledge" bar that Congress tried to remove in 1986.

On the other hand, the Courts of Appeals for the Fourth, Seventh and Eleventh Circuits have interpreted the term "based upon" as used in the public disclosure bar to mean "derived from."

Several Courts of Appeals have ruled that private exchanges of information, such as those between a government investigator and a potential fact witness, constitute "public disclosures" even when a relator is not part of the information exchange.

One Court of Appeals has ruled that production of documents or information during the discovery phase of a lawsuit is a "public disclosure" even if the material is not put on the public record of the judicial proceeding.

At least three Courts of Appeals have ruled that responses to FOIA requests are "public disclosures" that can deprive a court of jurisdiction even if the relator relies exclusively on his status as an insider to establish requisite elements of the fraud.

On the other hand, the Court of Appeals for the 9th Circuit has held that a response to a FOIA request is not a "public disclosure" within the meaning of the statute.

3. My Experience with the Public Disclosure Bar

The many court decisions that have interpreted the terms "public disclosure" and "based upon" in unduly broad terms have made relators reluctant to take otherwise prudent steps to confirm their allegations prior to filing suit, as these steps could generate disclosures from outside parties that might be deemed "public." Moreover, these decisions have led lower courts to bar meritorious allegations that never would have been uncovered or pursued by the government on its own.

For example, I have been consulted by clients and prospective clients with knowledge of a defendant's culpable practices, but without access to the inculpatory documents submitted to the government, who have suggested filing a FOIA request to obtain copies of the documents in question and thus confirm that the defendant actually submitted false claims. I have counseled such clients against filing FOIA requests because of the case law that poses a significant risk that the government's compliance with a FOIA request could be found to constitute a "public disclosure," potentially barring the client's lawsuit.

Case law that deters whistleblowers from confirming key facts before filing suit is not in the public interest. If flawed cases are filed as a result of incomplete or inaccurate understandings of the facts, executive and judicial branch time and resources, as well as the time and resources of the whistleblower, will be expended needlessly, and the whistleblower's career may be jeopardized. Moreover, this case law can prevent clients from meeting the requirements of other cases that require whistleblowers not only to allege how someone is defrauding the government, but also to present copies of the actual invoices or other claim documents submitted to the government.

In one instance our client assisted in the government's investigation, after we filed his qui tam action, by identifying categories of documents to be subpoenaed that would corroborate his allegations. When the government obtained the documents, the client reviewed and analyzed them at the government's request, in the privacy of a secure federal office. The documents corroborated the client's claims and furthered the investigation, and with the government's acquiescence the still-sealed complaint was amended to reflect specific examples of the corroborative facts. The court unsealed the case before the government's investigation was completed. Although the government's attorneys anticipated electing to intervene, they were not prepared to do so at that time and hoped we would be able to prosecute the case alone until the government was ready to intervene. After the complaint was unsealed, the court dismissed the case on the defendant's motion, ruling that a disqualifying "public disclosure" occurred when the client reviewed the documents to aid in the government's investigation.

The court's interpretation of "public disclosure" as encompassing post-filing disclosures by the government to the relator is particularly troubling in light of the Supreme Court's recent decision in Rockwell Int'l Corp. v. U.S., supra. In that decision, the Supreme Court looked to the final articulation of the legal claim that led to the judgment against the defendant to determine whether that claim was based upon publicly disclosed information.

When qui tam plaintiffs pursue cases declined by the United States, however, the final articulation of the legal claim will almost always encompass billing documentation that the qui tam plaintiff obtained from either the defendant or the government during discovery. Few insiders to fraud have access to all of the pertinent billing documentation. If the reasoning of the Rockwell court is ever combined with the reasoning of the judge in the case I just discussed, it could be the death knell for declined qui tam cases.

In my practice, I have seen how the courts' conflicting and unduly restrictive readings of this provision have been exploited to the fullest by defendants – parties that have no legitimate interest in the public disclosure question. The public disclosure provision was adopted for the government's benefit – i.e., to encourage to avoid sharing a recovery with an opportunistic relator who merely repeats in pleadings what is already widely known. It has nothing whatever to do with the defendant's culpability. It was not intended to shield defendants from liability merely because their misconduct was publicly exposed before the relator filed his lawsuit, and it flies in the face of the public interest to allow it to serve that distorted purpose.

Moreover, because courts consider "public disclosure" a jurisdictional bar, a defendant can use it to attack a relator regardless of whether the government considers the relator an opportunist from whom it wants to be protected, or a valued ally whose assistance and resources the government wishes to have on its side in the litigation. The government, for whose benefit the "public disclosure" bar was intended, should have – and exercise – the sole discretion to make that strategic decision. Again and again, defendants have raised this jurisdictional bar to force qui tam plaintiffs to incur the risk and expense of litigating this threshold issue, to delay adjudications of the merits of cases, and ultimately to avoid liability for defrauding the government. I have also had the experience of responding to "public disclosure" motions so lacking in merit as to suggest that they were filed either without a basic understanding of the law or with the hope of confusing or misleading the court. Congress could do no greater service in furtherance of the FCA than to amend this provision in the manner proposed in Senate Bill 2041.

4. The Proposed Amendments to the Public Disclosure Provision

The proposed amendments empower the government, and not the defendant, to seek the dismissal of opportunistic actions that merely repeat allegations already on the public record. Under the amendments, a FCA action could be dismissed due to a public disclosure only upon "timely" motion of the Attorney General. "Public disclosure" would be defined to include only disclosures on the public record and those that have been "disseminated broadly to the general public," with responses to Freedom of Information Act requests and exchanges with law enforcement expressly excluded from the definition. An action would be deemed to be "based upon" a public disclosure only when all elements of liability are "derived exclusively from" the public disclosure. The much-litigated "original source" language would drop out of the provision, as the new definition of "based upon" would have the effect of carving out complaints by original sources.

These changes, which endorse the interpretations in several of the opinions cited above, will conform the statute to original Congressional intent, leaving in place incentives for all but merely opportunistic relators. They will permit potential qui tam plaintiffs and their counsel to investigate diligently the merits of a potential case before filing suit without concern that such investigation will trigger the public disclosure bar. These changes will prevent defendants from delaying or obstructing litigation of the merits and wasting the resources of the government and the judiciary by repeated, often frivolous, challenges to the court's jurisdiction. Finally, they will empower the government, and not the defendant, to decide whether it is in the public interest for the relator to pursue a qui tam action notwithstanding public knowledge of the defendant's wrongdoing. As the recently decided Rockwell case illustrates, the government does not always favor a dismissal on "public disclosure" grounds but can be powerless to prevent it and retain the benefit of the relator's efforts and resources when the option to squelch the case lies with the defendant.

B. Clarifying that the FCA Protects All U.S. Government Money and Property

1. The Bill's Proposed Amendment of the Liability Provisions

The statute currently imposes liability on anyone who, among other things:

(1) knowingly presents, or causes to be presented, to an officer or employee of the United States Government or a member of the Armed Forces of the United States a false or fraudulent claim for payment or approval; or
(2) knowingly makes, uses, or causes to be made or used, a false record or statement to get a false or fraudulent claim paid or approved by the Government.

31 U.S.C. § 3729(a)(1) and (2).

The statute defines the term "claim" to mean "any request or demand, whether under a contract or otherwise, for money or property which is made to a contractor, grantee, or other recipient if the United States provides any portion of the money or property which is requested or demanded, or if the Government will reimburse such contractor, grantee, or other recipient for any portion of the money or property which is requested or demanded." 31 U.S.C. § 3729(c).

Notwithstanding the definition of "claim" set forth above, the Court of Appeals for the District of Columbia has ruled that FCA liability will lie only when the false claim has actually been presented to an employee or official of the United States. U.S. ex rel. Totten v. Bombardier Corp., 380 F.3d 488, 492-493 (D.C. Cir. 2004), cert. denied, 544 U.S. 1032 (2005). In the opinion of the D.C. Circuit, false claims submitted to a federal government agent, contractor or grantee are not claims presented to the United States even if the agent, contractor or grantee pays the claims with federal funding in order to carry out the goals of a federal program.

In Section Two, through amendments to 31 U.S.C. § 3729(a), S. 2041 would clarify that the FCA imposes liability for any knowing false claim that would inflict financial damage on the United States, regardless of whether the false claim is "presented" to a U.S. Government employee. Key to liability would be whether the defendant's misconduct ultimately would result in a loss to the United States, with false claims on government grantees, contractors and administrative agents considered within the ambit of the Act whenever the United States would suffer an economic loss as a result of the defendant's malfeasance.

Thus, revised Section 3729(a) expressly would protect "Government money or property" from knowing false claims, false statements made to get false claims paid, and the other categories of misconduct set forth in Section 3729. In new Section 3729(b)(2), the proposed amendments would define "Government money or property" to include not only money "belonging" to the United States, but also money that the United States provides a contractor, grantee, agent or other recipient "to be spent or used on the Government's behalf or to advance Government programs."

This amendment would overrule U.S. ex rel. Totten, supra, and its progeny. The amendment would embrace several recent judicial decisions that have held that the FCA should reflect Congress' intent to make a false claim actionable "although the claims were made to a party other than the Government, if the payment therefore would ultimately result in a loss to the United States." S. REP. 345 at 10. (See notes 11 and 12, infra.)

2. Congressional Intent Behind the 1986 Amendments

As noted above, the FCA defines the claims subject to the Act to include those "made to a contractor, grantee, or other recipient if the United States provides any portion of the money or property which is requested or demanded." 31 U.S.C. § 3729(c). In the legislative history to this provision, which Congress enacted in 1986, the Senate Judiciary Committee explained that the definition was added to clarify that:

> [a] false claim for reimbursement under the Medicare, Medicaid, or similar program is actionable under the act . . . A claim upon any Government agency or instrumentality, quasi-governmental corporation, or non-appropriated fund activity is a claim upon the United States . . . a claim is actionable although the claims or false statements were made to a party other than the Government, if the payment therefrom would ultimately result in a loss to the United States . . . a false claim to a recipient of a grant from the United States or to a State under a program financed in part by the United States, is a false claim to the United States.

S. REP. 345 at 9-10.

Moreover, the FCA applies to "circumstances where claims are submitted to state, local or private programs funded in part by the United States where there is significant Federal regulation and involvement." S. REP. 345 at 19-20.

3. The Totten Decision

Notwithstanding Congress' efforts in 1986 to make crystal clear that the FCA covers claims on grantees and quasi-governmental corporations, a divided panel of the Court of Appeals for the D.C. Circuit in U.S. ex rel. Totten, supra, ruled to the contrary, ignoring the the legislative history behind the definition of "claim." The court held in Totten that Sections 3729(a)(1) and (a)(2) of the FCA do not impose liability for false claims submitted to a government grantee or quasi-governmental corporation even if the entity paying the false claims uses federal money to do so. According to that court, such liability will arise only if the false claims are then resubmitted to a government official or employee. At issue in the Totten case were alleged false claims submitted to Amtrak, a quasi-governmental corporation that is also a federal government grantee that has received billions of dollars from the federal government.

Justice Roberts, the author of the Totten court's majority opinion, has acknowledged that this was a difficult decision for the Court of Appeals that reasonably could have gone either way. During his Senate confirmation hearings for the position of Supreme Court Justice, Senator Grassley grilled Justice Roberts on why he had ignored the 1986 legislative history when ruling as he did. Justice Roberts acknowledged:

[I]t's certainly possible that the majority in that case didn't get it right. And the dissent, that was a very strong dissent, did get it right. . I'm happy to concede that it was among the more difficult cases I've had over the past two years. Any time Judge Garland disagrees, you know you're in a difficult area. . . it's obviously to me, a case on which reasonable judges can disagree.

The Totten decision has led a number of lower courts to rule that the FCA may not be used to remedy misconduct involving knowing false claims unless the defendant is dealing directly with a U.S. government official. These lower court rulings effectively create "fraud free zones" in a vast array of situations in which the federal government uses an outside entity – such as an insurance company or a state agency - to administer its programs. These decisions fly directly in the face of the expressed legislative intent in that they hold that the FCA is not against defense subcontractor fraud, or against fraud on local and state programs, even those "funded in part by the United States where there is significant Federal regulation and involvement." S. REP. 345 at 19-20 (citing an area in which Congress intended the FCA to be applicable.)

4. The Impact of Totten

As a result of the Totten decision, not only are the courts dismissing cases that involve significant financial losses for the United States, they also are discouraging the qui tam bar from bringing such cases. I can speak from personal experience. In 2007, due in large part to the Totten ruling, I considered and rejected a case involving a federally-funded project that was to be carried out by a local governmental entity. The general contractor had submitted allegedly false claims to the local government entity, which had paid the claims without knowing of the fraud. Likewise, in 2006, I considered and rejected a case involving a state agency program with substantial federal funding for reasons that included the difficulty of proving that the state agency passed on the principal contractor's allegedly false claims to the United States.

With an increasing amount of our federal government's operations "outsourced" to private contractors, it is more important than ever that Congress clarify that the FCA is designed to protect federal assets – whether disbursed by a U.S. government official or by a third party. As the Department of Justice warned the Court of Appeals in its briefs in the Totten case, interpreting the Act to require presentment of the false claim to a federal employee leaves "'vast sums of federal monies' without FCA protection." 380 F.3d 488 at 502 (2004).

The proposed definition of "government money and property" is a sound one: the focus is on the intended use of the assets as much as the source of the assets – not only must the assets originate with the United States, they must also be assets that are being held by an outside entity specifically to be used on the Government's behalf or to advance government programs. Contrary to the spurious arguments raised by the defense bar in opposition to this provision, the definition does not encompass the salaries of government employees or Social Security checks paid to the aged. Once paid to government employees and Social Security recipients, funds that originated with the United States are no longer being held "on behalf of" the government or "to advance a government program."

5. Judicial Decisions Supporting the Proposed Clarification

This proposed amendment to the liability provisions, which would overrule the Totten Court's ruling that "presentment" to the United States is a precondition of FCA liability, finds support in compelling opinions issued by several highly respected federal judges. For example, in his dissent in the Totten case, Judge Merrick Garland opined that the Court's interpretation of Section 3729(a)(2) was "inconsistent" with the plain text of the statute, and "irreconcilable" with the legislative history. He noted that:

Under the Court's interpretation, the government cannot recover against a contractor that obtains money by presenting a false claim to a federal grantee – even if every penny paid to the contractor comes out of an account comprised wholly of federal funds – unless the grantee 're-presents' that false claim to a federal employee.

380 F.3d 488 at 502-03. Writing the majority opinion for the court, Judge Julia Gibbons of the 6th Circuit Court of Appeals also rejected the analysis of the majority in Totten. The case before the 6th Circuit involved alleged false claims by Allison Engine, Inc. as a subcontractor on a Department of Defense (DOD) contract. Overruling the district court's dismissal of the case due to the fact that the subcontractor was not in contractual privity with the federal government, Judge Gibbons ruled that:

Congress intended the 1986 amendments to overrule restrictive judicial interpretations of the FCA and increase the reach of the statute. By re-wording the statute and adding subsection (c), Congress accomplished this expansion, including making the FCA applicable to cases in which the government sustains a financial loss, regardless of whether the false claim is actually presented to the government. Reading a presentment requirement into subsections (a)(2) and (a)(3) is contrary to this purpose and contradicts the plain language of the statute.

The Supreme Court will consider the defendant's appeal of this Sixth Circuit ruling in its upcoming term.

C. Clarifying That the FCA Extends to Claims Against U.S.-Administered Funds

The language of the FCA is silent on whether it protects funds administered by the United States. As noted above, the Act speaks of claims "presented to" the United States "for payment or approval" and claims "paid or approved by the Government." 31 U.S.C. §3729(a)(1) and (2). As a matter of practice, the qui tam bar and the Department of Justice have interpreted the Act to protect U.S.-administered funds, and have enforced the Act accordingly. The United States has utilized the FCA to recover hundreds of millions of dollars from oil, gas and 18 mining companies that have underreported the royalties owed under leases on Indian land.

The availability of the Act as a remedy in these circumstances is now at risk. In a recent decision in a high profile case involving Iraq reconstruction fraud, a United States district court held that the FCA does not reach false claims on money administered but not owned by the U.S. Government. See U.S. ex rel. DRC, Inc. v. Custer Battles, LLC, 376 F. Supp. 2d 617, 636-641 (E.D. Va. 2005). This decision not only inhibits the use of the FCA to address Iraq reconstruction fraud, it also could negatively affect the ability of the government to pursue the many false claims cases involving fraud on oil, gas, mining and other leasehold interests administered by the U.S. on behalf of Native American tribal authorities.

In Section Two, S. 2041 would clarify that the FCA covers funds administered by the United States, such as funds of the Coalition Provisional Authority or Native American funds. The amendments do this by defining the "Government money or property" protected by the Act to include not only funds belonging to the United States or provided to a third party to be spent on the Government's behalf, but also funds managed by the United States for an administrative beneficiary, as that term is defined in new paragraph (b)(4).

When the Government affirmatively takes on the role of administering the assets of another entity, it does so because it sees its interests and goals as inextricably intertwined with the interests and goals of that other entity. In those situations, the FCA should apply since false claims on the administered fund damage the interests and goals of the United States. If Government-administered funds are not protected by the FCA, the interests of both parties are deprived of the protection of the Government's primary remedy against fraud.

D. Knowing Retention of U.S. Overpayments and Unauthorized Diversion of Government Funds or Property

In addition to imposing liability on those who knowingly make or cause false claims, or false statements in support of false claims, the FCA also imposes liability on anyone who:

> has possession, custody, or control of property or money used, or to be used, by the Government and, intending to defraud the Government or willfully to conceal the property, delivers, or causes to be delivered, less property than the amount for which the person receives a certificate or receipt.

31 U.S.C. § 3729(a)(4).

Through long term practice under the Act, qui tam counsel such as I have seen that this provision could be improved by express reference to those situations in which a recipient of government funds learns after receiving the money that it was overpaid or was ineligible to receive the money in the first place, and, knowing this, fails to report the overpayment or return the funds to the government. This situation comes up most frequently in the health care context, in which providers learn from employees that they have been overcharging the government for years (by using the wrong billing code, for example).

This provision also could be improved by addressing those situations in which a company submits a proper claim for government funds, and then diverts the funds for unauthorized purposes. Examples would include research institutions using government grant money for expenditures unrelated to the grant or defense contractors using up-front payments by the military to pay bribes or kickbacks.

By adding language to the liability provision found at 31 U.S.C. Section 3729(a)(4), the bill would clarify that the FCA covers situations in which a person who already has obtained government funds either diverts the funds to unauthorized uses after obtaining the funds, or holds onto the funds after learning that they were not entitled to receive them in the first place. Thus, the bill would amend Section 3729(a)(4) so that it imposes liability on anyone who:

> has possession, custody, or control of Government money or property and, intending . . . to retain overpayment [sic] or knowingly to convert the money or property, permanently or temporarily, to an unauthorized use, fails to deliver or return, or fails to cause the return or delivery of the money or property, or delivers, returns or causes to be delivered, or returned less money or property than the amount due or owed.

I support this amendment because it wisely anticipates the need for the Department of Justice to have a statutory mechanism in place to recover funds that have been advanced to an entity for one purpose, and are then employed for a second, unauthorized purpose, including, for example, bribes, kickbacks or personal enrichment. During wartime, funds are often disbursed on an emergent basis in advance of the work being performed, and without the usual required certifications of performance under the contract. This amendment would give the United States a means to recover from a contractor that knowingly used government money for an unauthorized purpose.

I also support the amendment because it implements the Supreme Court's admonition that Americans should "turn square corners" when doing business with the Government. Health care providers and others who learn after the fact that they have obtained government money to which they are not entitled should be required by law to return the money, and should be held accountable under the FCA if they fail to do so. With our Medicare, Medicaid and other Social Security programs struggling for financial solvency, it is imperative that we put in place all available checks on fraud.

E. Prohibiting Release of FCA Claims by Private Parties

The proposed legislation is aimed at a new tactic used by companies subject to internal accusations of fraud: terminating potential informants with severance packages that include covenants not to sue. While most jurisdictions strike down these covenants as contrary to public policy when a company tries to use them to bar a FCA action, the lack of clear language on this issue in the FCA creates opportunities for companies to discourage potential whistleblowers from coming forward. It also provides companies with an avenue to retaliate against those who do come forward, and to delay the progress of the FCA prosecutions they initiate, by seeking to enforce these covenants.

In my own practice, I have seen the chilling effect that these covenants can have on those considering suits under the FCA. I have been contacted by attorneys representing individuals who either have signed, or have been asked to sign, a covenant not to sue, and who were unsure whether such a covenant would bar their contemplated qui tam lawsuit. I am confident that many individuals never make that initial call to a lawyer due to their incorrect assumption that these covenants prevent them from suing their company even when doing so on behalf of the United States.

To address this issue, the bill adds a new provision stating that: "No claim for a violation of section 3729 may be waived or released by any action of any person, except insofar as such action is part of a court approved settlement of a false claim civil action brought under this section."

I strongly support this provision. First and foremost, it alerts potential whistleblowers early on – when they are considering whether even to call a lawyer – that private covenants cannot interfere with their ability to bring a FCA lawsuit on behalf of the United States. Prior to hiring a lawyer, potential informants are much more likely to consult the text of the FCA than they are likely to research and review the case law on contracts that violate public policy. As a result of this statutory change, more potential informants will come forward in the first instance. Second, with this amendment, once a case has been filed, defendants cannot rely on conflicting case law, or case law that they might try to distinguish, to penalize or bar a qui tam lawsuit.

F. Protecting Company Contractors and Agents from Retaliation and Protecting Steps Taken to Stop FCA Violations and Association with Whistle- Blowers

The FCA protects employees from retaliation through discrimination in the terms of their employment as a result of steps they have taken to further a qui tam action. Thus, the statute currently provides for monetary damages and other relief for:

> "Any employee who is discharged, demoted, suspended, threatened, harassed, or in any other manner discriminated against in the terms and conditions of employment by his or her employer because of lawful acts done by the employee on behalf of the employee or others in furtherance of an action under [Section 3730]. . . ."

S. 2041 would expand the class of protected persons to include contractors and agents, as well as employees. It also would expand the class of protected activity to include: i) steps taken towards stopping the violation of the FCA and, ii) association with those filing FCA actions or attempting to stop violations of the FCA.

These changes are badly needed. Many potential whistleblowers learn of violations of the FCA as contractors or agents of the defendant, rather than as employees. For example, many of the cases alleging fraud on Medicare or Medicaid are brought by physicians against the hospitals and clinics who employ them through contracts. These individuals are as deserving of protection from retaliation as those who fall strictly within the definition of an "employee." Moreover, the anti-retaliation provision encourages informants to come forward. While informants recognize they will become unemployable within their industries once it becomes known that they have blown the whistle, the anti-retaliation provision of the Act provides somewhat of an "insurance policy" against financial devastation and may serve to deter retaliation.

It is also good public policy to amend this provision so that it protects those who try to stop misconduct from the inside, by using internal compliance programs, for example. Whistleblowers should be supported in their efforts to seek to correct the defendant's misdeeds through appropriate corporate channels before taking the more extreme step of bringing a qui tam lawsuit. Most of the whistleblowers I have represented or considered representing were employees who observed improper practices, tried to put an end to them within the company or organization, and were ignored, rebuffed, threatened with termination, or terminated. Typically, they explored the possibility of a FCA lawsuit only after failing to bring about change from within.

The wording of S. 2041 regrettably drops some of the prior language of the statute which provided protection against retaliation for those who take steps toward filing a qui tam lawsuit. This language should be restored to the bill so that the existing protections are not inadvertently removed.

G. FCA's Statute of Limitations Applicable to Section 3730(h) Actions

Another important clarification in S. 2041 pertains to the appropriate statute of limitations for lawsuits brought under the FCA against those who retaliate against whistleblowers by discriminating against them in the terms of employment. Section 3730(h) of the FCA provides a remedy for whistleblowers suffering such retaliation. Section 3731(b)(1) of the Act permits any "civil action under Section 3730" to be brought by the later of six years from the violation of Section 3729, or three years from government discovery of the violation, not to exceed ten years from the violation.

The Supreme Court recently held that the language in the FCA's statute of limitations that provides that the period to bring a claim begins to run on the date of "the violation of Section 3729" means that Congress did not intend the FCA's statute of limitations to apply to anti-retaliation claims, which arise under Section 3730 rather than under Section 3729. See Graham County Soil & Water Conservation Dist. v. U.S. ex rel. Wilson, 545 U.S. 409, 415 (2005). The Supreme Court so ruled notwithstanding the fact that Congress drafted Section 3731 so that it expressly applies to "any" civil action brought under Section 3730. Identifying a number of state statutes of limitations as examples, the Supreme Court held that individuals bringing Section 3730(h) claims must comply with the state statute of limitations applicable to the most "analogous" sort of action available under state law.

The bill amends Section 3731(b) to provide expressly that the statute of limitations for anti-retaliation claims brought under Section 3730(h) of the Act is the same as the statute of limitations for qui tam actions brought on behalf of the United States. The proposed amendment is advisable to protect the viability of the anti-retaliation remedy in Section 3730(h). It is also advisable to alleviate the pressure on whistleblowers to file qui tam actions prematurely to comply with the extremely short statutes of limitations for wrongful discharge found in state law.

The effect of the Graham County decision is that many whistleblowers who have suffered retaliation will have to file their anti-retaliation claims within an extremely short period following the retaliatory action in order to invoke the FCA's remedy. State statutes of limitation for unlawful discharge are ordinarily quite short. In fact, in Texas, where I practice, it is possible that the 90 day statute of limitations for causes of action based on retaliation against public employees might apply; in Graham County, Justice Thomas, who wrote the majority opinion, identified this state statute along with one other as "the likely analogous state statutes of limitations." 545 U.S. at 419, n. 3 (citing to TEX. GOVT. CODE ANN. § 554.005 (West 2004)). Examples of other extremely short statutes of limitations considered analogous by the Graham County Court are the following:

Connecticut's 90 day statute of limitations for retaliation actions by whistleblowers (CONN. GEN. STAT. 31-51m (2007)),
Florida's 180 day statute of limitations for retaliation actions by public whistleblowers (FLA. STAT.§§ ch. 112.3187(8)(a) (2007), ch. 448.103(2007));
Michigan's 90 day statute of limitations for retaliation actions by whistleblowers (MICH. COMP. LAWS ANN. § 15.363(1) (West 2008));
New York's one year statute of limitations for actions to enforce a statute "given wholly or partly to any person who will prosecute" (N.Y. CIV. PRAC. LAW ANN. § 215(4) (West 2003)); and *Ohio's six month statute of limitations for retaliation actions by whistleblowers. (OHIO REV. CODE ANN. § 4113.52(D) (Lexis 2008)).

The reason this decision reduces the effectiveness of the anti-retaliation remedy is that it will force many potential whistleblowers to give up this remedy so that they do not forfeit their ability to pursue a qui tam action in the manner contemplated by the statute. Individuals with causes of action under Section 3730(h) ordinarily have potential causes of action under Section 3729. However, the investigation and preparation of a qui tam complaint almost always requires much more time and work than the preparation of an anti-retaliation complaint.

In my experience, it is the extremely rare qui tam case that can be put together from "soup to nuts" in the short periods of time found in many of the state statutes of limitations for retaliatory discharge. To file a qui tam case, an individual must first locate counsel who specializes in qui tam law. Given the significant financial risks of taking on these complex cases, potential qui tam plaintiffs often find it necessary to present their information to several successive attorneys over a period of many months before finding one who will take the case. During the process of trying to retain counsel, and thereafter, considerable effort is expended researching applicable program or contract rules, which are often complicated and difficult to identify. In addition, potential relators may spend months locating, assembling and analyzing the evidence of the false claims. Often these individuals approach other witnesses to ask for their cooperation in obtaining additional documents or testimony. With the federal government's investigative resources as overburdened as they are, skilled qui tam counsel always endeavor to present the government with as much evidence as possible at the time of the qui tam filing. The chances of government interest in the case increase exponentially with the quantity of probative evidence submitted alongside the filing.

While in theory a potential qui tam relator could file his wrongful termination case in a timely fashion, and then continue to work on preparing a possible qui tam case, this course of action has serious disadvantages. First and foremost, the Section 3730(h) action, which inevitably would discuss the misconduct about which the individual had complained internally, would have to be filed on the public record. The FCA does not provide for a seal on anti-retaliation claims. As a result, the defendant would learn that the individual had "blown the whistle" before the Department of Justice had had an opportunity to investigate the allegations using covert means, as contemplated by the seal on qui tam actions. Second, the public disclosure rulings discussed above pose a serious risk that the anti-retaliation case would be viewed as a "public disclosure" barring a later qui tam case "based" on the allegations set forth in the anti-retaliation case.

Accordingly, unless this proposed legislation is enacted, the Graham County decision will limit many potential informants to three undesirable alternatives: i) file a wrongful discharge case in open court, thereby prejudicing the ability of the U.S. government to investigate any later-filed qui tam action and risking the effect of the "public disclosure bar"; ii) forego the wrongful discharge claim so that the allegations of misconduct can be filed under seal as part of a carefully-prepared qui tam case; or, iii) rush to file a qui tam action before the running of the state statute of limitations on the anti-retaliation claim, without engaging in adequate investigation and research to substantiate the merits of the qui tam claim.

H. Relation Back of Government Complaints

The FCA provides for qui tam plaintiffs to file their cases under seal so that the United States may investigate the allegations and decide whether to intervene while the matter remains confidential. The statute provides for a sixty day period for the intervention decision, unless the court grants an extension of this time for "good cause shown." As a practical matter, the Government rarely, if ever, makes its intervention decision within sixty days. The Government ordinarily applies for repeated extensions of the seal, and makes its decision within two to five years of the original filing. The lengthy period of Government investigation is a product of several factors: i) the complicated and inherently secret nature of financial frauds, which often requires the Government to use multiple subpoenas and review hundreds of boxes of documents to uncover or confirm the truth; ii) the tendency of defendants to engage counsel who employ sophisticated tactics to delay the investigation and postpone the day of reckoning; and, iii) the increasingly scarce resources available to the Government to investigate the hundreds of qui tam cases filed every year.

When the Government does decide to intervene in a case, it typically files an amended complaint that reflects some of the additional information and evidence gathered in its investigation, and, in some cases, refines the legal theories set forth in the relator's complaint. Since the overall statutory scheme provides for the relator to sue "on behalf of" the United States, it has been reasonable, until recently, to assume that the Government's amended complaint "relates back" to the qui tam filing, for statute of limitations purposes, just as if the original filing had been filed by the Government itself. Federal Rule of Civil Procedure 15(c)(2) allows amended pleadings to relate back when "the claim or defense asserted in the amended pleading arose out of the conduct, transaction, or occurrence set forth or attempted to be set forth in the original pleading."

A recent Court of Appeals decision, however, casts doubt on the relation-back assumption. In U.S. v. Baylor Univ. Med. Ctr., 469 F.3d 263, 268-70 (2nd Cir. 2006), the Second Circuit ruled that the United States may not avail itself of Fed. R. Civ. P. 15(c)(2) when amending a qui tam plaintiff's complaint. The implication of this ruling is that the United States sometimes will be forced to forego a thorough investigation of the merits of qui tam allegations in order to ensure that it does not lose claims due to the running of the statute of limitations. No public policy purpose is served by such a rule if the defendant is on notice of the alleged wrongdoing, as it almost always is once the government's investigation is launched through subpoenas and witness interviews.

S. 2041 would add a new paragraph (b)(3) to Section 3731 to clarify that, when the United States intervenes in a qui tam action and files a complaint embodying allegations that arise out of the conduct, transaction or occurrence set forth or attempted to be set forth in the original qui tam pleading, the United States' complaint "relates back" to the date of the qui tam complaint for statute of limitations purposes. The new statutory language would be consistent with the rules on "relation back" of pleadings in non-qui tam cases, as set forth in Federal Rule of Civil Procedure 15(c)(2). As a practical matter, this amendment is necessary to preserve the FCA as an effective tool. With the shortage of investigative resources, it is now common for qui tam cases to remain under seal without a government intervention decision for three to five years. I have represented clients in at least two cases that remained under seal even longer. During this period of time, the statute of limitations is likely to run on many of the claims alleged in the qui tam complaint unless they are, in effect, tolled for the United States by the filing of the relator's claim on its behalf.

I. Delegation of CID Authority

The FCA was amended in 1986 to give the Department of Justice an investigative tool: civil investigative demands, or "CIDs," which are administrative subpoenas for documents, interrogatory responses and sworn testimony that may be used to investigate allegations of potential violations of the FCA. See 31 U.S.C. § 3733. Under the current statute, the Attorney General must review and issue every CID. 31 U.S.C. § 3733(a)(1). The Attorney General may not delegate this authority. Id.

The use of some form of Department of Justice compulsory process is increasingly necessary for effective investigation of FCA allegations. Program agencies are short on resources and often are unable to assign investigators even to patently meritorious cases, let alone issue Office of Inspector General subpoenas. Congress has enacted statutory restrictions on interviewing former and current employees of defendants without going through counsel, thereby making it difficult for the government's investigators to interview many of the key witnesses.

Regrettably, however, due to the statutory requirement that the Attorney General must personally issue every CID, the Department of Justice very rarely uses this investigatory tool. My understanding is that Assistant U.S. Attorneys and Main Justice trial attorneys are disinclined to request the issuance of CIDs because they have heard of CID request memos that languished in the bureaucracy for months without action. At one point just a few years ago, attorneys in the Commercial Litigation Branch advised one of my colleagues that CIDs sent to the Attorney General for approval and signature were not being acted upon; for over a year, they were neither reviewed nor approved. I am aware of very few instances in which the Department of Justice issued or even considered issuing a CID to investigate my clients' allegations.

S. 2041 would permit the Attorney General to delegate the authority to issue CIDs. This is a badly needed "fix" to the FCA that I understand is desired by both the qui tam bar and the Department of Justice.

II. Other Needed Changes

A. Permissible Uses of CID Material

There is a second reason why the Department of Justice has been reluctant to employ the CID authority. My understanding is that Department attorneys are concerned about language in the FCA that limits access to CID material to government "custodians" and "false claims law investigators." They see a risk that a court might conclude that such this language implicitly precludes them from showing the CID material to fact and expert witnesses, consultants and the parties. This is unfortunate because the qui tam relator and other witnesses and experts often are uniquely qualified to assess whether a defendant has responded fully to a CID, or to explain the meaning, function or context of a produced document. I have consistently been told by government attorneys, however, that they can not disclose materials obtained through CIDs to me or to my clients, even though they covet our assistance in reviewing the often voluminous materials for responsiveness and completeness, and need our help in analyzing the meaning and significance of the materials.

While statutory language does permit Department of Justice attorneys to make "official use" of CID material in "other cases and proceedings," they are disinclined to rely on this language since it references "other" cases and proceedings rather than "False Claims Act" cases and proceedings. Without express authority to disclose the CID material to fact witnesses, experts and the parties to an FCA proceeding, they fear that they may be unable to interpret accurately and efficiently the documents and information produced and, accordingly, that time spent on CID requests may be largely unproductive.

I urge the Committee to expand the bill to define the uses that the Department of Justice may make of CID material in false claims law proceedings. Surely, Congress intended the Department of Justice to use the material to develop further evidence, to litigate the case and/or to resolve the allegations. Accordingly, the statute should state clearly that the Department of Justice may use CID material for those purposes.

B. Clarifying that Qui Tam Cases May Proceed Without Billing Documents

The majority of Circuits have ruled that FCA complaints contain averments of fraud, and consequently must be pled with particularity pursuant to Federal Rule of Civil Procedure 9(b). Unfortunately, however, in addressing the question whether qui tam complaints satisfy Rule 9(b), many of these Circuit Courts have required a degree of detail that could not be known to anyone outside a defendant's billing or audit department, insisting that qui tam complaints not only describe the fraud scheme with particularity, but also describe the false claims submitted to the Government in such detail as essentially to require access to billing documents in order to provide claim numbers, dates, patient names, procedure codes, etc.

These rulings significantly undercut the viability of the FCA, rendering it extraordinarily difficult for many insiders with reliable knowledge of fraud to bring cases that will survive a motion to dismiss. For example, because compartmentalization of functions is common in most organizations, operational personnel who are knowledgeable about the organization's fraud scheme and how it works often have no involvement with the billing process and thus cannot provide such details as the dates on which the defendant sent false invoices to the government. Without such details, that person's qui tam complaint would be vulnerable to dismissal for lack of particularity under many court decisions. Courts apply the particularity requirements of traditional fraud cases to False Claims Act pleadings, but there is an important distinction between those two kinds of cases that should be noted and addressed. In a traditional fraud case, the plaintiff complains of the fraud perpetrated on him by the defendant. It is not surprising, therefore, that he is expected to allege in some detail the defendant's fraudulent interactions with him. In a False Claims Act case, on the other hand, the plaintiff complains of the fraud perpetrated by the defendant on a third party – the government. In that circumstance the plaintiff may be very knowledgeable about the fraud scheme and how it works, but he may quite understandably lack access to some of the transactional details he would possess if he were the defrauded party. Defendants are entitled to fair notice of the transgressions they are alleged to have committed, but hyper-technical pleading requirements that serve no purpose but to defeat False Claims Act actions without regard to the merits of a claim disserve both the remedial purposes of the Act and the public interest.

Congress should amend the Act to overrule these strict application decisions. Congress could do so without placing FCA cases outside the ambit of Fed. R. Civ. P. 9(b), by providing that a qui tam case may proceed so long as the particulars alleged in the complaint are sufficient to put the defendant on notice of the nature of the alleged misconduct, and that the specifics of the claims documentation need not be pled if other information serves this purpose.

End Notes

[1] S. 2041, 110th Cong., 1st Sess. (2007).

[2] FCA Implementation 1990, Hearing Before the Subcomm. on Admin. Law and Gov. Relations of the House Comm. on the Judiciary, 101st Cong., 2d Sess. 3 (1990) (statement of Sen. Grassley).

[3] U.S. ex rel. Springfield Terminal Ry. v. Quinn, 14 F.3d 645, 649 (D.C. Cir. 1994).

[4] Rockwell Int'l Corp. v. U.S., 127 S. Ct. 1397 (2007).

[5] See U.S. ex rel. Reagan v. E. Tex. Med. Ctr. Reg'l Healthcare Sys., 384 F.3d 168, 176 (5th Cir. 2004); Minn. Ass'n of Nurse Anesthetists v. Allina Health System Corp., 276 F.3d 1032 (8th Cir.), cert. denied, 537 U.S. 944 (2002); U.S. v. Board of Trustees of the Leland Stanford, Jr. Univ., 161 F.3d 533 (9th Cir. 1998), cert. denied, 526 U.S. 1066 (1999); U.S. ex rel. Findley v. FPC-Boron Employees' Club, 105 F.3d 675 (D.C. Cir.), cert. denied, 522 U.S. 865 (1997); U.S. ex rel. Precision Co. v. Koch Indus., Inc., 971 F.2d 548, 552 (10th Cir. 1992), cert. den. 507 U.S. 951 (1993); United St.

In: Fighting Fraud with Qui Tam and the False Claims Act ISBN: 978-1-61668-221-7
Editor: Ian M. Ortiz

Chapter 7

WRITTEN STATEMENT OF PAMELA H. BUCY, BAINBRIDGE PROFESSOR OF LAW, UNIVERSITY OF ALABAMA SCHOOL OF LAW

Pamela H. Bucy

S.2041, "The False Claims Act Correction Act of 2007," is likely to encourage more whistleblowers to bring actions under The False Claim Act (FCA).[2] In addition, because S.2041 also gives the United States Department of Justice (DOJ) greater authority to monitor frivolous qui tam actions, S. 2041 has the potential to enhance the quality of relators' actions and thereby protect defendants from inappropriate qui tam action. There are, however, some respects in which S. 2041 could be improved upon. This Statement addresses those.

I. OVERVIEW OF THE CIVIL FALSE CLAIMS ACT, 31 U.S.C. §3729 ET SEQ

The civil False Claims Act (FCA) creates a cause of action on the part of "any person" who believes that another person or entity has submitted false claims to the federal government. The FCA has been heralded as one of the most effective crime-fighting tools ever devised, and cursed as irresponsible and disruptive to a healthy economy.

Under the FCA, a person who believes that he has information and evidence that someone else (individual or company) has filed false claims against the federal government may file a lawsuit making such allegations. This plaintiff (termed a "qui tam relator") is required to file his lawsuit under seal (not even serving it on the defendant). The relator is also required to give a copy of the lawsuit to the United States Department of Justice (DOJ), along with a written report of "all material evidence and information" the relator possesses.[3]

The lawsuit stays under seal, often for two years or more, to allow DOJ to fully investigate the charges made by the relator. The secrecy provided by sealing the complaint not only protects a defendant's reputation if the relator's information amounts to nothing, but also facilitates DOJ's further investigation of the relator's information.

At the conclusion of its investigation, DOJ decides whether it will intervene in the lawsuit as an additional plaintiff. If it does, DOJ assumes "primary responsibility" for the case, although the relator remains as a plaintiff and is guaranteed a participatory role.[4]

In some cases, DOJ handles the entire case after intervening; in others, relators work hand-in-hand with government prosecutors. In some cases, relators and their attorneys assume the bulk of the investigative and litigative duties.

If DOJ does not join the lawsuit, the relator may continue pursuing the case, litigating it alone. Even if DOJ does not join a relator's case, it retains authority over the relator's lawsuit in several ways: DOJ monitors the case and may join it at any time, even for limited purposes, such as appeal; DOJ may settle or dismiss a relator's suit over the relator's objections as long as the relator has been given an opportunity in court to be heard; DOJ may seek limitations on the relator's involvement in the case, or seek alternative remedies (such as administrative sanctions) in lieu of the relator's lawsuit.

If the government joins the relator's case, the relator is guaranteed at least 15 percent of any judgment or settlement and the court can award more -- up to 25 percent. If the government does not join the lawsuit, the relator is guaranteed 25 percent and could receive up to 30 percent of the judgment. The amount within the statutory award depends upon the relator's helpfulness to the government. Because the FCA's damages and penalty provisions tend to generate exceptionally large judgments, relators' percentages involve substantial sums.

II. The FCA's Private-Public Partnership Makes the FCA an Effective Tool against Fraud

There are three primary reasons the FCA is so effective. First, it recognizes the value of "inside information of fraud and encourages those who have such information to come forward with it. Second, it effectively recruits legal talent who can supplement strapped prosecutive resources of DOJ. Third, it provides a mechanism for private citizens to report information to, and work with, law enforcement. This dialog has the potential, not yet fully realized, for controlling frivolous qui tam actions.

A. The Importance of Whistleblowers

In Detecting, Deterring and Combating Fraud Complex economic wrongdoing cannot be detected or deterred effectively without the help of those who are intimately familiar with it. Law enforcement will always be outsiders to organizations where fraud is occurring. They will not find out about such fraud until it is too late, if at all. When law enforcement does find out about such fraud, it is very labor intensive to investigate.

Fraud is usually buried in mountains of paper or digital documents. It is hidden within an organization. Many different people within an organization, in multiple offices, divisions, and corporate capacities, may have participated in the illegality. Because of the complex nature of economic crime and the diffuse nature of business environments, it may not be apparent, perhaps for years, that malfeasance is afoot. By then, victims will have been hurt, records and witnesses will have disappeared, and memories will have faded.

Given these facts, insiders who are willing to blow the whistle are the only effective way to learn that wrongdoing has occurred. Information from insiders is the only way to effectively and efficiently piece together what happened and who is responsible. Insiders can provide invaluable assistance during an investigation by identifying key records and witnesses, interpreting technical or industry information, providing expertise, and explaining the customs and habits of the business or industry. Help from an insider can save time and expense for both law enforcement and putative defendants by focusing the investigation on relevant areas.

Because of the valuable information brought by insiders, it is no surprise that government officials state: "Whistleblowers are essential to our operation. Without them, we wouldn't have cases."[5]

It can be a difficult decision to become a whistleblower because "[w]hat happens to whistleblowers shouldn't happen to a dog."[6] Personally and professionally, it can be a devastating experience to become a whistleblower. And, unlike the typical cooperating individual whose looming criminal liability is the impetus to cooperate with law enforcement, most whistleblowers have a choice. They have not participated in illegality and thus need not cooperate to obtain a "better bargain" for their own problems.

The FCA recognizes the difficulty of coming forward as a whistleblower, and in three ways encourages insiders to become whistleblowers. First, it awards whistleblowers who become relators in successful cases. This is simple market economics. Not only does the FCA guarantee such relators a share of judgements obtained and recovery of attorneys fees and litigation expenses, but it communicates, in this way, that whistleblowing is valuable. For whistleblowing to be seen as socially acceptable, rather than disloyal snitching or "tattling," it must be viewed with approval.[7] It is a human tendency to measure worth by material rewards.[8] Large financial awards to those who provide helpful inside information not only increase the attention whistleblowing gets and helps overcome the hardships it brings, they also affirm whistleblowing as a worthy endeavor.

B. The Resource of Legal Talent

In qui tam practice under the FCA, insiders potentially bring another resource to law enforcement: legal talent with skill and resources that can supplement DOJ resources. The large potential recoveries and statutory award of attorneys' fees under the FCA are incentive for top legal to represent relators. The structure of the FCA also has the potential to discourage inexperienced or unskilled relators' counsel. Every relator's goal is to convince DOJ to intervene as co-plaintiff in the case. To do so, relators' attorneys need to present to DOJ, prior to filing their complaint, a thorough, well thought out, carefully researched case describing exactly how the false claims were generated and how the fraud can be proven.

C. Mechanism for Cooperation

The FCA provides a protocol for whistleblowers to report their information and for law enforcement to evaluate their information. DOJ has a structured system in place for obtaining information from whistleblowers about potential fraud upon the government, for investigating this information, and for working with whistleblowers who become qui tam relators. The FCA allocate duties to both DOJ and relators. While the adequacy of DOJ resources to fully participate in this protocol is an open question, the point is a structured system exists for whistleblowers and law enforcement to work together to pursue potential fraud.

III. The Costs of the FCA's Private-Public Partnership

An honest appraisal of the FCA recognizes that for all of its benefits, the FCA's unusual partnering of private and public plaintiffs presents potential problems for businesses, regulatory authorities, and the judicial system.

The FCA presents problems for businesses. It is expensive for a company to respond to a allegations of fraud. Company employees are distracted from their normal duties when they have to gather subpoenaed records, respond to inquiries of investigators, or testify at hearings or depositions. When a fraud investigation becomes public, business expansions, corporate borrowing, and mergers may be put on hold, or lost as opportunities. Stock prices may fall and lay-offs may result, clients may leave, company stars may jump ship, company moral may plummet.

The FCA present problems for DOJ. It absorbs resources of DOJ and the agencies that investigate relators' allegations. Relators can end up driving some of DOJ's investigative agenda by filing cases. Relators may generate harmful precedent that binds DOJ and prevents DOJ from shaping the law. Whereas DOJ can choose which cases to pursue so as to present favorable legal theories and facts on appeal in efforts to develop helpful precedent and further the FCA, relators rarely will have this institutional interest in case law development.

Lastly, the FCA poses complications for the judicial system. Relators' actions often require the courts to referee disputes between relators and DOJ. To resolve these conflicts, courts find themselves delving into issues of prosecutive discretion and executive branch policy, issues that present separation of powers tensions.

IV. Ways in Which the FCA Currently Addresses the Costs of the Fca's Private-Public Prosecutor Partnership

The FCA currently includes four features which help address the tensions created by the FCA's unique private-public prosecutor partnership: (1) required dialog between relators and DOJ, (2) seal requirement, (3) DOJ's statutory authority to monitor and limit relators' involvement, (4) DOJ's authority to move for dismissal of frivolous actions. These features can neutralize the difficulties created for businesses, regulators, and the courts by this tension.

A. Required Dialog

The FCA requires that relators present their information of potential fraud to the DOJ prior to filing their complaint and also provide DOJ with a copy of their complaint and all relevant information and evidence they have after filing the complaint.[9] This required communication provides DOJ with the opportunity to corral frivolous relators' actions.

B. Seal Period

When relators file their lawsuits they are required to do so under seal, not even serving the defendants.[10] While the matter remains under seal, DOJ has the opportunity to investigate the allegations to determine if it will intervene as plaintiff, seek dismissal of the case, or seek some restrictions on the relator's involvement in the case. The initial secrecy surrounding qui tam complaints and the confidentiality of the reports relators file with DOJ help to protect defendants from reputational damage and the costs incurred in responding to a frivolous private action. DOJ can weed out frivolous allegations and refine credible allegations further protects defendants from reputational and financial damage that could result from unfounded or poorly pled private lawsuits.

C. DOJ Authority to Monitor Relators

The FCA gives DOJ considerable authority to monitor and control relators' conduct in FCA actions, whether or not DOJ intervenes. DOJ may move for extensions of the seal period to allow full investigation of relators' complaints and evidence,[11] seek restrictions on a relator's involvement in a case,[12] monitor lawsuits in which DOJ does not intervene by receiving copies of all pleadings filed, and depositions taken,[13] intervene at any time during a case "upon a showing of good cause,"[14] seek stays (in camera if necessary) in the relators' action if it interferes with Government investigations of related civil or criminal matters,[15] pursue the matter through any alternate remedy including administrative proceedings.[16]

D. DOJ Authority to Move for Dismissal

Of all of DOJ's supervisory powers over relators, the most important in protecting against frivolous qui tam actions is its authority to move for dismissal of a relator's lawsuit.[17] DOJ has utilized its authority to seek dismissal of qui tam actions sparingly. There is some logic to this approach: there is always a chance, however small, that the relator will prevail and collect a judgment, of which at least seventy percent will go to the government. Thus, economically it is advantageous for the government to remain a passive observer in the FCA actions it does not join.

E. Resources

It takes considerable DOJ resources to exercise its authority over relators' actions. If the FCA is to remain a powerful tool against fraud, such resources need to be allocated. Only by effective and thorough monitoring, can we have some assurance that the FCA's unique private-public partnership will further the public interest, protect defendants from frivolous actions, and preserve the long-term viability of the FCA.

V. How S.2041 Enhances the FCA's Effectiveness and How Revisions in S. 2041 Would Further Enhance the FCA's Effectiveness

A. The "Presentment" Clause

S. 2041, Section 2

S. 2041, Section 2 addresses the "presentment" issue raised in United States ex rel. Totten v. Bombardier Corp.,[18] and United States DRC v. Custer Battles.[19] In these decisions, courts held that liability under the FCA attaches only if the claim is "presented to an officer or employee of the United States Government." In both cases, the courts held that this meant the FCA did not apply to false claims submitted. In Totten,, the claims had been submitted to a "grantee" of federal funds; in Custer Battles, the claims were submitted to the Coalition Provisional Authority (CPA) established to rebuild and administer Iraq after Saddam Hussein's capture.[20]

Edward L. Totten brought a qui tam action alleging that defendants, Bombardier Corporation, and Envirovac, Inc., delivered defective rail cars to the National Railroad Passenger Corporation (Amtrak) and further, that they submitted false claims for payment of the rail cars by certifying that the cars met contractual specifications when they did not. Amtrack is not a federal governmental agency but a private entity which receives federal funds as a "grantee." As a grantee, Amtrak paid defendants with federal funds.[21]

While recognizing that the FCA's definition of "claim" specifically includes "claims presented to grantees,"[22] the DC Court of Appeals noted that the FCA, in § 3729(a)(1) also requires presentment of the claims "to an officer or employee of the United States Government."[23] Finding the language in § 37299(a)(1) controlling, the court held that presentment to a federal grantee did not fall within the FCA. The DC Circuit noted that the inconsistency in the FCA provisions was likely a "drafting error"[24] but held that Congress, not the courts, was the body to correct the error.[25]

In Custer Battles, the District Court for the Eastern District of Virginia examined three types of funds that financed the Coalition Provisional Authority (CPA) established to rebuild Iraq. The court found that Iraqi funds confiscated by the United States "vested" title in the United States and thus claims for "vested" funds were within the FCA.[26] The court further found that claims submitted for "seized" funds (Iraqi state assets, mostly currency and negotiable instruments, "seized" by Coalition Forces were within the FCA because even though the United States did not hold title to such funds, it had "dominion and control" over such funds,[27] and had the "discretion to direct [that their] expenditure [be] in the best interest of the United States."[28] Lastly, the court held that claims submitted for funds from the "Development Fund for Iraq" (DFI), funded from multiple sources including the United Nations and international donations, were not within the FCA because these were funds given to and belonging to the Iraqi people.[29] Clarifying the definition of 'Government money or property" will help resolve questions of blended funds.

Lastly, the Sixth Circuit has weighed in, holding in United States ex rel. Sanders v. Allison Engine Company, Inc. that the FCA, at least in §§ 3729(a)(2) and (a) (3), do not require presentment to an "officer or employee of the Government."[30] The Supreme Court has granted certiorari in this case.

By defining "Government money or property" as "money or property the United States Government provides, has provided, or will reimburse to a contractor, grantee, agent or other recipient to be spent or used on the Government's behalf or to advance Government programs,"[31]

S. 2041 makes clear that the FCA covers federal funds, whether disbursed by a grantee or directly by the federal government, and whether held by the federal government as a beneficiary for others.

S. 2041 does not, however, correct the "drafting error" identified by the D.C. Court of Appeals whereby one provision of the FCA (§ 3729(a)(1)) requires presentment of the claim to "an officer or employee of the United States Government," while another provision (§ 3739(c)) includes claims submitted to "grantees," who likely are not "officers or employees of the United States Government."

This anomaly should be corrected. Thus, I would recommend that § 3729(a)(1) be amended by substituting "knowingly makes, uses or causes to be made or used" for the language "knowingly presents, or causes to be presented."

B. Government Employees as Relators

S. 2041, Section 3

Section 3 of S. 2041 addresses a problem that has bedeviled courts for decades, i.e., whether government employees qualify to be relators. Utilizing different rationales, almost all courts have held that government employees whose duties include uncovering fraud, do not qualify as relators.[32]

S. 2041 permits a government employee to qualify as a relator when the government employee reports the fraud utilizing the designated protocol and no one does anything.[33] In this circumstance and after waiting at least 12 months, the employee may file an FCA action.

There are several noteworthy points about S. 2041, Section 3:

(1) The employees to whom this protocol applies are those who "learned of the information that underlies the alleged violation of § 3729 that is the basis of the action in the course of the person's employment by the United States." Thus, government employees who happen to learn of fraud independently of their government employment still qualify as relators. For obvious policy reasons (bringing forth important information of fraud) and to maintain equality with other

potential relators, this limitation is appropriate. This is also the approach taken, appropriately so, by the courts that have considered this scenario.[34]

(2) The employee must present "all necessary and specific material allegations" through the proscribed reporting chain. This requirement of specificity should prevent government employees from "gaming" the reporting protocol by reporting generalities, or holding back information, in hopes of filing their own FCA actions.
(3) The reporting mechanism set forth (to the agency inspector general, employee's supervisor and Attorney General) is multi-sourced and thus, the information is less likely to get overlooked.
(4) The proviso that the government employee may file an FCA action after 12 months from the time he reports the information as required if the Attorney General has not filed an FCA action is consistent with the FCA's terms and philosophy that qui tam actions should be able to proceed even if DOJ does not intervene.

Despite these positive aspects of this amendment, it should not be passed. There are significant policy problems in allowing government employees to file FCA actions when the information they use is information they obtain while serving as a government employee. The reporting protocols in S. 2041, which by the way should be required for government employees regardless of FCA issues, cannot overcome these problems.

(1) Access to confidential information. By virtue of their official position, government employees whose duty is to investigate fraud by government contractors, obtain access to confidential, proprietary, and privileged information of companies that serve as government contractors. These governmental officials also have access to internal governmental information including confidential and non-public records and experts. Access to all of this information is granted only because of the employee's governmental position. It is wrong for a government employee to use this access for his personal benefit.
(2) Damaged Credibility. Often the government auditor or agent who investigated fraud by a contractor is a key witness at any civil or criminal trial or administrative hearing. These individuals often testify as summary expert witnesses, explaining billing requirements and tracing how the defendant's conduct violated these requirements. When this individual has filed a lawsuit under the FCA in his own name and stands to profit personally from it, his credibility as a witness is ruined. This unfairly cripples any government case.
(3) Conflict of Interest. There are specific prohibitions against federal employees using "nonpublic government information...to further any private interest,"[35] participating in a government matter in which the employee has a financial interest,[36] using public office for private gain,[37] using government property or time for personal purposes,[38] and holding a financial interest that may conflict with the impartial performance of government duties[39]. There are also criminal penalties for federal government employees who participate in matters in which they have a financial interest.[40]

   When a government employee who obtains information of fraud by a government contractor in the course of the employee's duties, files an FCA action in his own name, all of the above regulations and statutes are violated. They are violated when the employee reviews documents, interviews witnesses, and discusses strategy and investigative direction with other government employees with expertise in such matters. Access to such information and expertise would not be available to the employee if he were a private citizen; he should not reap special benefit from the unique access he obtains by virtue of his employment.

(4) Erosion of Public Confidence. When potential defendants or witnesses know that a government employee who is investigating fraud may be working for himself and his own profit, they are less likely to come forward or voluntarily cooperate, or be fully forthcoming.

Also, the general public cannot help but look with scorn on a governmental system that allows its employees to personally profit from doing his job.

Summary: Section 3 of S. 2041 should not be passed, nor under any circumstance should government employees who obtain information about fraud in the course of their governmental duties be allowed to file qui tam actions.

C. Barred Actions

S. 2041, Section 4

S. 2041, Section 4, amends what is known as the FCA's "jurisdictional bar" provision. This provision, which seeks to ensure that relators' information in fact assists the government, is key to the FCA's goal of encouraging knowledgeable whistleblowers to bring forth helpful information about fraud upon the government. Since the 1986 amendments, this provision has generated the greatest amount of litigation of any FCA issue. While S. 2041 remedies inequities that have arisen given court decisions, principally Rockwell International Corporation v.United States ex rel. Stone,[41] it is not yet an optimal revision of "jurisdictional bar" provision.

S. 2041 makes three major changes to current "jurisdictional bar" provision: (1) it gives the Attorney General sole authority to raise the issue whether relators' information is based upon what is publicly known, (2) it cures the problem created by Rockwell, and (3) it redefines the definition of "public information."

(1) Authority to Challenge Relator's Eligibility as Plaintiff. S. 2041 assigns to the Attorney General sole authority to seek dismissal of a relator on the ground that the relator provides nothing new to the case.[42] Currently, this provision is "jurisdictional," which empowers any party, including defendants, to seek dismissal of a relator on this ground. For two reasons, this part of S. 2041, Section 3, makes sense. First, DOJ should assume a greater role in policing frivolous qui tam actions. This amendment consolidates and helps direct this duty to DOJ. Second, DOJ is uniquely situated to determine whether the allegations made by a relator are in fact based upon public information since assessing this often requires analysis of data available primarily to DOJ.

(2) The Rockwell Decision. In Rockwell, the Supreme Court in held that James Stone, the relator who brought a qui tam action against Rockwell International Corporation, was precluded from recovering any portion of the almost $5 million judgment

> awarded because the information Stone presented to DOJ when he initiated the case were not the ultimate facts upon which Rockwell was convicted.[43] By adding a wild card (the claims upon which the verdict will rest) to the existing unpredictability of litigation, this interpretation of the FCA will discourage knowledgeable individuals from becoming relators.

S. 2041 cures this problem by making clear that a relator is entitled to a portion of any recovery if the relator's information contributed to the "essential elements of liability."

Although S. 2041 cures the problem presented by Rockwell, it does so in a confusing way that will lead to significant practical problems. By focusing on "essential elements of liability" ie, what ultimately is proven in a case, S. 2041 adds to tensions between relators and DOJ. Linking relators' recoveries to the claims stay in the case all the way to judgment may well cause DOJ and relators to battle over what claims stay in a case or are heavily litigated during a trial. DOJ may be tempted to leverage the decision about claims into a decision about what percentage of the recovery relators will get. These disagreements will require more refereeing by the courts. This, in turn, will add to the separation of powers tensions already existing in FCA cases.

If S. 2041focused instead on the information the relator brings to DOJ initially rather than on the ultimate outcome of the case, the FCA will continue to encourage relators to come forward while also avoiding the inequity of Rockwell and the practical problems created by the current amendment. Instead of the suggestion in S. 2041, Section 3, 31 U.S.C. § 3730(e)(4)(A) should be amended as follows:

(4)(A) Upon timely motion of the Attorney General, a court shall dismiss an action or claim brought under section 3730(b) if the information supplied to the Attorney General by the relator is based exclusively on the public disclosure of allegations or transactions in ...."

(2) Changes to sources of "disqualifying public information" S. 2041 changes the definition of "public disclosure" in four ways. These changes impact relators' ability to bring FCA actions.

The first change to the definition of "public disclosure" in S. 2041 (at (4)(B)) is limiting public disclosures to "disclosures made on the public record or that have otherwise been disseminated broadly to the general public." There are three problems with this proposal. First, it is vague. "Public record" and "disseminated broadly to the general public" are unclear terms. No one: not relators, defense counsel, DOJ, or the courts, will have a clear sense of what these terms mean. The second reason this provision should not be enacted is that it is confusing when read with (4)(A), which sets forth a list of sources of public disclosure. Interpretative questions abound: Does 4(B) overrule 4(A), or supplement it? If there are conflicts in 4(A) and 4(B), which controls? For example, what if a "hearing" referred to in 4(A) is not on the "public record? " The third problem with this provision is that it is unnecessary. Section 4(A) lists the sources of public disclosure. There is no need to describe them again, this time generically, in 4(B).

The second change S. 2041 makes to the definition of public disclosure also limits the definition.

Specifically, 4(A) of S. 2041 provides that relators are disqualified if their information is based upon a "Federal criminal, civil, or administrative hearing" or a Federal administrative or General Accounting Office report, hearing, audit or investigation. Currently, the FCA is not limited to Federal matters. Thus with S. 2041, relators whose information is based upon state or possibly international criminal, civil or administrative matters would qualify as relators as long as the relator's information is not otherwise barred (because it had been disclosed, for example, in the news media).

This is an appropriate proposal. The point of the FCA is to encourage individuals who have knowledge of fraud upon the federal government to come forward with their information. Trolling through the overwhelming amount of information publicly available to find instances, even large instances, of fraud upon the federal government, is not a job that federal law enforcement officials can do alone. There is too much information and not enough investigative resources. To encourage knowledgeable individuals (ie, "professional relators" who specialize in such data gathering endeavors) to seek out information about fraud upon the federal government about which federal law enforcement officials are not aware, is good policy.

Notably, there are two significant restrictions on this "trolling-through-state-proceedings" opportunity that will limit possible abuse. The first restriction is the requirement that the information brought by a relator has not been disclosed in the news media. If the facts from the state proceeding have appeared in the news media, the information is public and the relator is disqualified. Second, a number of state agencies, Medicaid for example, are statutorily and contractually obligated to report instances of fraud involving federal funds to the federal government. When these state agencies fulfill their federal obligation to report such fraud, they will do so in a "federal administrative report" which the current amendment similarly includes as public information. Once such a report is made to federal authorities by a state office, the relator is disqualified.

The third change S. 2041 makes in the definition of "public disclosure" is excluding information obtained from "a Freedom of Information Act [FOIA] request."[44] Like the limitation of public disclosure to "Federal" sources of information," this proposal will expand relators' ability to bring actions. It will encourage "professional relators" to seek and research FOIA data sources, thereby supplementing law enforcement's investigative resources. Because any such FOIA search efforts are still subject to existing limitations on what is public disclosure, namely, information in the news media or disclosed in various hearings, reports or audits, this FOIA "carve-out," should result in helpful but not duplicative assistance from relators.

The fourth change S. 2041 makes to the definition of "public disclosure" is excluding information obtained from "exchanges with law enforcement and other Government employees."[45] Like the other limitations to the definition of public disclosure proposed by S. 2041, this information is still subject to the caveat that it is nevertheless public information if this information is reported in media or in hearings, audits or reports.

This change in the definition of "public disclosure" should not be made. It will be helpful only in a few instances (when all government employees at issue are ignoring their duties) and could generate considerable mischief (encouraging would-be relators to pester government employees for information). For these two reasons it should not be included.

Lastly, S. 2041 does not make a change to the "jurisdictional bar" provision that should be made. Neither current § 3730(e)(4)(A) nor S.2041, 4(A), includes "investigation" in the list of sources that constitute public disclosure. Both refer to "public disclosure...in a criminal, civil or administrative hearing" and later to a "congressional, administrative, or Government Accounting Office report, hearing, audit, or investigation...." The term "investigation should be added in both places for the obvious reason that sometimes investigations will become public. Allowing relators to file suit based upon a publicly disclosed investigation would be parasitic to the government's existing effort.

In summary, therefore, S. 2041, Section 4 at 4(A) and (B) should state:[46]

(4)(A) Upon timely motion of the Attorney General, a court shall dismiss an action or claim brought under section 3730(b) if the allegations relating to all essential elements of liability of the action or claim are information supplied by the relator is based exclusively on the public disclosure of allegations or transactions in a Federal criminal, civil or administrative hearing or investigation, in a congressional, Federal administrative, or Government Accountability Office report, hearing, audit or investigation or from the news media.

(B) In this paragraph:

(i) The term 'public disclosure' includes only disclosures made on the public record or that have otherwise been disseminated broadly to the general public.

(ii) The person bringing the action does not create a public disclosure by obtaining information from a Freedom of Information Act request or from information exchanges with law enforcement and other Government employees if such information does not otherwise qualify as publicly disclosed.

(iii) An action or claim is based on public disclosure only if the person bringing the action derived his knowledge of all essential elements of liability of the action or claim alleged in his complaint from the public disclosure.

D. Relief From Retaliatory Actions

S. 2041, Section 5

Section 5 makes two major changes in the protection against retaliatory actions. First, section 5 expands the coverage of individuals who are entitled to seek relief from an "employee" to "employee, government contractor or agent." This is an appropriate expansion of the FCA. It reflects the reality of who is, can be, and should be, relators under the FCA.

The second major change made by section 5 concerns the description of conduct which activates the protection of the FCA. The current FCA provides protection for "lawful acts ...in furtherance of an action under this section, including investigation for, initiation of, testimony for, or assistance in an action filed or to be filed under this section." S. 2041 replaces this language with the following: "lawful acts...in furtherance of other efforts to stop 1 or more violations of this chapter."

S. 2041's proposed change in the conduct protected is problematic. The amendment is confusing and raises multiple interpretative difficulties. What exactly is an "effort" to "stop" a "violation"? Is reporting the problem internally sufficient "effort"? Or is reporting to law enforcement agencies necessary to qualify for protection? Must a person report to the correct agency or just make a reasonable attempt to report to the appropriate agency? How much information must be reported to constitute an "effort"? Is "effort" satisfied only by filing an

FCA action? Does "violation" mean the defendant must be found liable before the protection is activated? Depending on the interpretation of these terms, S. 2041 could be too narrow (providing protection only the filing of FCA actions and only when defendants are actually found liable) or too broad (reporting vague suspicions internally).

It seems more prudent to retain the current language with minor amendments to it to clarify issues over which courts have struggled. For example, while most courts hold that it is not necessary to actually file an FCA action to obtain protection under the FCA,[47] the matter is not completely settled. The applicable statute of limitations for retaliatory claims was resolved by the Supreme Court but only by applying a default rule of statutory construction. The Court held that the statute of limitations for a 3730(h) action runs from the date of retaliation rather than from the date of the FCA violation.[48] Because the facts concerning the violation of the FCA will enter into the issues of retaliation, the activating event for statute of limitation purposes should be the FCA violation. In addition, a 10-year statute of limitations is consistent with S. 2041, Section 6.

In summary, S. 2041, Section 5 should amend 31 U.S.C. § 3730(h) as follows:[49]

(1) **In General** – Any employee, government contractor, or agent shall be entitled to all relief necessary to make that employee, government contractor whole, if that employee, government contractor or Agent is discharged, demoted, suspended, threatened, harassed, or in any other manner discriminated against in the terms and conditions of employment because of lawful acts done by the employee, government contractor, or agent in furtherance of other efforts to stop 1 or more violations of this subchapter in furtherance of an action under this section, not necessarily including filing an action under this Section but including investigation for, initiation of, testimony for, or assistance in an action filed or to be filed under this section.

(2) **Relief** – Relief under (1) shall include reinstatement with the same seniority status that employee, government contractor, or agent would have had but for the discrimination, 2 times the amount of back pay, interest on the back pay, and compensation for any special damages sustained as a result of the discrimination, including litigation costs and reasonable attorneys' fees. An action under this subsection may be brought in the appropriate district court of the United States for the relief provided in this subsection.

E. Statute of Limitations

S. 2041, Section 6

This amendment replaces the dual 3 and 10 year provision to a simplified 10 year standard for all cases. It also provides that when the government intervenes in a case brought by a relator, pleadings relate back and do not change the original filing date as long as "the claim of the Government arises out of the conduct, transactions, or occurrences set forth, or attempted to be set forth, in the prior complaint...." This amendment is appropriate and should be enacted. Doing so will clarify what have been an unnecessarily confusing aspects of FCA practice.

F. Civil Investigative Demands

S. 2041, Section 7

Civil Investigative Demands (CIDs) permit DOJ to obtain, prior to filing suit, "any documentary material or information relevant to a false claims law investigation." CIDs have great potential, allowing DOJ to fully investigate a matter before deciding whether to intervene. Full use of CIDs help DOJ weed out frivolous qui tam actions.

As currently drafted, the FCA has been interpreted by DOJ to perrmit only the Attorney General, Deputy Attorney General, or Assistant Attorney General to authorize CIDs. This is unworkable. S. 2041 provides that the Attorney General "or his designee" may authorize CIDs. This is an appropriate amendment for it recognizes the practicalities of DOJ delegation of duties.

DOJ has also interpreted the FCA as prohibiting sharing with relators information obtained by virtue of CIDs. S. 2041 addresses this issue and allows such sharing of information "if the Attorney General, or his designee, "determine it to be necessary as part of any false claims act investigation. This amendment should be adopted for it recognizes the investigative needs and potential of the private-public partnership created by the FCA.

End Notes

[1] Portions of this written statement are excerpted from Pamela H. Bucy, Games and Stories: Game Theory and the Civil False Claims Act, 31 FLA. ST. U. L. REV. 603 (2004); Pamela H. Bucy, Private Justice, 76 S. CAL. L. REV. 1 (2002); Pamela H. Bucy, Information as a Commodity in the Regulatory World, 39 HOUS. L. REV. 905 (2002).

[2] 31 U.S.C. § 3729 et seq.

[3] 31 U.S.C. § 3730(b)(2) (2002).

[4] Id. at § 3730(b)(4)(B).

[5] Justin Gillis, Whistleblowing: What Price Among Scientists? WASH. POST, Dec. 28, 1995, at A21 (quoting Lawrence J. Rhoades, a division direction at the U.S. Department of Health and Human Services, which polices federal health research for scientific misconduct).

[6] Jane Bryan Quinn, When Whistleblowing Backfires, WA. POST, May 24, 1998, at H2.

[7] As Professors Robert Frank and Philip Cook note, "the recognition and approval of others is a profound source of human recognition." ROBERT H. FRANK & PHILIP J. COOK, THE WINNER TAKE-ALL SOCIETY 113 (1995).

[8] FRANK & COOK at 113.

[9] 31 U.S.C. § 3730(b)(2).

[10] 31 U.S.C. § 3730(b)(2).

[11] 31 U.S.C. § 3730(b)(3).

[12] Id. at § 3730(c)(2)(C),(D).

[13] Id. at § 3730(3).

[14] Id.

[15] Id. at § 3730(4).

[16] Id.

[17] 31 U.S.C. § 3730(c)(2)(A).

[18] 380 F.3d. 488 (D.C. 2004)

[19] 376 F. Supp. 2d 628 (E.D. Va. 2006) (appeal filed, No. 07-1220, 4th Cir.)

[20] Id. at 618.

[21] 380 F. 3d. at 490-91.

[22] Id. at 492; See 31 U.S.C. § 3729 (c): "CLAIM DEFINED – For purposes of this section, 'claim' includes any request or demand, whether under a contract or otherwise, for money or property which is made to a contractor, grantee or other recipient if the United States Government provides any portion of the money or property which is requested or demanded, or if the Government will reimburse such contractor, grantee, or other recipient for any portion of the money or property which is requested or demanded." (emphasis added)

[23] 380 F.3d at 492; See 31 U.S.C. § 3729 (a)(1): Any person who...knowingly presents, or causes to be presented, to an officer or employee of the United States Government...a false or fraudulent claims for payment or approval." (emphasis added)
[24] Id. at 496.
[25] "[O]ur job is reading statutes as written, not rewriting them "in an effort to achieve that which congress is perceived to have failed to do." Id. at 497
[26] Id. at 641.
[27] Id. at 644.
[28] Id. at 645.
[29] Id. at 646-647.
[30] 471 F.3d 610 (6th Cir. 2006).
[31] S. 2041, Section 2.
[32] See, e.g., LeBlanc, 913 F2d 17 (1st Cir.)(on the ground that such a relator does not qualify as an original source as required in the FCA if the information in the complaint is known to the government); Fine, 72 F.3d 740 (9th Cir.)(on the ground that the relator did not "voluntarily" provide the information in his complaint to the government as required in the FCA).
[33] S. 2041 specifies that the employee must report "all ...necessary and specific material allegations" to relevant inspector general, the employee's supervisor and the Attorney General" or to the employee's supervisor and the Attorney General if the employee's agency does not have an inspector general.
[34] United States ex rel. Givler v. Smith, 760 F. Supp 72 (E.D. PA 1991); United States ex rel McDowell v. McDonnell Douglas, 755 F. Supp 1038, 1040 (M.D. Ga. 1991)
[35] 5 C.F.R. §§ 2635.101(b)(3), 2635.7039(a).
[36] 5 C.F.R. §§ 2635.402, 2635.501, 2635.502.
[37] 5 C.F.R.§§ 2635.101(b)(7), 2635.702.
[38] 5 C.F.R. §§ 2635.704, 2635.705.
[39] 5 C.F.R. §§ 2635.403.
[40] 18 U.S.C. § 201.
[41] 549 U.S. ____, 127 S. Ct. 1397 (2007).
[42] S. 2041(4)(A).
[43] 127 S. Ct. at 1397.
[44] S. 2041(4)(B).
[45] S. 2041
[46] The underlined portion is the additional language I propose to S. 2041, Section 4, at 4(A) and (B).
[47] United States ex rel. Karvelas v. Melrose-Wakefield Hosp., 360 F.3d 220, 235 (1st Cir. 2004); Dookeran v. Mercy Hospital, 281 F.3d 105, 108 (3d Cir. 2002).
[48] United States ex rel. Wilson. Graham County Soil & Water Conserv., 545 U.S. 409 (2005).
[49] Underlined portion is additional to S. 2041 and also is identical to existing § 3730(h) except for the italicized portion which is new to both.

In: Fighting Fraud with Qui Tam and the False Claims Act
Editor: Ian M. Ortiz
ISBN: 978-1-61668-221-7

Chapter 8

THE FALSE CLAIMS ACT, THE *ALLISON ENGINE* DECISION, AND POSSIBLE EFFECTS ON HEALTH CARE FRAUD ENFORCEMENT

Jennifer Staman

SUMMARY

The False Claims Act (FCA), an important tool for combating fraud against the U.S. government, generally provides that a person who knowingly submits, or causes to be submitted, a false or fraudulent claim for payment to the U.S. government may be subject to civil penalties and damages. Recently, the Supreme Court examined the scope of the FCA in *Allison Engine v. United States ex rel. Sanders,* in which a former employee of a subcontractor brought an action against other subcontractors who had allegedly submitted a false claim to the prime contractor on a U.S. defense contract. The Court struck down the FCA claim against the subcontractors, holding that a demonstration that a false claim was paid for with government funds, without more, does not establish liability under 31 U.S.C. §§ 3729(a)(2) and (a)(3). Under these sections, the Court found that a plaintiff must prove that the defendant intended to defraud the government (and not just a recipient of government funds) when it submitted or agreed to make use of the false claim. Given that the FCA is frequently invoked in the health care context, it has been questioned how this decision could affect these cases. This report provides an overview of the FCA and the *Allison Engine* decision, analyzes how this decision could affect certain FCA health care claims, and discusses proposed legislation that would amend the False Claims Act (*i.e.,* the False Claims Act Clarification Act of 2009 (S. 458), the False Claims Act Correction Act of 2009 (H.R. 1788), and the Fraud Enforcement and Recovery Act of 2009 (S. 386)), which could limit the application of the *Allison Engine* decision.

FALSE CLAIMS ACT

The federal False Claims Act (FCA), codified at 31 U.S.C. §§ 3729-3733, provides for judicial imposition of civil monetary penalties and damages for the knowing submission of false claims to the U.S. government.[1] The FCA, as amended, is considered a vital tool used by the U.S. government to recover losses due to fraud, and, in particular, it has been utilized with respect to false claims made to defraud government health care programs such as Medicare and Medicaid. Reports indicate that in FY2007, the U.S. government recovered $2 billion dollars in settlements and judgments in FCA cases, and more than 75% of these recoveries were from health care entities.[2]

Under three key provisions of the FCA, civil liability may be imposed on any person that

(1) knowingly presents, or causes to be presented, to an officer or employee of the United States Government or a member of the Armed Forces of the United States a false or fraudulent claim for payment or approval [31 U.S.C. § 3729(a)(1)];
(2) knowingly makes, uses, or causes to be made or used, a false record or statement to get a false or fraudulent claim paid or approved by the Government [31 U.S.C. § 3729(a)(2)]; or
(3) conspires to defraud the Government by getting a false or fraudulent claim allowed or paid [31 U.S.C. 3729(a)(3)].

Penalties under the FCA include treble damages, plus an additional penalty of $5,500 to $11,000 for each false claim filed.

Civil actions may be brought in federal district court under the False Claims Act by the Attorney General or by a private person referred to as a relator (*i.e.*, a "whistleblower"), for the person and for the U.S. government, in what is termed a *qui tam* action. The ability to initiate a *qui tam* action has been viewed as a powerful weapon against fraud, in that it may be initiated by a private party who may have direct and independent knowledge of any misconduct. Popularity of *qui tam* actions brought under the FCA may be attributed in large part to the fact that successful relators can receive between 15% and 30% of the monetary proceeds of the action or settlement that are recovered by the government.

OVERVIEW OF THE *ALLISON ENGINE* DECISION

In *Allison Engine Co. v. U.S. ex. rel. Sanders*, the Navy contracted with two shipyards to build destroyers. The shipyards subcontracted with Allison Engine Company to build generator sets (Gen-Sets), which would provide electrical power for the destroyers. Allison Engine subcontracted with General Tool Company (which also used a subcontractor) to manufacture different parts needed for the Gen-Sets. The Navy's contracts with the shipyards required that all parts of the destroyers, including the Gen-Sets, be constructed in accordance with Navy specifications. This requirement was included in the contracts with the subcontractors. In addition, the contracts required that each Gen-Set come with a certificate of conformance that certified the unit met the Navy's requirements. All of the money used to pay the contractors for the work on the Gen-Sets ultimately came from the U.S. Treasury.

Former employees of General Tool Company, Roger Sanders and Roger Thacker (the relators), brought actions against Allison Engine Company and other subcontractors under §§ 3729(a)(1)- (3) of the FCA, alleging fraud with respect to the construction of the Gen-Sets. The relators contended that the subcontractors knew that there were defects in the construction of the Gen-Sets and that the Gen-Sets did not conform to Navy specifications. Still, the subcontractors submitted invoices to the shipyards for payment, which constituted "false or fraudulent claims" paid by the government in violation of the FCA.[3]

During the jury trial before the district court, the relators produced evidence that the subcontractors had issued certificates of conformance containing false statements that the Gen- Sets complied with Navy requirements, as well as invoices that the subcontractors presented to the shipyards. However, the relators did not provide evidence of the subcontractors or the shipyards submitting a false claim to the Navy. While the subcontractors argued that the relators' claim failed because there was no demonstration that the false claims were presented to the government, the relators asserted that their claim under the FCA was sufficient because government funds had been used to pay the invoices that were presented to the shipyards.[4] The district court agreed with the subcontractors and granted their motion for judgment as a matter of law. The court concluded that in order to sustain a claim under § § 3729(a)(1) and (a)(2) of the FCA, there must be a showing that a false claim was presented to the U.S. government.[5]

On appeal, the Sixth Circuit reversed the district court in relevant part and found the subcontractors liable under the FCA.[6] The court of appeals evaluated the statutory language and found that, while liability under § 3729(a)(1) depends on whether a claim has been presented to the government, the language in §§ 3729(a)(2) and (a)(3) contains no indication that presentment is required, so as long as there is a showing that the claim was paid with government funds. The court of appeals opined that the legislative history of the FCA supported this view.[7] Additionally, while the Sixth Circuit articulated that § 3729(a)(2) requires a "causal connection" between the defendant's false statement and the payment or approval of the claim by the government, the court focused its decision on the idea that proof of presentment is not required in order to bring a successful FCA claim under § 3729(a)(2) and (a)(3).

The Supreme Court granted certiorari on the issue of whether false claims for federal government money made by subcontractors are actionable under § 3729(a)(2) or § 3729(a)(3) of the FCA, if the claims were not presented to the U.S. government. In a unanimous decision, the Supreme Court vacated the Sixth Circuit decision and remanded the case for further proceedings.[8] While the Court held that a false claim does not have to be presented to the government under § § 3729(a)(2) and (a)(3), the Court found that under § 3729(a)(2), a plaintiff "must prove that the defendant intended that the false record or statement be material to the Government's decision to pay or approve the false claim."[9] Similarly, under § 3729(a)(3), a plaintiff must demonstrate that the conspirators agreed to make use of the false record or statement in an effort to defraud the government, and that the statement would have a material effect on the government's decision to pay the false or fraudulent claim.

The Court found that the language of § 3729(a)(2) did not support the Sixth Circuit's finding that a plaintiff can establish liability under the FCA by showing that a false statement resulted in the use of government funds to pay a false or fraudulent claim. The Court pointed to the language of the subsection, in particular, the phrase " to get a false claim paid by the government." As the Court articulated, "'[t]o get' denotes purpose, and thus a person must have the purpose of getting a false claim 'paid or approved by the Government' in order to be liable under § 3729(a)(2)."[10] Without this element of intent, the Court elaborated, the reach of the FCA would expand beyond its role of "combating fraud against the government." Further, the Court explained that "[r]ecognizing a cause of action under the FCA for fraud directed at private entities would threaten to transform the FCA into an all-purpose antifraud statute."[11]

Additionally, the Court agreed with the Sixth Circuit that, while a plaintiff must present a claim to the government under § 3729(a)(1), § 3729(a)(2) does not require proof that a defendant's false record or statement was submitted to the government, but instead that the defendant submitted the claim for the purpose of getting the claim paid by the government. The Court also found that under § 3729(a)(3) it is not necessary to show that conspirators presented a false claim to the government, but instead that conspirators agreed that the false record or statement would have a material effect on the government's decision to pay the claim.

RAMIFICATIONS OF *ALLISON ENGINE* DECISION ON HEALTH CARE CASES

As mentioned above, the FCA is often invoked due to fraud in federal health care programs such as Medicare and Medicaid. Although *Allison Engine* does not address its application to health care cases, there has been speculation over how the case could affect FCA health care litigation, especially since claims for payment from federal health care programs like Medicare and Medicaid can be paid for with federal funds, but are often paid through some type of intermediary. Some commentators have suggested that *Allison Engine* could make it more difficult for plaintiffs to bring an FCA claim against health care entities.[12] While lower courts have begun to evaluate cases in light of the *Allison Engine* decision, it remains to be seen whether the decision will have a significant effect on health care litigation under the FCA.

The Social Security Act gives private entities a large role in the administration of Medicare, which includes making coverage determinations, as well as processing and paying claims. For example, under Medicare Parts A and B, non-government organizations contract to serve as the fiscal agent between health care providers and the federal government.[13] It has been proposed that on the basis of *Allison Engine*, defendants may be able to argue for dismissal of an FCA claim by alleging that the claim at issue was merely relied upon by the private entities that processed and paid the claim; that the claim was not submitted with the purpose of inducing payment by the government;[14] or that the falsehoods were not material to the government's decision to pay the claim.[15] On the other hand, a plaintiff may be able to argue that health care providers and others submitting a Medicare claim are fully aware that, while they are submitting a claim to a contractor, the claims are ultimately paid by Medicare. This awareness could possibly demonstrate an intent to defraud the government, as opposed to a private contractor.[16]

Perhaps a more difficult question is how *Allison Engine* will affect Medicaid claims. Medicaid is a state-administered program that is jointly financed by states and the federal government. When some Medicaid beneficiaries receive care from a health care provider, the provider bills the state Medicaid program for the services.[17] Other Medicaid enrollees receive their care through managed care organizations (MCO), entities that are usually paid monthly, in advance for each enrollee. Typically, the state pays the provider or MCO from a combination of state funds and federal funds, which the Centers for Medicare and Medicaid Services (CMS) advances to the state each quarter. The state later files an expenditure report with CMS in which the state may claim federal reimbursement for Medicaid expenditures, and there is a reconciliation of the expenditures with the federal advance.[18] Applying the reasoning of *Allison Engine*, it has been suggested that plaintiffs will have difficulty proving that a defendant intended to defraud the federal government when the claim was submitted to a state Medicaid program.[19]

However, it still seems possible that plaintiffs may be able to bring successful FCA claims for Medicaid fraud under the reasoning of *Allison Engine*. For example, if a plaintiff could demonstrate that a defendant intended a state Medicaid program to rely on a false record or statement in order to receive federal reimbursement, a court may be willing to find that the plaintiff meets the requirements of § 3729(a)(2). In *United States ex. rel. Romano v. New York Presbyterian Hospital*,[20] one of the first court opinions to rely on the Supreme Court's decision in *Allison Engine*, the relator alleged that the defendant hospital was liable under the FCA for its complicity in submitting false bills to Medicaid.[21] The hospital argued that it was entitled to summary judgment because, as a matter of law, it could not have violated the FCA's requirement of presentment to a federal officer "for payment or approval" because the Medicaid claims were submitted to and approved by state agencies. The court denied the hospital's motion for summary judgment and found that based on the *Allison Engine* decision, the question to be addressed was whether or not the hospital acted with the requisite intent when it submitted false claims to state Medicaid agencies, and this was a question of fact to be determined at trial.

PROPOSED LEGISLATION IN THE 111TH CONGRESS

Members of the 111th Congress have introduced legislation which would make several changes to the FCA and could, if enacted, make it easier for certain plaintiffs to bring an FCA claim. These bills include the False Claims Act Clarification Act of 2009 (S. 458), introduced by Senator Grassley, and the False Claims Act Correction Act of 2009 (H.R. 1788), introduced by Representative Berman. According to congressional reports accompanying similar versions of these bills from the 110th Congress, the legislation aims to clarify the meaning of several provisions of the FCA due to "restrictive" judicial interpretations of the statute that are said to run contrary to congressional intent.[22] In addition, the Fraud Enforcement and Recovery Act of 2009 (S. 386, as reported in the Senate), which was introduced by Senator Leahy and Senator Grassley to enhance federal enforcement capabilities to counteract mortgage fraud, securities fraud, and fraud with respect to federal financial assistance, would also amend the FCA to "clarify that the False Claims Act was intended to extend to any false or fraudulent claim for government money or property, whether or not the claim is presented to a government official or employee ... and whether or not the defendant specifically intended to defraud the U.S. government."[23]

Proposed amendments to the FCA included in S. 458, H.R. 1788, and S. 386 (which all contain similar, but not identical, provisions) could potentially limit the application of *Allison*

Engine. For example, section 2 of S. 458 would amend 31 U.S.C. § 3729(a)(2) to provide that a person who "knowingly makes or uses ... a false record or statement to get a false or fraudulent claim paid or approved" can be liable to the government for penalties.[24] The bills all remove the phrase "by the government" from § 3729(a)(2), presumably for the purpose of clarifying that this section of the FCA covers false claims which are paid for by private parties with government grant or contract funds. While S. 458 and H.R. 1788 retain the phrase "to get," which the *Allison Engine* Court relied on as a basis for its determination that must be an element of intent to defraud the government in a successful § 3729(a)(2) claim, S. 386 would amend § 3729(a)(2) to provide that any person who "knowingly makes, uses, or causes to be made or used, a false record or statement *material to* a false or fraudulent claim" is liable under the FCA.[25] According to a Senate report, the purpose of this language is to eliminate the intent requirement articulated in *Allison Engine*.[26] Depending on how a court interprets what records or statements are "material to" a false claim, relators may have a considerably greater opportunity to bring an FCA claim in cases where a false claim was submitted to a recipient of government funds. However, it should be noted that while all three bills could make it easier for a relator to bring a claim under § 3729(a)(2) in situations where the false claim was not submitted directly to the government, under these bills a relator still must prove that a defendant *knowingly* made or used the false or fraudulent claim.[27]

End Notes

[1] Recoveries under the FCA have amounted to over $20 billion since 1986 (when substantial changes were made to the FCA). See Department of Justice Press Release, Justice Department Recovers $2 Billion for Fraud Against the Government in Fy 2007; More Than $20 Billion Since 1986, *available at* http://www.usdoj.gov/ opa/pr/ 2007/ November/07 _civ _873.html.

[2] *Id. See also* Robert Wolin and B. Scott McBride, *The Feds Pick Up a New Cudgel*, National Law Journal (August 11, 2008).

[3] United States ex rel. Sanders v. Allison Engine Co., 471 F.3d 610, 613 (6th Cir. 2006).

[4] United States ex rel. Sanders v. Allison Engine Co., 2005 U.S. Dist. LEXIS 5612 (S.D. Ohio 2005).

[5] *Id.* at 3 1-32. The district court also found with respect to § 3729(a)(3), the relators' claim failed because they had not demonstrated that there was a false or fraudulent claim.

[6] United States ex rel. Sanders v. Allison Engine Co., 471 F.3d 610 (6th Cir. 2006).

[7] According to the court, the legislative history indicated, among other things, that the FCA "is intended to reach all fraudulent attempts to cause the Government to pay out sums of money." *Id.* (*quoting* S.Rept. 99-435 (1986), reprinted in 1986 U.S.C.C.A.N. 5266).

[8] Allison Engine Co. v. United States ex rel. Sanders, 128 S. Ct. 2123 (2008).

[9] *Id.* at 2126.

[10] *Id.* at 2128.

[11] *Id.* at 2130.

[12] *See generally* Katherine M. Keefe and Susan L. Fields, Health Care Providers Face Unprecedented New Regulatory, Compliance and Enforcement Challenges, New Jersey Law Journal, Vol. 193, Issue 11 (September 15, 2008) (*Allison Engine* case a "potential victory for health care providers"); *See also*, Supreme Court Narrows Scope of False Claims Act, Implications for Medicare, Medicaid, Health Care Collector (August 2008). *But see* Judith A. Thorn, *High Court Rules Relators Must Show Intent to Defraud Government Under FCA*, BNA Health Care Fraud Report (June 18, 2008) (comments of Fredrick M. Morgan, that *Allison Engine* decision "was mostly anticlimactic in terms of the issues raised"). *See also* United States ex rel. Snapp, Inc. v. Ford Motor Co., 532 F.3d 496, 509 (6th Cir. 2008) (in a qui tam action concerning whether the defendant automobile manufacturer fraudulently induced the federal government to contract with the manufacturer by inflating the extent of the manufacturer's dealings with small and minority-owned businesses, court acknowledged that "in light of the Supreme Court's recent decision in *Allison Engine Co. v. United States ex rel. Sanders*, the law in this Circuit is now less friendly to qui tam plaintiffs than it was prior to that decision.").

[13] *See e.g.,* 42 U.S.C. § 1395kk-1 (addressing the authority and functions of a Medicare administrative contractor).

[14] *See e.g.,* United States ex rel. Thomas v. Bailey, 2008 U.S. Dist. LEXIS 91221 (E.D. Ark. 2008) (relator claimed, among other things, that company selling spinal surgery devices and others caused hospitals to present false or fraudulent claims for payment to Medicare and other federal health care programs under §§3729(a)(2) and (a)(3); court relied on *Allison Engine* and found that amended complaint failed to state a claim under these sections because the complaint did not identify any false records or statements made or used to get a false claim paid, nor did it allege a conspiracy which was specifically intended to defraud the government).

[15] *See* Supreme Court Narrows Scope of False Claims Act, Implications for Medicare, Medicaid, Health Care Collector (August 2008). *See also* Robert T. Rhoad, Supreme Court's Allison Engine Decision's Potential Impact On False Claims Act Enforcement In Healthcare Cases, ABA Health eSource, Vol. 4, Number 12 (August 2008).

[16] Ian Hennessey and Diana Gustin, *U.S. Supreme Court Decision Limits False Claims Act*, East Tennessee Medical News (August 2008).

[17] For a description of the Medicaid payment process, see GAO Report GAO-05-748, *Medicaid Financing, States' Use of Contingency-Fee Consultants to Maximize Federal Reimbursements Highlights Need for Improved Federal Oversight*, June 2005.

[18] *Id.*

[19] Memorandum from Harry Silver, Laurence Freedman and Laura Laemmle-Weidenfeld, Allison Engine Decision (June 13, 2008) *available at* http://www.pattonboggs.com/files/News/41ac72e6-e74a-4023-9f17-19b6cffb82e5/Presentation/NewsAttachment/3bc9457f-5ea0-446f-b3c6-1c66c19d1b67/Allison_Memo_HarrySilver.pdf.

[20] 571 F. Supp. 2d 473 (S.D.N.Y. 2008).

[21] *Id.* at 474.

[22] *See, e.g.*, S.Rept. 110-507 (2008).

[23] Press Release, Leahy, Grassley Introduce Anti-Fraud Legislation, Bill Would Give Federal Government More Resources To Combat Mortgage Fraud (Feb. 5, 2009), available at http://leahy.senate

[24] Section 2 of H.R. 1788 provides that a person who "knowingly makes or uses ... a false record or statement to get a false or fraudulent claim *for Government money or property* paid or approved" will be liable under the FCA. "Government money or property," as defined by the bill, includes money or property belonging to the United States government, or money or property that the government has provided to a contractor, grantee, agent, or other recipient (or for which the U.S. government will reimburse these entities) that is spent on the government's behalf or to advance a government program.

[25] Emphasis added. S. 386 defines the term "material" as "having a natural tendency to influence, or be capable on influencing, the payment or receipt of money or property."

[26] *See* S.Rept. 111-10 (2009). It should be noted that while S. 386 generally applies to conduct occurring on or after the date of enactment, it would make the amendments to § 3729(a)(2) retroactive to the date of the *Allison Engine* decision (i.e., June 7, 2008). It has been suggested that giving the legislation retroactive effect would be subjected to challenge in the courts. See Richard O. Duvall , Allison V. Feierabend , Christopher A. Myers and John P. Rowley III, United States: The Expansion Of The Civil False Claims Act Under S. 386, available at http://www.mondaq.com/article.asp? articleid=77 124. An analysis of the retroactivity of this provision is outside the scope of this report.

[27] "Knowingly" is defined by the current version of the FCA, as well as each of the three bills discussed above, as meaning that a person, with respect to information — (1) has actual knowledge of the information; (2) acts in deliberate ignorance of the truth or falsity of the information; or (3) acts in reckless disregard of the truth or falsity of the information, and no proof of specific intent to defraud is required. 31 U.S.C. § 3729(b).

In: Fighting Fraud with Qui Tam and the False Claims Act ISBN: 978-1-61668-221-7
Editor: Ian M. Ortiz

Chapter 9

QUI TAM: THE FALSE CLAIMS ACT AND RELATED FEDERAL STATUTES

Charles Doyle

SUMMARY

Qui tam enlists the public in the recovery of civil penalties and forfeitures. It rewards with a portion of the recovered proceeds those who sue in the government's name. A creature of antiquity, once common, today qui tam lives on in federal law only in the False Claims Act and in two minor examples found in patent and Indian protection laws.

The False Claims Act, expanded by the Fraud Enforcement and Recovery Act of 2009, P.L. 111- 21 (S. 386), 123 Stat. 1617 (2009), now proscribes: (1) presenting a false claim; (2) making or using a false record or statement material to a false claim; (3) possessing property or money of the U.S. and delivering less than all of it; (4) delivering a certified receipt with intent to defraud the U.S.; (5) buying public property from a federal officer or employee, who may not lawfully sell it; (6) using a false record or statement material to an obligation to pay or transmit money or property to the U.S., or concealing or improperly avoiding or decreasing an obligation to pay or transmit money or property to the U.S.; (7) conspiring to commit any such offense. Additional liability may also flow from any retaliatory action taken against whistleblowers under the False Claims Act. Offenders may be sued for triple damages, costs, expenses, and attorneys fees in a civil action brought either by the United States or by a relator (whistleblower or other private party) in the name of the United States.

If the government initiates the suit, others may not join. If the government has not brought suit, a relator may do so, but must give the government notice and afford it 60 days to decide whether to take over the litigation. If the government declines to intervene, a prevailing relator's share of any recovery is capped at 30%; if the government intervenes, the caps are lower and depend upon the circumstances. Relators in patent and Indian protection qui tam cases are entitled to half of the recovery.

Federal qui tam statutes have survived two types of constitutional challenges—those based on defendants' rights in criminal cases and those based on the doctrine of separation of powers. The courts have found the rights required in criminal cases inapplicable, because qui tam actions are civil matters. They have generally rejected standing arguments, because relators stand in the shoes of the United States in whose name qui tam actions are brought. They have rejected appointments clause arguments, because relators hold no appointed office. They have rejected take care clause arguments, because the residue of governmental control over qui tam actions is considered constitutionally sufficient.

INTRODUCTION

Qui tam is the process whereby an individual sues or prosecutes in the name of the government and shares in the proceeds of any successful litigation or settlement. Although frequently punitive, it is generally a civil procedure. Unlike antitrust, RICO, and other federal punitive damage, private attorney general provisions,[1] the individual need not have been a victim of the misconduct giving rise to the litigation. The name qui tam is the shortened version of an oft abbreviated Latin phrase which roughly translates to "he who prosecutes for himself as well as for the King."[2] Qui tam comes to us from before the dawn of the common law. Reviled at various times throughout the ages as a breeding ground for "viperous vermin"[3] and parasites,[4] legislative bodies have authorized it when they consider the enforcement of some law beyond the unaided capacity or interest of authorized law enforcement officials.[5] Best known of the contemporary members of the line is the federal False Claims Act (31 U.S.C. 3729-3733), recently amended in the Fraud Enforcement and Recovery Act of 2009, P.L. 111-21, 123 Stat. 1617 (2009). Since 1986, False Claims Act recoveries have totaled an amount in excess of $20 billion.[6]

This is a brief discussion of the constitutional questions raised by qui tam provisions; of the history of such provisions; and of the three existing, active federal qui tam statutes—the False Claims Act, 31 U.S.C. 3729-3733; the false marking patent statute, 35 U.S.C. 292; and the Indian protection provisions of 25 U.S.C. 201.

BACKGROUND

Qui Tam in England

The earliest cited example of a qui tam provision is the 695 declaration of King Wihtred of Kent, which stated that "If a freeman works during the forbidden time [*i.e.*, the Sabbath], he shall forfeit his *healsfang*, and the man who informs against him shall have half the fine, and [the profits arising] from the labour."[7] By the fourteenth, fifteenth, and sixteenth century, qui tam statutes had become a common feature of English law.[8] They brought with them, however, unintended consequences. They gave rise to a class of bounty hunters who unscrupulously exploited weaknesses in the system. "Old statutes which had been forgotten were unearthed and used as means to gratify ill-will. Litigation was stirred up simply in order that the informer might compound [*i.e.,* settle] for a sum of money. Threats to sue were easy means of levying blackmail."[9] Coke in his *Third Part of the Institutes of the Laws of England* devotes a chapter to the reform legislation designed to control the practices of these "vexatious relators, informers, and promoters," whom he classifies as *turbidum hominum genus* (a class of unruly men)[10] and as a species among the classes of "viperous vermin"[11]—a class was so unpopular that Queen Elizabeth I at one time found it necessary to issue a proclamation shielding its members from mob violence. [12] Legislative reform, however, appears to have been effective, because a century and a half after Coke's comments, Blackstone describes qui tam without criticism, expect to note a statutorily-cured abuse.[13]

Early American Experience

Qui tam was no stranger to colonial America nor to the early Republic. Colonial legislatures enacted qui tam statutes of their own,[14] and colonial courts heard qui tam cases arising under these statutes,[15] as well as under English law. [16] Qui tam statutes dot the work of the first Congresses of the new Republic,[17] and qui tam cases appear among the cases of the early federal courts.[18] By the turn of the twentieth century, qui tam statutes had largely fallen into disuse in this country, although they often remained on the books.

CONTEMPORARY FEDERAL QUI TAM STATUTES

In *Stevens*, the Supreme Court identified four contemporary federal qui tam statutes: the False Claims Act, the Patent Act, and two Indian protection laws.[19] One of the Indian protection statutes, 25 U.S.C. 81, has since been amended so that it no longer authorizes a qui tam action. Of the others, the False Claims provision is by far the most often invoked.

Congress has enacted a number of other statutes, beyond those with obvious qui tam markings, which might be similarly characterized. The Supreme Court observed in *United States ex rel. Marcus v. Hess* that "statutes providing for a reward to informers which do not specifically either authorize or forbid the informer to institute the action are construed to authorize him to sue."[20] The suggestion encouraged environmentalists to bring qui tam actions based on an informer- reward provision in the Rivers and Harbors Act. The lower courts were not particularly receptive to the suggestion.[21] In fact thus far, they have generally refused to recognize the authority to bring a qui tam action under the Rivers and Harbors Act.[22]

Yet the Court mentioned the suggestion again in *Vermont Agency of Natural Resources v. United States ex rel. Stevens,*[23] and in citing the existing qui tam-specific statutes, pointed out two of the qui tam-silent informer-reward statutes.[24] The lower federal courts, however, continue to maintain that "Congress must *explicitly* create *qui tam* statutes."[25]

FALSE CLAIMS ACT

Civil War Origins

The False Claims Act originated as the Act of March 2, 1863, 12 Stat. 696 (1863). Its brief legislative history is devoted almost exclusively to a subsequently abandoned proposal that all offenders, both military and civilian, be tried by courts martial.[26] Senator Howard, the sponsor and floor manager of the bill in the Senate, provided the only explicit explanation of the qui tam provision:

> The other clauses which follow, and which prescribe the mode of proceeding to punish persons who are not in the military service of the United States, I take it, are open to no serious objection. The effect of them is simply to hold out to a confederate a strong temptation to betray his coconspirator, and bring him to justice. The bill offers, in short, a reward to the informer who comes into court and betrays his coconspirator, if he be such; but it is not confined to that class. Even the district attorney, who is required to be vigilant in the prosecution of such cases, may be also the informer, and entitle himself to one half the forfeiture under the *qui tam* clause, and to one half of the double damages which may be recovered against the person committing the act. In short, sir, I have based the fourth, fifth, sixth, and seventh sections upon the old-fashion idea of hold out a temptation, and "setting a rogue to catch a rogue," which is the safest and most expeditious way I have ever discovered of bringing rogues to justice.[27]

As enacted, the statute prohibited various frauds against the government, including making or presenting false claims, false vouchers, false oaths, forged signatures, theft, embezzlement, and conspiracy.[28] The proscriptions applied to both military personnel and civilians.[29] Civilian offenders faced a sentence of imprisonment of from one to five years or a fine of not less than $1,000 nor more than $5,000.[30] They also faced civil liability in the amount of $2,000, double the amount of damage sustained by the United States, and costs.[31] Any person might bring suit in the name of the United States to recover the civil penalties, although the suit could only be settled with the consent of the court and federal prosecutors.[32] The private parties, known as relators,[33] were entitled to half of the penalty recovered and costs, if successful.[34] The qui tam provisions were codified in the Revised Statutes[35] and continued relatively unchanged until 1943 when the Attorney General sought to have them repealed.[36]

1943 Amendments

On August 28, 1942, Attorney General Biddle requested repeal of the qui tam provisions in identical letters to the Speaker of the House and the Chairman of the Senate Judiciary Committee.[37] He explained that:

> The reasons advanced by Senator Howard for the enactment of these sections are no longer pertinent. Recent experience shows that plaintiffs in informers' suits not only fail to furnish to the United States the information which is the basis of their actions, but on the contrary, at times base the litigation on information which has been secured by the Government in the regular course of law enforcement. Such plaintiffs at times not only use information contained in indictments returned against the defendant, but also seek to use Government files to prove their cases. Consequently, informers' suits have become mere parasitical actions, occasionally brought only after law-enforcement offices have investigated and prosecuted persons guilty of a violation of law and solely because of the hope of a large reward.[38]

He also referred to a court of appeals decision that seemed to reflect judicial condemnation of the qui tam provisions.[39] The Senate passed the repeal proposal with little debate at the close of the 77th Congress.[40] The House acted with similar dispatch and passed a comparable bill when it convened in the 78th Congress.[41] In the interim, however, the Supreme Court had repudiated the lower court opinion which the Attorney General had cited.[42] Moreover, opposition to repeal had developed in the Senate.[43] As a consequence, the Senate Judiciary Committee recommended curtailing, rather than repealing, the false claim qui tam provisions.[44] The two Houses ultimately concurred and passed Public Law 78-213, 57 Stat. 608 (1943).

The legislation required relators to provide the government with the evidence upon which their litigation was based and to allow the government 60 days to intervene.[45] It precluded qui tam suits based on information already within the government's possession,[46] and it reduced the relator's share of a successful suit from 50% to no more than 25% (no more than 10% should the government litigate the case).[47]

1986 Amendments

The 1943 amendments addressed reform of those qui tam procedures seen as rewarding the unworthy and obstructing other law enforcement efforts. The 1986 amendments reinvigorated qui tam procedures in the face of the evidence of extensive fraud against the United States.[48] They reflected a fairly wide array of concerns. Changes included:

an explicit cause of action for reverse false claims (false statements calculated to reduce an obligation to pay the United States),[49]
a cause of action for retaliation against whistleblowers,[50]
an increase in sanctions from a penalty of not more than $2,000 and double damages to a penalty of not less than $5,000 nor more than $10,000 and treble damages,[51]
an increase in the maximum award available to qui tam relators from not more than 25% to not more than 30%,[52]
an express definition of the knowledge required for a violation and declaration that a specific intent was unnecessary,[53]
a specific preponderance-of-the-evidence burden of proof standard,[54]
a declaration that states might act as qui tam relators,[55]
a revised jurisdictional bar for qui tam suits based on matters of public knowledge,[56]
an expanded statute of limitations,[57] and
an authorization for government use of civil investigative demands.[58]

2009 Amendments

The amendments of the Fraud Enforcement and Recovery Act of 2009 reinforced the 1986 amendments, particularly in instances where judicial developments evidenced a need for clarification.[59] Modifications included:

elimination of language suggesting that a false claim must be submitted directly to a federal officer or employee,[60]

addition of a specific materiality element defined to encompass those false statements having natural tendency to influence payment,[61]

expansion of the conspiracy proscription to apply to all of the substantive False Claims Act violations,[62] and

enlargement of the reverse false claims offense to cover not only false statements but any improper avoidance. [63]

Current State of the Law

Persons Who May Be Liable

The False Claims Act declares that any "person" who violations its prohibitions may incur liability. It does not define the term "person." As a general rule, federal law understands the term to "include corporations, companies, associations, firms, partnerships, societies, and joint stock companies, as well as individuals," 1 U.S.C. 1. Local governments are considered persons for purposes of False Claims Act suits brought by private parties,[64] but states[65] and Indian tribes are not.[66] The statute also denies federal courts jurisdiction over certain False Claims Act suits brought by private parties against Members of Congress, members of the federal judiciary, senior federal officials, or members of the armed forces.[67]

Who May Bring an Action

The False Claims Act is designed to allow private individuals to sue on behalf of the government, but any False Claims Act litigation takes place in the shadow of the government's prerogatives. The action is brought in the name of the United States. The Attorney General may bring an action for violations, 31 U.S.C. 3730(a). Although a private party may also bring such an action, 31 U.S.C. 3730(b), the government may elect to assume primary responsibility for the litigation from the beginning, 31 U.S.C. 3730(c)(1). If it initially chooses not to do so, the government is nevertheless free to intervene later in the proceedings upon a showing of cause, 31 U.S.C. 3730(c)(3). The government is likewise free to move to dismiss or settle the litigation over the objections of the relator, as long as the relator is given an opportunity to be heard, 31 U.S.C. 3730(c)(2)(A), (B). The government may also petition the court to limit the relator's participation in the litigation in the interest of a more effective presentation of the action.[68]

A relator may not bring a False Claims Act action based on public information or information from official proceedings, unless the relator is the original source of the information.[69] In addition, the False Claims Act features a first-to-file bar which precludes a second relator from bringing a later copycat action.[70] The bar extends to any claims that allege the same material or essential elements of the same underlying fraud.[71] Furthermore, a member of the armed forces may not bring an action against another member based on the defendant's service.[72] On the other hand, even though relators are often referred to as private parties, government employees may bring a False Claims Act qui tam action as long as one of the statutory bars does not apply.[73]

Basis for Liability

Seven forms of misconduct give rise to civil liability under section 3729. They occur when anyone:

(A) knowingly presents, or causes to be presented, a false or fraudulent claim for payment or approval;
(B) knowingly makes, uses, or causes to be made or used, a false record or statement material to a false or fraudulent claim;
(C) conspires to commit a violation of subparagraph (A), (B), (D), (E), (F), or (G);
(D) has possession, custody, or control of property or money used, or to be used, by the Government and knowingly delivers, or causes to be delivered, less than all of that money or property;
(E) is authorized to make or deliver a document certifying receipt of property used, or to be used, by the Government and, intending to defraud the Government, makes or delivers the receipt without completely knowing that the information on the receipt is true;
(F) knowingly buys, or receives as a pledge of an obligation or debt, public property from an officer or employee of the Government, or a member of the Armed Forces, who lawfully may not sell or pledge property; or
(G) knowingly makes, uses, or causes to be made or used, a false record or statement material to an obligation to pay or transmit money or property to the Government, or knowingly conceals or knowingly and improperly avoids or decreases an obligation to pay or transmit money or property to the Government, 31 U.S.C. 3729.

Additional liability may also flow from any retaliatory action taken against those who seek to stop violations of the False Claims Act, 31 U.S.C. 3730(h).

Presentation of a False or fraudulent claim (31 U.S.C. 3279(a)(1)(A))

Prior to enactment of the Fraud Enforcement and Recovery Act of 2009 (2009 Act),[74] this section was designated 31 U.S.C. 3279(a)(1) and read, "(a) Any person who—knowingly presents, or causes to be presented, to an officer or employee of the United States Government or member of the Armed Forces of the United States a false or fraudulent claim for payment or approval."[75] The language had been construed in the D.C. Circuit's *Totten* opinion to mean that liability "only attach[ed] if the claim [was] 'presented to an officer or employee of the Government.'"[76] Congress removed the reference to federal government employees and members of the armed services in order to clarify "that direct presentment is not required for liability to attach."[77] The claims encompassed within section 3729(a)(1)(A) are those presented to the federal government, its employees or agents, as well as those presented to others for payment, directly or indirectly, out of federal funds.[78] Liability, however, does not flow from simple negligence;[79] a defendant must be shown to have known, been deliberately ignorant of, or recklessly disregarded the false or fraudulent nature of the record or statement.[80]

Use of false records or statements material to a false or fraudulent claim (31 U.S.C. 3279(a)(1)(B))

Before the 2009 Act's amendments, this section reached, "Any person who ... (2) knowingly makes, uses, or causes to be made, or used, a false record or statement to get a false or fraudulent claim *paid or approved by the Government*."[81] The 2009 Act amended the section to negate the Supreme Court's suggestion in *Allison Engine* [82] that liability under its provisions required proof that "a defendant must intend that the Government itself pay the claim."[83] The 2009 Act also made materiality a specific element of section 3729(a)(1)(B), thus requiring that the false record or statement have "a natural tendency to influence, or be capable of influencing, the payment or receipt of money or property."[84] At the time of enactment, most but not all of the lower courts to consider the issue believed that section 3729 contained an implicit materiality requirement.[85]

Conspiracy to commit liability triggering misconduct (31 U.S.C. 3279(a)(1)(C))

At one time, this section (then referred to as section 3279(a)(3)) imposed civil liability upon those who conspired "to defraud the Government by getting a false or fraudulent claim allowed or paid."[86] To some, this meant that liability for substantive misconduct and conspiracy did not correspond. For example, although civil liability might be incurred under then section 3279(a)(7) for false statements calculated to conceal an obligation to pay the United States (reverse false claims), a reverse false claims conspiracy might not be thought to result in liability since it would not constitute a conspiracy to get a "claim allowed or paid," as the language of the conspiracy prohibition then required.[87] The 2009 Act resolved the incongruity by recasting the section to establish liability for conspiracy to engage in any misconduct covered by the substantive pronouncements in section 3729(a)(1) not just the misconduct described in sections 3729(a)(1)(A) and 3729(a)(1)(B)(the only two sections to expressly refer to claims).[88]

Short-changing the government on the transfer of funds or other property (31 U.S.C. 3729(a)(1)(D))

The 2009 Act streamlined this section, eliminating the receipt requirement and substituting a knowledge element for one that once insisted on willful concealment or an intent to defraud. Where the section once declared:

> Any person who ... (4) has possession, custody, or control of property or money used, or to be used, by the Government and, intending to defraud the Government or willfully to conceal the property, delivers, or causes to be delivered, less property than the amount for which the person receives a certificate or receipt ... is liable.... 31 U.S.C. 3729(a)(4)(2006 ed. & Supp. II).

It now states:

> Any person who ... (D) has possession, custody, or control of property or money used, or to be used, by the Government and knowingly delivers, or causes to be delivered, less than all of that money or property ... is liable.... 31 U.S.C. 3729(a)(1)(D).

Issuing a false government receipt (31 U.S.C. 3729(a)(1)(E))

Section 3729(a)(1)(E)(previously designated section 3729(a)(5)) establishes civil liability for any individual, authorized to certify receipt of property on behalf of the government, who knowingly certifies falsely.[89]

Unlawful purchase of government property (31 U.S.C. 3729(a)(1)(F))

Section 3729(a)(1)(F)(once section 3729(a)(6)) creates civil liability for those who purchase government property, or who accept government property as security, from a government officer or employee or member of the armed forces who has no authority to sell or pledge the property.[90]

Reverse false claims (31 U.S.C. 3729(a)(1)(G))

The 2009 Act rewrote and substantially changed the scope of section 3729(a)(1)(G)(once section 3729(a)(7)), the so-called reverse false claims section. It is "described as a 'reverse false claims' provision because the financial obligation that is the subject of the fraud flows in the opposite of the usual direction."[91] Instead of attempting to obtain money or property from the government, the misconduct is designed to avoid providing money or property to the government. In its present state, the section covers two forms of misconduct: (1) making or using a false statement or record material to an obligation to provide the government with money or property, and (2) knowingly concealing or improperly avoiding or decreasing an obligation to provide the government with money or property. The first prong is the traditional form; the 2009 Act added the second.

The Committee report accompanying passage of the 2009 Act explained that the addition was designed for greater symmetry with sections 3729(a)(1)(A) and 3729(a)(1)(B). Where those sections speak of misconduct calculated to induce excessive payments by the government, section 3729(a)(1)(G) speaks of misconduct calculated to avoid full payment to the government. Sections 3729(a)(1)(B) and (A) condemn making false statements and submitting false claims to induce payment by the government; section 3729(a)(1)(G) was crafted to condemn making false statements and engaging in other improper conduct calculated to avoid full payment of the government. Until passage of the 2009 Act, section 3729(a)(1)(G)(then styled section 3729(a)(7)) only covered false statements, but had no false presentation counterpart.[92] The section was amended in hopes of filling the gap:

> Any person who ... (G) knowingly makes, uses, or causes to be made or used, a false record or statement *material* to an obligation to pay or transmit money or property to the Government, or *knowingly conceals or knowingly and improperly avoids or decreases an obligation to pay or transmit money or property to the Government* is liable.... 31 U.S.C. 3729(a)(1)(G)(language added by the 2009 Act in italics).[93]

The new language does more than fill gaps. Unlike section 3729(a)(1)(A), it creates civil liability for not only false or fraudulent claims, but for "any knowing and improper conduct." Moreover, unlike section 3729(a)(1)(A), it establishes liability without insisting on either direct or indirect presentation.[94] Nor need the misconduct involve a false or fraudulent statement or record; conscious or recklessly improper conduct will suffice.[95]

Although the term "improper" is not defined, the 2009 Act added a new definition of "obligation" which considerably enlarges the scope of the false statement and the improper avoidance prongs of section 3729(a)(1)(G). Parsed to its constituent parts, the definition states:

obligation means

1. an established duty
2. whether fixed or not fixed
3. arising from
   a. an express or implied
      (i) contractual,
      (ii) grantor-grantee, or
      (iii) licensor-licensee relationship
   b. a fee-based or similar relationship
   c. statute or regulation, or
   d. the retention of any overpayment.[96]

Earlier courts, operating without the benefit an explicit definition, had often construed the term "obligation" more narrowly. Some courts had found that the reverse false claims section did not "extend to the potential or contingent obligations to pay the government fines or penalties which [had] not been levied or assessed ... and which [did] not arise out of an economic relationship between the government and the defendant (such as a lease or a contract or the like)."[97] Although a few had held that the obligation need not always be fixed,[98] most had "held that in order to create liability under (a)(7), the obligations must be fixed and definite at the time of the false claim."[99] The 2009 Act codified a more expansive view:

> The term 'obligation' is now defined under new Section 3729(b)(3) and includes fixed and contingent duties owed to the Government—including fixed liquidated obligations such as judgments, and fixed, unliquidated obligations such as tariffs on imported goods.... By including contingent obligations such as, 'imposed contractual, quasi-contractual, grant-or-grantee, licensor-licensee, fee-based, or similar relationships, this new section reflects the Committee's view, ... that an 'obligation' arises across the spectrum of possibilities from the fixed amount debt obligation where all particulars are defined to the instance where there is a relationship between the Government and a person that results in a duty to pay the Government money, whether or not the amount owed is yet fixed.[100]

It remains to be seen whether the section includes false statements or improper conduct calculated to mitigate the extent of a future fine or penalty assessment not constituting an obligation, contingent or fixed, at the time of the statement or conduct.

Retaliatory actions (31 U.S.C. 3730(h))

The False Claims Act has for some time encouraged insiders to report and cooperate with efforts to investigate and prosecute violations of the Act by offering them protection against retaliation. Until passage of the 2009 Act, the False Claims Act condemned retaliation by employers against employees and mentioned some of the protected forms of assistance. The courts concluded that only employees might claim the section's protection and that it exposed only employers to liability.[101] The 2009 Act expanded section 3730(h) to specifically include employees, contractors, and agents and eliminated references to employers and specific examples of protected assistance:

> Any employee, contractor, or agent shall be entitled to all relief necessary to make that employee, contractor, or agent whole, if that employee, contractor, or agent [who] is discharged, demoted, suspended, threatened, harassed, or in any other manner discriminated against in the terms and conditions of employment [by his or her employer] because of lawful acts done by the employee, contractor, or agent on behalf of the employee, contractor, or agent or associated others in furtherance of other efforts to stop 1 or more violations of this subchapter [an action under this section, including investigation for, initiation of, testimony for, or assistance in action filed or to be filed under this section, shall be entitled to all relief necessary to make the employee whole]. 31 U.S.C. 3730(h) (language added in the 2009 Act appears in italics; language eliminated within brackets in bold).

Congress clearly intended to expand the protection to section 3730(h) to include contractors and agents. It remains to be seen whether the courts will conclude that it intended also to expand liability under the section beyond employers to include supervisors, contractors, and agents of an employer.

Penalties and Awards

If a court finds a defendant liable under section 3729, it may award treble damages; a statutory penalty ranging from $5,000 to $10,000; the government's litigation costs; and a relator's expenses, attorneys' fees, and costs.[102] The court may reduce its damage award to no less than double damages if it finds that a defendant made prompt disclosure and provided full cooperation before judicial or administrative proceedings began.[103] If a court finds an individual has been the victim of retaliation in violation of section 3730(h), it may order the defendant to pay the individual's attorneys' fees, litigation costs, and twice the amount of "back pay, interest on back pay, and compensation for special damages sustained as a consequence" of the retaliation, 31 U.S.C. 3730(h)(2).

If the False Claims Act action succeeds, relators are entitled to a share in the proceeds of up to 30%. If the government has not participated in the litigation, they are entitled to an award of from 25% to 30%.[104] If the government has participated in the litigation, they are entitled to an award of from 15% to 25%,[105] reduced to no more than 10% when their claim was based primarily on public information.[106] In any case, they are also entitled to attorneys' fees, expenses, and costs, but may be denied any award if they participated in the underlying fraud.[107]

If the defendant prevails in an False Claims Act action in which only a private relator has taken part, the court may award the defendant attorneys' fees and expenses, should it conclude that the action was clearly frivolous, vexatious, or brought to harass.[108] The test for whether attorneys' fees and expenses are appropriate is said to be analogous to that used for prevailing defendants under 42 U.S.C. 1988.[109] Such awards are thought to be appropriate only under "rare and special circumstances,"[110] when the relator's action is meritless, groundless, or without foundation;[111] when allegations are bereft of factual support or when there is no reasonable chance of success;[112] or when brought or pursued for an improper motive.[113]

Procedure

The False Claims Act states that prosecution of a violation of section 3729 must begin within six years, although there is an exception for undiscovered fraud which extends the deadline to 10 years as long as the action is brought within three years of discovery.[114] The courts are divided over the question of whether this extension is available to private parties or only in cases initiated by the government.[115] In the case of litigation for retaliatory misconduct under section 3730(h)(rather than one of section 3729's proscriptions), parties must look to the most closely analogous statute of limitations under state law, since the sole explicit False Claims Act provision applies only to causes of action under section 3729.[116]

Until recently, some courts had held that the statute of limitations in cases where the government elected to intervene did not relate back to the time of the relator's original complaint.[117] The 2009 Act added a new subsection to section 3731 to afford the government the advantage of the date of the relator's complaint as a cut-off date for statute of limitations purposes.[118] Thus, a complaint, which would be time barred as of the date of the government's intervention, survives, if it would not be time barred on the date of the relator's earlier original complaint.

For private litigants, the process begins with a complaint filed under seal with the federal court in the district in which a violation occurred or in which any of the defendants are found, resides, or does business, 31 U.S.C. 3730(b)(2), 3732(a). Thereafter, relators must deliver all their material evidence and information to the government, 31 U.S.C. 3730(b)(2). The government has 60 days, or until the end of a longer period of any extensions granted by the court for cause, in which to decide whether intervene, 31 U.S.C. 3730(b)(2), (3), (4). The government has at its disposal civil investigative demand authority which allows it to compel the production of material and testimony in its investigations, 31 U.S.C. 3733.

After the government has made its initial determination of whether to intervene, the defendants are served and have 20 days in which to respond, 31 U.S.C. 3730(b)(3). The government, or in its absence the relator, must prove damages and all of the elements of the asserted violation by a preponderance of the evidence.[119] A defendant, however, may not contest the presence of any elements of any violation which has been established or conceded against him in parallel criminal proceedings.[120] Although they sue in the name of the United States, relators are bound by the 30- day deadline for appellate review rather than the 60-day deadline available to the government.[121]

PATENT ACT (35 U.S.C. 292)

(a) Whoever, without the consent of the patentee, marks upon, or affixes to, or uses in advertising in connection with anything made, used, offered for sale, or sold by such person within the United States, or imported by the person into the United States, the name or any imitation of the name of the patentee, the patent number, or the words "patent," "patentee," or the like, with the intent of counterfeiting or imitating the mark of the patentee, or of deceiving the public and inducing them to believe that the thing was made, offered for sale, sold, or imported into the United States by or with the consent of the patentee; or

Whoever marks upon, or affixes to, or uses in advertising in connection with any unpatented article, the word "patent" or any word or number importing that the same is patented for the purpose of deceiving the public; or

Whoever marks upon, or affixes to, or uses in advertising in connection with any article, the words "patent applied for," "patent pending," or any word importing that an application for patent has been made, when no application for patent has been made, or if made, is not pending, for the purpose of deceiving the public–

Shall be fined not more than $500 for every such offense.

(b) Any person may sue for the penalty, in which event one-half shall go to the person suing and the other to the use of the United States. 35 U.S.C. 292.

Section 292 is recognized as a qui tam statute.[122] The party bringing the action need not be a victim; it may be prosecuted by anyone who can satisfy constitutional standing requirements.[123] In order to prevail under the most commonly prosecuted prongs of the statute, the relator must establish by a preponderance of the evidence that: "(1) an article was falsely marked or advertised with the word 'patent' or any word or number that imports that the article is patented, (2) the article so marked or advertised was an unpatented article, and (3) the marking or advertisement was made with the intent to deceive the public."[124] The first element (falsely marked) may include conditional statements or marks , *e.g.*, "may be covered by one or more U.S. or foreign pending or issued patents."[125] Proof the first and third elements (falsely marked and intent to deceive) are frequently intertwined. Thus, "the fact of misrepresentation coupled with proof that the party making it had knowledge of its falsity is enough to warrant drawing the inference that there was a fraudulent intent."[126] On the other hand, "an intent to deceive the public will not be inferred if the facts show no more than that the erroneous patent marking was the result of mistake," inadvertence, or innocent oversight.[127] As for the second element, a product is "unpatented" when no patent, foreign or domestic, is pending or has been issued for it or for a portion of it; or when any of the patents asserted on his behalf do not in fact cover it; or when any patent which once covered it has expired.[128]

Unlike qui tam actions under the False Claims Act, actions to enforce section 292 are subject to the general five-year statute of limitations found in 28 U.S.C. 2462.[129] Section 292 qui tam actions differ from those brought under the False Claims Act with respect to the recovery of attorneys' fees as well. Section 292 makes no mention of attorneys' fees, although they may be available to either party in exceptional cases under the general remedies provisions of 35 U.S.C. 285.[130]

Indian Protection (25 U.S.C. 201)

All penalties which shall accrue under Title 28 of the Revised Statutes shall be sued for and recovered in an action in the nature of an action of debt, in the name of the United States, before any court having jurisdiction of the same, in any State or Territory in which the defendant shall be arrested or found, the one half to the use of the informer and the other half to the use of the United States, except when the prosecution shall be first instituted on behalf of the United States, in which case the whole shall be to their use. 25 U.S.C. 201.

Section 201 dates from 1834 and authorizes qui tam actions for violations of five separate statutes: (1) unlawful purchase of land from an Indian nation or tribe, 25 U.S.C. 177 (Rev. Stat. §2116); (2) driving livestock to feed on Indian land, 25 U.S.C. 179 (Rev. Stat. §2117); (3) settling on or surveying Indian land, 25 U.S.C. 180 (Rev. Stat. §2118); (4) setting up a distillery in Indian country, 25 U.S.C. 251 (Rev. Stat. §2141); and (5) trading in Indian country without a license, 25 U.S.C. 264 (Rev. Stat. 2133).[131]

Qui tam actions under section 201 are relatively rare and appear to have arisen most often under sections 264 (unlicensed trading) and 179 (grazing). In *Hall*, the section 264 relators' action survived a standing challenge,[132] but was dismissed for failure to join an indispensible party—the tribe, which had contracted for gambling equipment and services from an unlicensed supplier.[133] In *Keith*, the relator's action was dismissed after the court concluded that "bureaucratic nonfeasance" made it impossible to obtain the required trader's license.[134] Relators were somewhat more successful in *Hornell*, where the court upheld recovery of the monetary penalty, but declined to affirm confiscation of the station wagon that was the object of the unlicensed sale.[135]

Section 179 prohibits grazing horses, mules, or cattle on Indian land without permission and sets the penalty at $1 per head. The circuits are divided over the question of whether the Secretary of the Interior may by regulation set the penalty at $1 per head for each day of violation.[136] Federal district courts have jurisdiction exclusive of the states for enforcement of the penalties under section 179, but they may abstain from exercising jurisdiction in favor of enforcement in a tribal court of jurisdiction.[137]

There may be some question whether the monetary penalty established in section 177 may be enforced by a qui tam action under section 201. Section 201 applies to "penalties which shall accrue under Title 28 of the Revised Statutes,"(*i.e.,* Rev. Stat. §§2039-2157). Section 177 appears in Title 28 of the Revised Statutes as section 2116. Thus, on its face, section 201 permits a qui tam action to recover the penalties accruing under section 177.

In *Harlan*, however, the Eighth Circuit stated in dicta that "25 U.S.C. § 177 appears to deal directly with cases where, as here, a person attempts to lease tribal lands without express approval of the federal government.... The statute makes violators subject to a fine of $1,000, *but has no provision entitling relators to bring actions under it. See James v. Watt*, 716 F.2d 71 (1st Cir. 1983)."[138] The issue in *Harlan* was whether the qui tam provisions then found in 25 U.S.C. 81, relating to contracts for services which required government approval, extended to sharecrop agreements. The court referred to section 177 "simply ... to demonstrate that a broad and general policy to oversee all contracts by Indians need not be accomplished though 25 U.S.C. §81 alone." The *James* case, which the court cites, held that an individual tribal member, suing as a victim of a violation of section 177, may only do so as a representative of his tribe and not on his own behalf. [139] It says nothing of whether he may do so on behalf of the United States qui tam.

The application of section 201 to the penalties under section 177 seems clear on its face, but the contrary statement in *Harlan* seems equally clear.

CONSTITUTIONAL CONCERNS

Qui tam evokes constitutional issues of two classes. First, to what extent may qui tam defendants claim the constitutional protections available to defendants in criminal cases? Second, is qui tam compatible with the Constitution's allocation of powers among the three branches of government? At first glance, the first question seems the least troubling. The rights available in criminal proceedings exist precisely because the proceedings are criminal. The Sixth Amendment rights— the right to counsel; to call and confront witnesses; to informed of the nature of the charges against him; to trial in the place where the offense occurred; and to a speedy and public trial before an impartial jury—apply only to "the accused" in criminal proceedings.[140] Thus, they are inapplicable to federal qui tam proceedings which are civil in nature.[141] Rights found elsewhere in the Constitution, however, often turn upon whether the government's action may be or must be considered punitive. Here the answers are bit less clear.

Double Jeopardy

For example, in the context of the False Claims Act, it was once thought that the Fifth Amendment's double jeopardy clause applied to "actions intended to authorize criminal punishment to vindicate public justice" but not to "civil, remedial actions brought primarily to protect the government from financial loss," *United States ex rel. Marcus v. Hess*, 317 U.S. 537, 548, 549 (1943). It was further thought that a legislatively established civil remedy should not be considered a criminal penalty for double jeopardy purposes unless its purpose or effect was so excessive as to belie its civil designation, *Rex Trailer Co. v. United* States, 350 U.S. 148, 154 (1956).

But then the Court seemed to make a rule of the exception when it declared that, "under the Double Jeopardy Clause a defendant who already has been punished in a criminal prosecution may not be subjected to an additional civil sanction to the extent that the second sanction may not fairly be characterized as remedial, but only as a deterrent or retribution," *United States v. Halper*, 490 U.S. 435, 448-49 (1989).[142] Nine years later, however, the Court withdrew from the broad implications of *Halper* whose analysis it characterized as "ill considered," *Hudson v. United States*, 522 U.S. 93, 101 (1997). The appropriate test, the Court declared,[143] is one exemplified in its pre-*Halper* case law:

> Whether Congress, in establishing the penalizing mechanism, indicate[] either expressly or impliedly a preference for one label or the other. Second, where Congress has indicated an intention to establish a civil penalty, [was] the statutory scheme ... so punitive either in purpose or effect as to negate that intention. In regard to this latter inquiry, we have noted that only the clearest proof could suffice to establish the unconstitutionality of a statute on such a ground.[144]

The Court has looked to the due process standards listed in *Kennedy v. Mendoza-Martinez*, 372 U.S. 144, 168-69 (1963), when defendants seek to satisfy the daunting "clearest proof" test.[145] Although *Hudson* was not a qui tam case, later lower federal court qui tam cases consider it dispositive.[146]

Excessive Fines

The Supreme Court implied in *Hudson* that the problems which drove its *Halper* analysis might more appropriately be judged by Eighth Amendment excessive fines standards.[147] The Eighth Amendment states that "[e]xcessive bail shall not be required, nor excessive fines imposed, nor cruel and unusual punishments inflicted," U.S. Const. Amend. VIII. In other contexts, the Supreme Court has determined that the excessive fines clause "does not constrain an award of money damages in a civil suit when the government neither has prosecuted the action nor has any right to receive a share of the damages awarded."[148] The clause does apply to "the government's power to extract payments ... as punishment for some offense."[149] The critical question is not whether the procedure for extracting the payment is classified as civil or criminal or whether it serves some additional remedial purposes; if the payment constitutes punishment, it is a "fine" and as a general matter may not be excessive.[150] A fine is excessive, in the eyes of the Court, "if it is grossly disproportionate to the gravity of the defendant's offense."[151]

In the qui tam context, subsequent lower court reported cases ordinarily treat False Claims Act qui tam penalties as punishment and consequently subject to excessive fines clause analysis.[152] They have generally concluded, however, that the fines imposed in the cases before them were not excessive for Eighth Amendment purposes.[153]

Due Process

Two Supreme Court cases suggest that permitting individuals with a personal interest to prosecute in the name of the United States may present due process issues. In *Marshall v. Jerrico, Inc.*, the Court rejected the argument that an administrative agency's receipt of civil penalties which it assessed and collected posed a due process risk of biased prosecution.[154] In the course of its opinion, however, the Court noted that it "need not say with precision what limits there may be on a financial or personal interest of one who performs a prosecutorial function. In particular, we need not say whether different considerations might be held to apply if the alleged biasing influence contributed to prosecutions against particular persons, rather than to a general zealousness in the enforcement process."[155] That fact pattern surfaced in *Young v. United States ex rel. Vuitton et Fils S.A.*, but the issue splintered the Court.

Young and Vuitton were engaged in trademark litigation which had resulted in the issuance of an order enjoining Young from manufacturing or distributing counterfeit versions of Vuitton's product line.[156] Upon a showing of probable cause to believe that Young had violated the injunction, the court appointed Vuitton's lawyers to prosecute the criminal contempt.[157] Five members of the Supreme Court agreed that Young's subsequent conviction should be overturned because, "counsel for a party that is the beneficiary of a court order may not be appointed as prosecutor in a contempt action alleging a violation of that order."[158] Four members of the Court felt this was so because the appointment of an interested prosecutor constituted error which undermined confidence in the integrity of the criminal proceeding.[159] One of the four went so far as to assert that the failure to appoint a disinterested prosecutor constituted a due process violation.[160] A fifth Justice merely concurred in the result, because he felt that the lower court's appointment of a prosecutor—disinterested or not—was invalid on separation of powers grounds.[161]

Lower federal courts thereafter confronted with due process challenges to qui tam have rejected them based on the fact that relators press their claims as private civil litigants and thus do not exercise government power subject to due process clause restrictions on criminal prosecutions.[162]

Separation of Powers

Is qui tam legislation compatible with the Constitution's allocation of powers among the three branches? The Constitution allocates federal governmental authority among three coordinated branches. It vests all legislative powers in Congress, executive power in the President, and the judicial power of the United States in the federal courts.[163] It declares that Congress shall have the power to make all laws, necessary and proper, for carrying into execution its own powers and those of the executive and judicial branches.[164] It empowers Congress to remove by impeachment the President, the Vice President, and any civil officer of the United States for treason, bribery, or other high crimes and misdemeanors.[165] It requires the advice and consent of the Senate for the appointment of ambassadors, public ministers and consuls, judges of the Supreme Court, and all other officers of the United States (except for those inferior officers whose appointment has been otherwise provided for by law).[166] It instructs the President "to take care that the laws be faithfully executed."[167]

The Constitution authorizes the President to recommend legislation to Congress and to call Congress into extraordinary session.[168] Legislation may not become law until presented to the President for his approval, and in the case of his disapproval only upon the vote of a super majority in each House.[169] The Constitution says little about how the President may or must exercise the executive authority of the United States. It names the President commander in chief of the armed forces.[170] It empowers the President to nominate, and with Senate advice and consent to appoint, ambassadors, public ministers, consuls, judges of the Supreme Court, and all other officers of the United States (except for those inferior officers whose appointment has been otherwise provided for by law).[171] It permits the President to grant pardons and reprieves with respect to offenses against the United States and to require executive department heads to provide him with written opinions on matters relevant to their duties.[172] It authorizes the President to receive ambassadors and other public ministers.[173] Finally, the Constitution defines those cases and controversies to which the judicial power of the United States extends.[174]

This "system of separation of powers and checks and balances ... was regarded by the Framers as a self-executing safeguard against the encroachment or aggrandizement of one branch at the expense of the other[s]."[175] Yet, in this interwoven fabric of governmental authority, the Framers realized that "[w]hile the Constitution diffuses power the better to secure liberty, it also contemplates that practice will integrate the dispersed powers into a workable government. It enjoins upon its branches separateness but interdependence, autonomy but reciprocity."[176]

Commentators and litigants have questioned whether the qui tam is at odds with these basic constitutional principles.[177] Their concerns are three. First, the Constitution grants the federal courts the judicial power over "cases and controversies." This is thought to require at least two parties with conflicting interests, presented in a context suitable for judicial resolution, *i.e.*, standing in a case or controversy. Yet, relators come to court with no interest of their own, only a contingent personal interest.[178] Second, the Constitution instructs the President to see that the laws are faithfully executed. Yet, without his approval or unrestricted control, relators may initiate and prosecute litigation.[179] Third, the President is vested with the authority to appoint officers of the United States and, with the courts and heads of departments, to appoint inferior officers. Yet, relators, who engage in activities otherwise reserved to officers and inferior officers of the United States, are appointed neither by the President, the courts, nor by the head of any department.[180]

Each of the constitutional challenges to the False Claims Act's qui tam provisions faces an apparent hurdle. Qui tam statutes were fairly common at the time of the drafting of the Constitution. Qui tam statutes were enacted by the early Congresses, populated by men responsible for drafting and ratifying the new Constitution. Although enactment in an early Congress is hardly a sure mark of constitutionality,[181] action there "provides contemporaneous and weighty evidence of the Constitution's meaning."[182] Thus, critics face the problem of explaining how a process, which the Framers did not consider unconstitutional, should now be so construed.

Standing

History plays a significant role in determining whether standing exists. Standing requires (1) a concrete injury to the plaintiff's interest, (2) attributable to the defendant, (3) and amenable to judicial relief.[183] When it put standing challenges to rest in *Vermont Agency of Natural Resources v. United States ex rel. Stevens*, the Supreme Court observed that:

> [T]he long tradition of *qui tam* actions in England and the American colonies ... is particularly relevant to the constitutional standing inquiry since ... Article III's restriction of the judicial power to "Cases" and "Controversies" is properly understood to mean "cases and controversies of the sort traditionally amenable to, and resolved by, the judicial process."[184]

On the more perplexing matter of the relator's injury, the *Stevens* Court found the injury to the United States sufficient to establish False Claims Act relator standing. With respect to the government's share of the fruits of successful litigation, the Court found standing in the relator as an agent of the defrauded United States.[185] With respect to the relator's share, it considered him the assignee of that portion of the interest of the United States.[186]

Relator standing is in greater doubt in cases where tangible injury to the United States is less obvious. In the case of the false marking section of the Patent Act, at least one court has held that the relator must show either an injury to himself or an injury to the United States for which he might be the agent/assignee, *i.e.*, "an actual or imminent injury in fact to competition, to the United States economy, or [to] the public that could be assigned to him as a qui tam plaintiff or be vindicated through this litigation."[187]

The *Stevens* Court resolved the issue of qui tam standing, but it "express[ed] no view on the question of whether *qui tam* suits violate Article II, in particular the Appointments Clause of §2 and the 'take Care' Clause of §3," *Id.* at 778 n.8.

Appointments clause

> . . . [The President] shall nominate, and by and with the Advice and Consent of the Senate, shall appoint Ambassadors, other public Ministers and Consuls, Judges of the supreme Court, and all other Officers of the United States, whose Appointments are not herein otherwise provided for, and which shall be established by Law: but the Congress may by Law vest the Appointment of such inferior Officers, as they think proper, in the President alone, in the Courts of Law, or in the Heads of Departments. U.S. Const. Art. II, §2, cl. 2.

The appointments clause issue in qui tam cases flows from apparently contradictory language in two Supreme Court cases. In the more recent, *Buckley v. Valeo*, the Court seemed to conclude that only officers appointed under Article II could be vested with conducting civil litigation on behalf of the United States:

> We hold that these provisions of the Act, vesting in the Commission primary responsibility for conducting civil litigation in the courts of the United States for vindicating public rights, violate Art. II, §2, cl. 2, of the Constitution. Such functions may be discharged only by persons who are "Officers of the United States" within the language of that section.[188]

Yet, earlier Court decisions suggested that the appointments clause applied only to those purported to hold an "office of the United States," and that Congress might authorize the performance of services in the name of the United States by those who did so without the attributes of office, selected other than under Article II. The line begins with *United States v. Hartwell* which found that a Treasury Department clerk was an officer of the United States for purposes of an embezzlement statute. The Court noted that the defendant had been appointed in a manner consistent with Article II to a position that "embraced the ideas of tenure, duration, emolument, and duties" and for which the duties were continuing and permanent rather than occasional or temporary.[189]

The second case, *United States v. Germaine*, likewise involved a penal statute applicable to "officers of the United States." The Court concluded that the defendant, a surgeon paid to conduct and report on the results of examinations of applicants and recipients of federal pensions, was not an officer of the United States.[190] The Court supported its view by noting that the defendant filled no office; his duties were occasional and intermittent; he kept no place of business for the public use; he gave no bond; he took no oath; he was but an agent employed by the Commissioner of Pensions to obtain information needed for the performance of the Commissioner's duties.[191]

The Court used the same mode of analysis in *Auffmordt v. Heden*, when it concluded that appraisers called upon in the event of a customs dispute were not officers of the United States and consequently their selection other than under the Article II formula did not invalidate their efforts.[192]

The Court in *Buckley* distinguished rather than repudiated *Germaine* and *Affmordt*, but it did so in manner that does not necessarily resolve the qui tam issue:

> [The term] "Officers of the United States" does not include all employees of the United States, but there is no claim made that the Commissioners are employees of the United States rather than officers. Employees are lesser functionaries subordinate to officers of the United States, see *Auffmordt v. Hedden,* 137 U.S. 310, 327 (1890); *United States v. Germaine*, *supra*,

whereas the Commissioners, appointed for a statutory term, are not subject to the control or direction of any other executive, judicial, or legislative authority.[193]

The Court later affirmed the *Buckley* assertion that only officers appointed in conformity with Article II could "exercis[e] significant authority pursuant to the laws of the United States."[194] Yet in *Freytag*, it acknowledged the existence of various classes empowered other than by Article II appointment who performed services in the name of the United States. There it distinguished Tax Court special trial judges (inferior officers) from special masters (not officers) along the lines suggested in *Germaine* rather than based on a relative degree of independence mentioned in *Buckley*:

> The office of special trial judge is established by Law, and the duties, salary, and means of appointment for that office are specified by statute. These characteristics distinguish special trial judges from special masters, who are hired by Article III courts on a temporary, episodic basis, whose positions are not established by law, and whose duties and functions are not delineated in a statute. Furthermore, special trial judges perform more than ministerial tasks. ... [T]he special trial judges exercise significant discretion. *Freytag v. Commissioner*, 501 U.S. at 881-82 (internal citations omitted).

Although the Court has thus far "express[ed] no view on the question of whether *qui tam* suits violate Article II, in particular the Appointments Clause of §2,"[195] the lower federal courts generally see no appointments clause impediments, because they do not consider qui tam relators officers of the United States:

> The procedural requirements of the Appointments Clause only apply to the appointment of officers. Thus, the threshold question that we face is whether *qui tam* relators are "officers" for purposes of Article II. We conclude that they are not; *qui tam* relators do not serve in any office of the United States. There is no legislatively created office of informer or relator under the FCA. Relators are not entitled to the benefits of officeholders, such as drawing a government salary. And they are not subject to the requirement, noted long ago by the Supreme Court, that the definition of an officer "embraces the ideas of tenure, duration, emolument, and duties, and the latter were continuing and permanent, not occasional or temporary." *United States v. Germaine*, 99 U.S. 508, 511-12 (1878); *see also Auffmordt v. Hedden*, 137 U.S. 310, 327 (1890).[196]

Take care

Unlike the appointments clause, the take care clause does not vest authority in the President. Instead, it imposes a responsibility upon him. The Framers, however, allocated powers among the branches so as to prevent Congress or the courts from undermining or unduly interfering with the President's ability to perform his constitutional duties, including the duty to take care to see that the laws are faithfully executed.[197] *Morrison v. Olson* presents a question perhaps most closely analogous to the one of whether qui tam statutes undermine or unduly interfere with the President's ability to fulfill his responsibilities under the take care clause. The case involved the constitutionality of the independent counsel provisions of the Ethics in Government Act.[198] The statute permitted judicial appointment of a special prosecutor (independent counsel) under limited circumstances to investigate and in some instances to criminally prosecute senior executive branch officials.[199]

It was suggested that the Act impermissibly "reduc[ed] the President's ability to control the prosecutorial powers wielded by the independent counsel," both specifically when it precluded removal of the special prosecutor except for cause and as a general matter.[200] The Court disagreed. It began by noting that the Constitution's "system of separation of powers and checks and balances" was crafted "as a self-executing safe-guard against the encroachment or aggrandizement of one branch at the expense of the other."[201] It found that the Act presented no such threat.[202] The Court then ran through an abbreviated check list of features which might be said to restrict the Executive's prosecutorial control as well as those which appeared to re-enforce his control.

It acknowledged that under the Act the President's agent, the Attorney General: (1) did not select the special prosecutor; (2) did not define the scope of the special prosecutor's inquiry; and (3) could not remove the special prosecutor without cause.[203] On the other hand, (1) a special prosecutor could be selected only upon the Attorney General's unreviewable request; (2) the court defined the special prosecutor's scope of authority based upon the facts contained in that request; and (3) the Attorney General might remove the special prosecutor for cause.[204] All of which indicated to the Court that "the Act give[s] the Executive Branch sufficient control over the independent counsel to ensure that the President is able to perform his constitutionally assigned duties."

Lower court False Claims Act qui tam cases decided in *Morrison*'s shadow generally reached the same conclusion—the False Claims Act affords the Executive Branch sufficient control to turn aside a take care clause challenge—although they often concede that the control factors of the two were not the same.[205]

Appendix

False Claims Act (Text)

False Claims Act (Text)

31 U.S.C. 3729

(a) Liability for certain acts.–

(1) In general.– Subject to paragraph (2), any person who –

(A) knowingly presents, or causes to be presented, a false or fraudulent claim for payment or approval;

(B) knowingly makes, uses, or causes to be made or used, a false record or statement material to a false or fraudulent claim;

(C) conspires to commit a violation of subparagraph (A), (B), (D), (E), (F), or (G);

(D) has possession, custody, or control of property or money used, or to be used, by the Government and knowingly delivers, or causes to be delivered, less than all of that money or property;

(E) is authorized to make or deliver a document certifying receipt of property used, or to be used, by the Government and, intending to defraud the Government, makes or delivers the receipt without completely knowing that the information on the receipt is true;

(F) knowingly buys, or receives as a pledge of an obligation or debt, public property from an officer or employee of the Government, or a member of the Armed Forces, who lawfully may not sell or pledge property; or

(G) knowingly makes, uses, or causes to be made or used, a false record or statement material to an obligation to pay or transmit money or property to the Government, or knowingly conceals or knowingly and improperly avoids or decreases an obligation to pay or transmit money or property to the Government, is liable to the United States Government for a civil penalty of not less than $5,000 and not more than $10,000, as adjusted by the Federal Civil Penalties Inflation Adjustment Act of 1990 (28 U.S.C. 2461 note; P.L. 104-410), plus 3 times the amount of damages which the Government sustains because of the act of that person.

(2) Reduced damages.–If the court finds that–

(A) the person committing the violation of this subsection furnished officials of the United States responsible for investigating false claims violations with all information known to such person about the violation within 30 days after the date on which the defendant first obtained the information;

(B) such person fully cooperated with any Government investigation of such violation; and

(C) at the time such person furnished the United States with the information about the violation, no criminal prosecution, civil action, or administrative action had commenced under this title with respect to such violation, and the person did not have actual knowledge of the existence of an investigation into such violation, the court may assess not less than 2 times the amount of damages which the Government sustains because of the act of that person.

(3) **Costs of civil actions.**–A person violating this subsection shall also be liable to the United States Government for the costs of a civil action brought to recover any such penalty or damages.

(b) **Definitions.**–For purposes of this section–

(1) the terms "knowing" and "knowingly" –

(A) mean that a person, with respect to information–

(i) has actual knowledge of the information;

(ii) acts in deliberate ignorance of the truth or falsity of the information; or

(iii) acts in reckless disregard of the truth or falsity of the information; and

(B) require no proof of specific intent to defraud;

(2) the term "claim" –

(A) means any request or demand, whether under a contract or otherwise, for money or property and whether or not the United States has title to the money or property, that—

(i) is presented to an officer, employee, or agent of the United States; or

(ii) is made to a contractor, grantee, or other recipient, if the money or property is to be spent or used on the Government's behalf or to advance a Government program or interest, and if the United States Government—

(I) provides or has provided any portion of the money or property requested or demanded; or

(II) will reimburse such contractor, grantee, or other recipient for any portion of the money or property which is requested or demanded; and

(B) does not include requests or demands for money or property that the Government has paid to an individual as compensation for Federal employment or as an income subsidy with no restrictions on that individual's use of the money or property;

(3) the term "obligation" means an established duty, whether or not fixed, arising from an express or implied contractual, grantor-grantee, or licensor-licensee relationship, from a fee-based or similar relationship, from statute or regulation, or from the retention of any overpayment; and

(4) the term "material" means having a natural tendency to influence, or be capable of influencing, the payment or receipt of money or property.

(c) **Exemption from disclosure.** –Any information furnished pursuant to subsection (a)(2) shall be exempt from disclosure under section 552 of title 5.

(d) **Exclusion**. –This section does not apply to claims, records, or statements made under the Internal Revenue Code of 1986.

[(e) Redesignated (d)]

31 U.S.C. 3730

(a) **Responsibilities of the Attorney General.** –The Attorney General diligently shall investigate a violation under section 3729. If the Attorney General finds that a person has violated or is violating section 3729, the Attorney General may bring a civil action under this section against the person.

(b) Actions by private persons. –

(1) A person may bring a civil action for a violation of section 3729 for the person and for the United States Government. The action shall be brought in the name of the Government. The action may be dismissed only if the court and the Attorney General give written consent to the dismissal and their reasons for consenting.

(2) A copy of the complaint and written disclosure of substantially all material evidence and information the person possesses shall be served on the Government pursuant to Rule 4(d)(4) of the Federal Rules of Civil Procedure. The complaint shall be filed in camera, shall remain under seal for at least 60 days, and shall not be served on the defendant until the court so orders. The Government may elect to intervene and proceed with the action within 60 days after it receives both the complaint and the material evidence and information.

(3) The Government may, for good cause shown, move the court for extensions of the time during which the complaint remains under seal under paragraph (2). Any such motions may be supported by affidavits or other submissions in camera. The defendant shall not be required to respond to any complaint filed under this section until 20 days after the complaint is unsealed and served upon the defendant pursuant to Rule 4 of the Federal Rules of Civil Procedure.

(4) Before the expiration of the 60-day period or any extensions obtained under paragraph (3), the Government shall–

(A) proceed with the action, in which case the action shall be conducted by the Government; or

(B) notify the court that it declines to take over the action, in which case the person bringing the action shall have the right to conduct the action.

(5) When a person brings an action under this subsection, no person other than the Government may intervene or bring a related action based on the facts underlying the pending action.

(c) Rights of the parties to qui tam actions. –

(1) If the Government proceeds with the action, it shall have the primary responsibility for prosecuting the action, and shall not be bound by an act of the person bringing the action. Such person shall have the right to continue as a party to the action, subject to the limitations set forth in paragraph (2).

(2)(A) The Government may dismiss the action notwithstanding the objections of the person initiating the action if the person has been notified by the Government of the filing of the motion and the court has provided the person with an opportunity for a hearing on the motion.

(B) The Government may settle the action with the defendant notwithstanding the objections of the person initiating the action if the court determines, after a hearing, that the proposed settlement is fair, adequate, and reasonable under all the circumstances. Upon a showing of good cause, such hearing may be held in camera.

(C) Upon a showing by the Government that unrestricted participation during the course of the litigation by the person initiating the action would interfere with or unduly delay the Government's prosecution of the case, or would be repetitious, irrelevant, or for purposes of harassment, the court may, in its discretion, impose limitations on the person's participation, such as–

(i) limiting the number of witnesses the person may call;

(ii) limiting the length of the testimony of such witnesses;

(iii) limiting the person's cross-examination of witnesses; or

(iv) otherwise limiting the participation by the person in the litigation.

(D) Upon a showing by the defendant that unrestricted participation during the course of the litigation by the person initiating the action would be for purposes of harassment or would cause the defendant undue burden or unnecessary expense, the court may limit the participation by the person in the litigation.

(3) If the Government elects not to proceed with the action, the person who initiated the action shall have the right to conduct the action. If the Government so requests, it shall be served with copies of all pleadings filed in the action and shall be supplied with copies of all deposition transcripts (at the Government's expense). When a person proceeds with the action, the court, without limiting the status and rights of the person initiating the action, may nevertheless permit the Government to intervene at a later date upon a showing of good cause.

(4) Whether or not the Government proceeds with the action, upon a showing by the Government that certain actions of discovery by the person initiating the action would interfere with the Government's investigation or prosecution of a criminal or civil matter arising out of the same facts, the court may stay such discovery for a period of not more than 60 days. Such a showing shall be conducted in camera. The court may extend the 60-day period upon a further showing in camera that the Government has pursued the criminal or civil investigation or proceedings with reasonable diligence and any proposed discovery in the civil action will interfere with the ongoing criminal or civil investigation or proceedings.

(5) Notwithstanding subsection (b), the Government may elect to pursue its claim through any alternate remedy available to the Government, including any administrative proceeding to determine a civil money penalty. If any such alternate remedy is pursued in another proceeding, the person initiating the action shall have the same rights in such proceeding as such person would have had if the action had continued under this section. Any finding of fact or conclusion of law made in such other proceeding that has become final shall be conclusive on all parties to an action under this section. For purposes of the preceding sentence, a finding or conclusion is final if it has been finally determined on appeal to the appropriate court of the United States, if all time for filing such an appeal with respect to the finding or conclusion has expired, or if the finding or conclusion is not subject to judicial review.

(d) Award to qui tam plaintiff. –

(1) If the Government proceeds with an action brought by a person under subsection (b), such person shall, subject to the second sentence of this paragraph, receive at least 15 percent but not more than 25 percent of the proceeds of the action or settlement of the claim, depending upon the extent to which the person substantially contributed to the prosecution of the action. Where the action is one which the court finds to be based primarily on disclosures of specific information (other than information provided by the person bringing the action) relating to allegations or transactions in a criminal, civil, or administrative hearing, in a congressional, administrative, or Government Accounting Office report, hearing, audit, or investigation, or from the news media, the court may award such sums as it considers appropriate, but in no case more than 10 percent of the proceeds, taking into account the significance of the information and the role of the person bringing the action in advancing the case to litigation. Any payment to a person under the first or second sentence of this paragraph shall be made from the proceeds. Any such person shall also receive an amount for reasonable expenses which the court finds to have been necessarily incurred, plus reasonable attorneys' fees and costs. All such expenses, fees, and costs shall be awarded against the defendant.

(2) If the Government does not proceed with an action under this section, the person bringing the action or settling the claim shall receive an amount which the court decides is reasonable for collecting the civil penalty and damages. The amount shall be not less than 25 percent and not more than 30 percent of the proceeds of the action or settlement and shall be paid out of such proceeds. Such person shall also receive an amount for reasonable expenses which the court finds to have been necessarily incurred, plus reasonable attorneys' fees and costs. All such expenses, fees, and costs shall be awarded against the defendant.

(3) Whether or not the Government proceeds with the action, if the court finds that the action was brought by a person who planned and initiated the violation of section 3729 upon which the action was brought, then the court may, to the extent the court considers appropriate, reduce the share of the proceeds of the action which the person would otherwise receive under paragraph (1) or (2) of this subsection, taking into account the role of that person in advancing the case to litigation and any relevant circumstances pertaining to the violation. If the person bringing the action is convicted of criminal conduct arising from his or her role in the violation of section 3729, that person shall be dismissed from the civil action and shall not receive any share of the proceeds of the action. Such dismissal shall not prejudice the right of the United States to continue the action, represented by the Department of Justice.

(4) If the Government does not proceed with the action and the person bringing the action conducts the action, the court may award to the defendant its reasonable attorneys' fees and expenses if the defendant prevails in the action and the court finds that the claim of the person bringing the action was clearly frivolous, clearly vexatious, or brought primarily for purposes of harassment.

(e) Certain actions barred. –

(1) No court shall have jurisdiction over an action brought by a former or present member of the armed forces under subsection (b) of this section against a member of the armed forces arising out of such person's service in the armed forces.

(2)(A) No court shall have jurisdiction over an action brought under subsection (b) against a Member of Congress, a member of the judiciary, or a senior executive branch official if the action is based on evidence or information known to the Government when the action was brought.

(B) For purposes of this paragraph, "senior executive branch official" means any officer or employee listed in paragraphs (1) through (8) of section 101 (f) of the Ethics in Government Act of 1978 (5 U.S.C. App.).

(3) In no event may a person bring an action under subsection (b) which is based upon allegations or transactions which are the subject of a civil suit or an administrative civil money penalty proceeding in which the Government is already a party.

(4)

(A) No court shall have jurisdiction over an action under this section based upon the public disclosure of allegations or transactions in a criminal, civil, or administrative hearing, in a congressional, administrative, or Government Accounting Office report, hearing, audit, or investigation, or from the news media, unless the action is brought by the Attorney General or the person bringing the action is an original source of the information.

(B) For purposes of this paragraph, "original source" means an individual who has direct and independent knowledge of the information on which the allegations are based and has voluntarily provided the information to the Government before filing an action under this section which is based on the information.

(f) Government not liable for certain expenses. –The Government is not liable for expenses which a person incurs in bringing an action under this section.

(g) Fees and expenses to prevailing defendant. –In civil actions brought under this section by the United States, the provisions of section 24 12(d) of title 28 shall apply.

(h) Relief from retaliatory actions. –

(1) In general. –Any employee, contractor, or agent shall be entitled to all relief necessary to make that employee, contractor, or agent whole, if that employee, contractor, or agent is discharged, demoted, suspended, threatened, harassed, or in any other manner discriminated against in the terms and conditions of employment because of lawful acts done by the employee, contractor, or agent on behalf of the employee, contractor, or agent or associated others in furtherance of other efforts to stop 1 or more violations of this subchapter.

(2) Relief. –Relief under paragraph (1) shall include reinstatement with the same seniority status that employee, contractor, or agent would have had but for the discrimination, 2 times the amount of back pay, interest on the back pay, and compensation for any special damages sustained as a result of the discrimination, including litigation costs and reasonable attorneys' fees. An action under this subsection may be brought in the appropriate district court of the United States for the relief provided in this subsection.

31 U.S.C. 3731

(a) A subpena requiring the attendance of a witness at a trial or hearing conducted under section 3730 of this title may be served at any place in the United States.

(b) A civil action under section 3730 may not be brought–

(1) more than 6 years after the date on which the violation of section 3729 is committed, or

(2) more than 3 years after the date when facts material to the right of action are known or reasonably should have been known by the official of the United States charged with responsibility to act in the circumstances, but in no event more than 10 years after the date on which the violation is committed, whichever occurs last.

(c) If the Government elects to intervene and proceed with an action brought under 3730(b), the Government may file its own complaint or amend the complaint of a person who has brought an action under section 3730(b) to clarify or add detail to the claims in which the Government is intervening and to add any additional claims with respect to which the Government contends it is entitled to relief. For statute of limitations purposes, any such Government pleading shall relate back to the filing date of the complaint of the person who originally brought the action, to the extent that the claim of the Government arises out of the conduct, transactions, or occurrences set forth, or attempted to be set forth, in the prior complaint of that person.

(d) In any action brought under section 3730, the United States shall be required to prove all essential elements of the cause of action, including damages, by a preponderance of the evidence.

(e) Notwithstanding any other provision of law, the Federal Rules of Criminal Procedure, or the Federal Rules of Evidence, a final judgment rendered in favor of the United States in any criminal proceeding charging fraud or false statements, whether upon a verdict after trial or upon a plea of guilty or nolo contendere, shall estop the defendant from denying the essential elements of the offense in any action which involves the same transaction as in the criminal proceeding and which is brought under subsection (a) or (b) of section 3730.

31 U.S.C. 3732

(a) Actions under section 3730.—Any action under section 3730 may be brought in any judicial district in which the defendant or, in the case of multiple defendants, any one defendant can be found, resides, transacts business, or in which any act proscribed by section 3729 occurred. A summons as required by the Federal Rules of Civil Procedure shall be issued by the appropriate district court and served at any place within or outside the United States.

(b) Claims under state law.—The district courts shall have jurisdiction over any action brought under the laws of any State for the recovery of funds paid by a State or local government if the action arises from the same transaction or occurrence as an action brought under section 3730.

(c) Service on State or local authorities.—With respect to any State or local government that is named as a co-plaintiff with the United States in an action brought under subsection (b), a seal on the action ordered by the court under section 3730(b) shall not preclude the Government or the person bringing the action from serving the complaint, any other pleadings, or the written disclosure of substantially all material evidence and information possessed by the person bringing the action on the law enforcement authorities that are authorized under the law of that State or local government to investigate and prosecute such actions on behalf of such governments, except that such seal applies to the law enforcement authorities so served to the same extent as the seal applies to other parties in the action.

31 U.S.C. 3733

(a) **In general. –**

(1) **Issuance and service.** –Whenever the Attorney General, or a designee (for purposes of this section), has reason to believe that any person may be in possession, custody, or control of any documentary material or information relevant to a false claims law investigation, the Attorney General, or a designee, may, before commencing a civil proceeding under section 3730(a) or other false claims law, or making an election under section 3730(b), issue in writing and cause to be served upon such person, a civil investigative demand requiring such person—

(A) to produce such documentary material for inspection and copying,

(B) to answer in writing written interrogatories with respect to such documentary material or information,

(C) to give oral testimony concerning such documentary material or information, or

(D) to furnish any combination of such material, answers, or testimony.

The Attorney General may delegate the authority to issue civil investigative demands under this subsection. Whenever a civil investigative demand is an express demand for any product of discovery, the Attorney General, the Deputy Attorney General, or an Assistant Attorney General shall cause to be served, in any manner authorized by this section, a copy of such demand upon the person from whom the discovery was obtained and shall notify the person to whom such demand is issued of the date on which such copy was served. Any information obtained by the Attorney General or a designee of the Attorney General under this section may be shared with any qui tam relator if the Attorney General or designee determine it is necessary as part of any false claims act investigation.

(2) **Contents and deadlines. –**

(A) Each civil investigative demand issued under paragraph (1) shall state the nature of the conduct constituting the alleged violation of a false claims law which is under investigation, and the applicable provision of law alleged to be violated.

(B) If such demand is for the production of documentary material, the demand shall–

(i) describe each class of documentary material to be produced with such definiteness and certainty as to permit such material to be fairly identified;

(ii) prescribe a return date for each such class which will provide a reasonable period of time within which the material so demanded may be assembled and made available for inspection and copying; and

(iii) identify the false claims law investigator to whom such material shall be made available.

(C) If such demand is for answers to written interrogatories, the demand shall–

(i) set forth with specificity the written interrogatories to be answered;

(ii) prescribe dates at which time answers to written interrogatories shall be submitted; and

(iii) identify the false claims law investigator to whom such answers shall be submitted.

(D) If such demand is for the giving of oral testimony, the demand shall—

(i) prescribe a date, time, and place at which oral testimony shall be commenced;

(ii) identify a false claims law investigator who shall conduct the examination and the custodian to whom the transcript of such examination shall be submitted;

(iii) specify that such attendance and testimony are necessary to the conduct of the investigation;

(iv) notify the person receiving the demand of the right to be accompanied by an attorney and any other representative; and

(v) describe the general purpose for which the demand is being issued and the general nature of the testimony, including the primary areas of inquiry, which will be taken pursuant to the demand.

(E) Any civil investigative demand issued under this section which is an express demand for any product of discovery shall not be returned or returnable until 20 days after a copy of such demand has been served upon the person from whom the discovery was obtained.

(F) The date prescribed for the commencement of oral testimony pursuant to a civil investigative demand issued under this section shall be a date which is not less than seven days after the date on which demand is received, unless the Attorney General or an Assistant Attorney General designated by the Attorney General determines that exceptional circumstances are present which warrant the commencement of such testimony within a lesser period of time.

(G) The Attorney General shall not authorize the issuance under this section of more than one civil investigative demand for oral testimony by the same person unless the person requests otherwise or unless the Attorney General, after investigation, notifies that person in writing that an additional demand for oral testimony is necessary.

(b) Protected material or information. –

(1) In general. –A civil investigative demand issued under subsection (a) may not require the production of any documentary material, the submission of any answers to written interrogatories, or the giving of any oral testimony if such material, answers, or testimony would be protected from disclosure under–

(A) the standards applicable to subpoenas or subpoenas duces tecum issued by a court of the United States to aid in a grand jury investigation; or

(B) the standards applicable to discovery requests under the Federal Rules of Civil Procedure, to the extent that the application of such standards to any such demand is appropriate and consistent with the provisions and purposes of this section.

(2) Effect on other orders, rules, and laws. –Any such demand which is an express demand for any product of discovery supersedes any inconsistent order, rule, or provision of law (other than this section) preventing or restraining disclosure of such product of discovery to any person. Disclosure of any product of discovery pursuant to any such express demand does not constitute a waiver of any right or privilege which the person making such disclosure may be entitled to invoke to resist discovery of trial preparation materials.

(c) Service; jurisdiction. –

(1) By whom served. –Any civil investigative demand issued under subsection (a) may be served by a false claims law investigator, or by a United States marshal or a deputy marshal, at any place within the territorial jurisdiction of any court of the United States.

(2) Service in foreign countries. –Any such demand or any petition filed under subsection (j) may be served upon any person who is not found within the territorial jurisdiction of any court of the United States in such manner as the Federal Rules of Civil Procedure prescribe for service in a foreign country. To the extent that the courts of the United States can assert jurisdiction over any such person consistent with due process, the United States District Court for the District of Columbia shall have the same jurisdiction to take any action respecting compliance with this section by any such person that such court would have if such person were personally within the jurisdiction of such court.

(d) Service upon legal entities and natural persons. –

(1) Legal entities. –Service of any civil investigative demand issued under subsection (a) or of any petition filed under subsection (j) may be made upon a partnership, corporation, association, or other legal entity by–

(A) delivering an executed copy of such demand or petition to any partner, executive officer, managing agent, or general agent of the partnership, corporation, association, or entity, or to any agent authorized by appointment or by law to receive service of process on behalf of such partnership, corporation, association, or entity;

(B) delivering an executed copy of such demand or petition to the principal office or place of business of the partnership, corporation, association, or entity; or

(C) depositing an executed copy of such demand or petition in the United States mails by registered or certified mail, with a return receipt requested, addressed to such partnership, corporation, association, or entity at its principal office or place of business.

(2) Natural persons. –Service of any such demand or petition may be made upon any natural person by–

(A) delivering an executed copy of such demand or petition to the person; or

(B) depositing an executed copy of such demand or petition in the United States mails by registered or certified mail, with a return receipt requested, addressed to the person at the person's residence or principal office or place of business.

(e) Proof of service. –A verified return by the individual serving any civil investigative demand issued under subsection (a) or any petition filed under subsection (j) setting forth the manner of such service shall be proof of such service. In the case of service by registered or certified mail, such return shall be accompanied by the return post office receipt of delivery of such demand.

(f) Documentary material. –

(1) Sworn certificates. –The production of documentary material in response to a civil investigative demand served under this section shall be made under a sworn certificate, in such form as the demand designates, by–

(A) in the case of a natural person, the person to whom the demand is directed, or

(B) in the case of a person other than a natural person, a person having knowledge of the facts and circumstances relating to such production and authorized to act on behalf of such person. The certificate shall state that all of the documentary material required by the demand and in the possession, custody, or control of the person to whom the demand is directed has been produced and made available to the false claims law investigator identified in the demand.

(2) Production of materials. –Any person upon whom any civil investigative demand for the production of documentary material has been served under this section shall make such material available for inspection and copying to the false claims law investigator identified in such demand at the principal place of business of such person, or at such other place as the false claims law investigator and the person thereafter may agree and prescribe in writing, or as the court may direct under subsection (j)(1). Such material shall be made so available on the return date specified in such demand, or on such later date as the false claims law investigator may prescribe in writing. Such person may, upon written agreement between the person and the false claims law investigator, substitute copies for originals of all or any part of such material.

(g) Interrogatories. –Each interrogatory in a civil investigative demand served under this section shall be answered separately and fully in writing under oath and shall be submitted under a sworn certificate, in such form as the demand designates, by–

(1) in the case of a natural person, the person to whom the demand is directed, or

(2) in the case of a person other than a natural person, the person or persons responsible for answering each interrogatory.

If any interrogatory is objected to, the reasons for the objection shall be stated in the certificate instead of an answer. The certificate shall state that all information required by the demand and in the possession, custody, control, or knowledge of the person to whom the demand is directed has been submitted. To the extent that any information is not furnished, the information shall be identified and reasons set forth with particularity regarding the reasons why the information was not furnished.

(h) Oral examinations. –

(1) Procedures. –The examination of any person pursuant to a civil investigative demand for oral testimony served under this section shall be taken before an officer authorized to administer oaths and affirmations by the laws of the United States or of the place where the examination is held. The officer before whom the testimony is to be taken shall put the witness on oath or affirmation and shall, personally or by someone acting under the direction of the officer and in the officer's presence, record the testimony of the witness. The testimony shall be taken stenographically and shall be transcribed. When the testimony is fully transcribed, the officer before whom the testimony is taken shall promptly transmit a copy of the transcript of the testimony to the custodian. This subsection shall not preclude the taking of testimony by any means authorized by, and in a manner consistent with, the Federal Rules of Civil Procedure.

(2) Persons present. –The false claims law investigator conducting the examination shall exclude from the place where the examination is held all persons except the person giving the testimony, the attorney for and any other representative of the person giving the testimony, the attorney for the Government, any person who may be agreed upon by the attorney for the Government and the person giving the testimony, the officer before whom the testimony is to be taken, and any stenographer taking such testimony.

(3) Where testimony taken. –The oral testimony of any person taken pursuant to a civil investigative demand served under this section shall be taken in the judicial district of the United States within which such person resides, is found, or transacts business, or in such other place as may be agreed upon by the false claims law investigator conducting the examination and such person.

(4) Transcript of testimony. –When the testimony is fully transcribed, the false claims law investigator or the officer before whom the testimony is taken shall afford the witness, who may be accompanied by counsel, a reasonable opportunity to examine and read the transcript, unless such examination and reading are waived by the witness. Any changes in form or substance which the witness desires to make shall be entered and identified upon the transcript by the officer or the false claims law investigator, with a statement of the reasons given by the witness for making such changes. The transcript shall then be signed by the witness, unless the witness in writing waives the signing, is ill, cannot be found, or refuses to sign. If the transcript is not signed by the witness within 30 days after being afforded a reasonable opportunity to examine it, the officer or the false claims law investigator shall sign it and state on the record the fact of the waiver, illness, absence of the witness, or the refusal to sign, together with the reasons, if any, given therefor.

(5) Certification and delivery to custodian. –The officer before whom the testimony is taken shall certify on the transcript that the witness was sworn by the officer and that the transcript is a true record of the testimony given by the witness, and the officer or false claims law investigator shall promptly deliver the transcript, or send the transcript by registered or certified mail, to the custodian.

(6) Furnishing or inspection of transcript by witness. –Upon payment of reasonable charges therefor, the false claims law investigator shall furnish a copy of the transcript to the witness only, except that the Attorney General, the Deputy Attorney General, or an Assistant Attorney General may, for good cause, limit such witness to inspection of the official transcript of the witness' testimony.

(7) Conduct of oral testimony. –

(A) Any person compelled to appear for oral testimony under a civil investigative demand issued under subsection (a) may be accompanied, represented, and advised by counsel. Counsel may advise such person, in confidence, with respect to any question asked of such person. Such person or counsel may object on the record to any question, in whole or in part, and shall briefly state for the record the reason for the objection. An objection may be made, received, and entered upon the record when it is claimed that such person is entitled to refuse to answer the question on the grounds of any constitutional or other legal right or privilege, including the privilege against self-incrimination. Such person may not otherwise object to or refuse to answer any question, and may not directly or through counsel otherwise interrupt the oral examination. If such person refuses to answer any question, a petition may be filed in the district court of the United States under subsection (j)(1) for an order compelling such person to answer such question.

(B) If such person refuses to answer any question on the grounds of the privilege against self- incrimination, the testimony of such person may be compelled in accordance with the provisions of part V of title 18.

(8) Witness fees and allowances. –Any person appearing for oral testimony under a civil investigative demand issued under subsection (a) shall be entitled to the same fees and allowances which are paid to witnesses in the district courts of the United States.

(i) Custodians of documents, answers, and transcripts. –

(1) Designation. –The Attorney General shall designate a false claims law investigator to serve as custodian of documentary material, answers to interrogatories, and transcripts of oral testimony received under this section, and shall designate such additional false claims law investigators as the Attorney General determines from time to time to be necessary to serve as deputies to the custodian.

(2) Responsibility for materials; disclosure. –

(A) A false claims law investigator who receives any documentary material, answers to interrogatories, or transcripts of oral testimony under this section shall transmit them to the custodian. The custodian shall take physical possession of such material, answers, or transcripts and shall be responsible for the use made of them and for the return of documentary material under paragraph (4).

(B) The custodian may cause the preparation of such copies of such documentary material, answers to interrogatories, or transcripts of oral testimony as may be required for official use by any false claims law investigator, or other officer or employee of the Department of Justice. Such material, answers, and transcripts may be used by any such authorized false claims law investigator or other officer or employee in connection with the taking of oral testimony under this section.

(C) Except as otherwise provided in this subsection, no documentary material, answers to interrogatories, or transcripts of oral testimony, or copies thereof, while in the possession of the custodian, shall be available for examination by any individual other than a false claims law investigator or other officer or employee of the Department of Justice authorized under subparagraph (B). The prohibition in the preceding sentence on the availability of material, answers, or transcripts shall not apply if consent is given by the person who produced such material, answers, or transcripts, or, in the case of any product of discovery produced pursuant to an express demand for such material, consent is given by the person from whom the discovery was obtained. Nothing in this subparagraph is intended to prevent disclosure to the Congress, including any committee or subcommittee of the Congress, or to any other agency of the United States for use by such agency in furtherance of its statutory responsibilities.

(D) While in the possession of the custodian and under such reasonable terms and conditions as the Attorney General shall prescribe–

(i) documentary material and answers to interrogatories shall be available for examination by the person who produced such material or answers, or by a representative of that person authorized by that person to examine such material and answers; and

(ii) transcripts of oral testimony shall be available for examination by the person who produced such testimony, or by a representative of that person authorized by that person to examine such transcripts.

(3) Use of material, answers, or transcripts in other proceedings. – Whenever any attorney of the Department of Justice has been designated to appear before any court, grand jury, or Federal agency in any case or proceeding, the custodian of any documentary material, answers to interrogatories, or transcripts of oral testimony received under this section may deliver to such attorney such material, answers, or transcripts for official use in connection with any such case or proceeding as such attorney determines to be required. Upon the completion of any such case or proceeding, such attorney shall return to the custodian any such material, answers, or transcripts so delivered which have not passed into the control of such court, grand jury, or agency through introduction into the record of such case or proceeding.

(4) Conditions for return of material. –If any documentary material has been produced by any person in the course of any false claims law investigation pursuant to a civil investigative demand under this section, and—

(A) any case or proceeding before the court or grand jury arising out of such investigation, or any proceeding before any Federal agency involving such material, has been completed, or

(B) no case or proceeding in which such material may be used has been commenced within a reasonable time after completion of the examination and analysis of all documentary material and other information assembled in the course of such investigation,

the custodian shall, upon written request of the person who produced such material, return to such person any such material (other than copies furnished to the false claims law investigator under subsection (f)(2) or made for the Department of Justice under paragraph (2)(B)) which has not passed into the control of any court, grand jury, or agency through introduction into the record of such case or proceeding.

(5) Appointment of successor custodians. –In the event of the death, disability, or separation from service in the Department of Justice of the custodian of any documentary material, answers to interrogatories, or transcripts of oral testimony produced pursuant to a civil investigative demand under this section, or in the event of the official relief of such custodian from responsibility for the custody and control of such material, answers, or transcripts, the Attorney General shall promptly–

(A) designate another false claims law investigator to serve as custodian of such material, answers, or transcripts, and

(B) transmit in writing to the person who produced such material, answers, or testimony notice of the identity and address of the successor so designated.

Any person who is designated to be a successor under this paragraph shall have, with regard to such material, answers, or transcripts, the same duties and responsibilities as were imposed by this section upon that person's predecessor in office, except that the successor shall not be held responsible for any default or dereliction which occurred before that designation.

(j) Judicial proceedings. –

(1) Petition for enforcement. –Whenever any person fails to comply with any civil investigative demand issued under subsection (a), or whenever satisfactory copying or reproduction of any material requested in such demand cannot be done and such person refuses to surrender such material, the Attorney General may file, in the district court of the United States for any judicial district in which such person resides, is found, or transacts business, and serve upon such person a petition for an order of such court for the enforcement of the civil investigative demand.

(2) Petition to modify or set aside demand. –

(A) Any person who has received a civil investigative demand issued under subsection (a) may file, in the district court of the United States for the judicial district within which such person resides, is found, or transacts business, and serve upon the false claims law investigator identified in such demand a petition for an order of the court to modify or set aside such demand. In the case of a petition addressed to an express demand for any product of discovery, a petition to modify or set aside such demand may be brought only in the district court of the United States for the judicial district in which the proceeding in which such discovery was obtained is or was last pending. Any petition under this subparagraph must be filed—

(i) within 20 days after the date of service of the civil investigative demand, or at any time before the return date specified in the demand, whichever date is earlier, or

(ii) within such longer period as may be prescribed in writing by any false claims law investigator identified in the demand.

(B) The petition shall specify each ground upon which the petitioner relies in seeking relief under subparagraph (A), and may be based upon any failure of the demand to comply with the provisions of this section or upon any constitutional or other legal right or privilege of such person. During the pendency of the petition in the court, the court may stay, as it deems proper, the running of the time allowed for compliance with the demand, in whole or in part, except that the person filing the petition shall comply with any portions of the demand not sought to be modified or set aside.

(3) Petition to modify or set aside demand for product of discovery. –

(A) In the case of any civil investigative demand issued under subsection (a) which is an express demand for any product of discovery, the person from whom such discovery was obtained may file, in the district court of the United States for the judicial district in which the proceeding in which such discovery was obtained is or was last pending, and serve upon any false claims law investigator identified in the demand and upon the recipient of the demand, a petition for an order of such court to modify or set aside those portions of the demand requiring production of any such product of discovery. Any petition under this subparagraph must be filed–

(i) within 20 days after the date of service of the civil investigative demand, or at any time before the return date specified in the demand, whichever date is earlier, or

(ii) within such longer period as may be prescribed in writing by any false claims law investigator identified in the demand.

(B) The petition shall specify each ground upon which the petitioner relies in seeking relief under subparagraph (A), and may be based upon any failure of the portions of the demand from which relief is sought to comply with the provisions of this section, or upon any constitutional or other legal right or privilege of the petitioner. During the pendency of the petition, the court may stay, as it deems proper, compliance with the demand and the running of the time allowed for compliance with the demand.

(4) Petition to require performance by custodian of duties. – At any time during which any custodian is in custody or control of any documentary material or answers to interrogatories produced, or transcripts of oral testimony given, by any person in compliance with any civil investigative demand issued under subsection (a), such person, and in the case of an express demand for any product of discovery, the person from whom such discovery was obtained, may file, in the district court of the United States for the judicial district within which the office of such custodian is situated, and serve upon such custodian, a petition for an order of such court to require the performance by the custodian of any duty imposed upon the custodian by this section.

(5) Jurisdiction. –Whenever any petition is filed in any district court of the United States under this subsection, such court shall have jurisdiction to hear and determine the matter so presented, and to enter such order or orders as may be required to carry out the provisions of this section. Any final order so entered shall be subject to appeal under section 1291 of title 28. Any disobedience of any final order entered under this section by any court shall be punished as a contempt of the court.

(6) Applicability of federal rules of civil procedure. –The Federal Rules of Civil Procedure shall apply to any petition under this subsection, to the extent that such rules are not inconsistent with the provisions of this section.

(k) Disclosure exemption. –Any documentary material, answers to written interrogatories, or oral testimony provided under any civil investigative demand issued under subsection (a) shall be exempt from disclosure under section 552 of title 5.

(l) Definitions. –For purposes of this section–

(1) the term "false claims law" means–

(A) this section and sections 3729 and 3732; and

(B) any Act of Congress enacted after the date of the enactment of this section which prohibits, or makes available to the United States in any court of the United States any civil remedy with respect to, any false claim against, bribery of, or corruption of any officer or employee of the United States;

(2) the term "false claims law investigation" means any inquiry conducted by any false claims law investigator for the purpose of ascertaining whether any person is or has been engaged in any violation of a false claims law;

(3) the term "false claims law investigator" means any attorney or investigator employed by the Department of Justice who is charged with the duty of enforcing or carrying into effect any false claims law, or any officer or employee of the United States acting under the direction and supervision of such attorney or investigator in connection with a false claims law investigation;

(4) the term "person" means any natural person, partnership, corporation, association, or other legal entity, including any State or political subdivision of a State;

(5) the term "documentary material" includes the original or any copy of any book, record, report, memorandum, paper, communication, tabulation, chart, or other document, or data compilations stored in or accessible through computer or other information retrieval systems, together with instructions and all other materials necessary to use or interpret such data compilations, and any product of discovery;

(6) the term "custodian" means the custodian, or any deputy custodian, designated by the Attorney General under subsection (i)(1);

(7) the term "product of discovery" includes–

(A) the original or duplicate of any deposition, interrogatory, document, thing, result of the inspection of land or other property, examination, or admission, which is obtained by any method of discovery in any judicial or administrative proceeding of an adversarial nature;

(B) any digest, analysis, selection, compilation, or derivation of any item listed in subparagraph (A); and

(C) any index or other manner of access to any item listed in subparagraph (A); and

(8) the term "official use" means any use that is consistent with the law, and the regulations and policies of the Department of Justice, including use in connection with internal Department of Justice memoranda and reports; communications between the Department of Justice and a Federal, State, or local government agency, or a contractor of a Federal, State, or local government agency, undertaken in furtherance of a Department of Justice investigation or prosecution of a case; interviews of any qui tam relator or other witness; oral examinations; depositions; preparation for and response to civil discovery requests; introduction into the record of a case or proceeding; applications, motions, memoranda and briefs submitted to a court or other tribunal; and communications with Government investigators, auditors, consultants and experts, the counsel of other parties, arbitrators and mediators, concerning an investigation, case or proceeding.

Notes

[1] 15 U.S.C. 15 (antitrust), 18 U.S.C. 1964 (racketeer influenced and corrupt organizations (RICO)); examples of other punitive damage provisions include 15 U.S.C. 1679g (consumer credit protection), 18 U.S.C. 2710 (wrongful disclosure of video tape rental or sales records), 18 U.S.C. 2520 (communications privacy), 18 U.S.C. 2724 (state motor vehicle record privacy), 47 U.S.C. 551 (cable subscriber privacy). Other federal private attorney general statutes permit suit by those who are not victims. These allow the award of attorney's fees, but unlike qui tam provisions they do not call for the private plaintiff to share any damage or penalty award with the government, *e.g.*, 33 U.S.C. 1365 (water pollution control), 42 U.S.C. 4911 (noise control).

[2] Blackstone explained that the phrase "qui tam" comes from a longer one which he abbreviated to "*qui tam pro domino rege, &c, quam pro seipso in hac parte sequitur,* " III BLACKSTONE, COMMENTARIES ON THE LAWS OF ENGLAND 160 (1768)(transliteration supplied). Taking the "&c" into account, the phrase might read in full, "he who brings this following matter for my Lord the King and who as well who brings this following matter for himself." In any event, later courts and commentators usually drop at least the "&c" from Blackstone's quote, see *e.g.*, *Vermont Agency of Natural Resources v. United States ex rel. Stevens*, 529 U.S. 768 n. 1 (2000)("*qui tam pro domino rege quam pro seipso in hac parte sequitur*"); Beck, *The False Claims Act and the English Eradication of* Qui Tam *Legislation*, 78 NORTH CAROLINA LAW REVIEW 539, 541 n. 3 (2000)(same); *The History and Development of Qui Tam*, 1972 WASHINGTON UNIVERSITY LAW QUARTERLY 81, 83 ("*Qui tam* is the accepted abbreviation of the phrase '*qui tam pro domino rege quam pro seipso* '").

[3] COKE, THE THIRD PART OF THE INSTITUTES OF THE LAWS OF ENGLAND 194 (1628).

[4] S. Rept. No. 77-1708, at 2 (1942), and H. Rept. No. 78-263 at 2 (1943), each quoting from a letter by Attorney General Biddle.

[5] *E.g.*, 132 *Cong. Rec.* 20535 (1986)(remarks of Sen. Grassley urging enactment of an anti-fraud qui tam measure)("There is no question that the current state of affairs begs for reform. Fraud allegations are climbing at a steady rate while the Justice Department's own economic crime council last year terms the level of enforcement in defense procurement fraud inadequate").

[6] *The False Claims Act Correction Act (S. 2041): Strengthening the Government's Most Effective Tool Against Fraud for the 21st Century: Hearing Before the Senate Comm. on the Judiciary*, 110th Cong., 2d Sess. 1 (2008)(statement of Sen. Leahy).

[7] Translated in Attenborough, THE LAWS OF THE EARLIEST ENGLISH KINGS 27 (1963); described in Plucknett, EDWARD I AND CRIMINAL LAW 31-2 (1960), and Beck, *The False Claims Act and the English Eradication of* Qui Tam *Legislation*, 78 NORTH CAROLINA LAW REVIEW 539, 567 (2000).

[8] *E.g.*, 12 EDWARD II, ch. 6 (1318), 1 STATS. OF THE REALM 177, 178 (" ... no officer in City or in Borough ... shall . merchandise for Wines ... And if any do, and be thereof convict[ed], the Merchandize whereof he is convict[ed] shall be forfeit[ed] to the King, and the third part thereof shall be delivered to the Party that sued the Offender, as the King's Gift ... "); 22 EDWARD IV, ch. 8 (1482), 2 STATS. OF THE REALM 468, 476 (export violations required the offender to forfeit the contraband or its value and the statute provided that "our Lord the King to have as well the one Half of all such Merchandise forfeited and seised, as the one half of all Sums of Money which shall be recovered by Action in the Form aforementioned, [to pursue] for Value of any such Goods so forfeited; and the Person or Persons which shall seise or sue in the Form aforesaid, to have the other Half of the same ... "); 32 HENRY VIII, ch. 9, §3 (1540), 3 STATS. OF THE REALM 753, 753 (suborning perjury was made subject to a £10 penalty and "Th[e] one moytie [i.e., half] thereof to the King our sourveraine lorde and th[e] other moytie to him that w[i]ll sue for the same by action of de[b]t[,] bill[,] playnte or information in any of the Kinges Courtis ... ").

[9] IV HOLDSWORTH, A HISTORY OF ENGLISH LAW 356 (1903). Coke strikes a similar note and adds the evils of forum shopping to a defendant's inconvenience, expense, and disadvantage, COKE, THE THIRD PART OF THE INSTITUTES OF THE LAWS OF ENGLAND 192, 194 (1628)("First, many penall laws obsolete, and in time grown apparently impossible, or inconvenient to be performed, remained as snares, whereupon the relator, informer, or promooter did vex and entangle the subject ... The second mischief was, that common informers ... drew all informations for any offence, in any place within the realm of England against any penall law to some of the kings courts as Westminister, to the intolerable charge, vexation, and trouble of the subject ... The third mischief was, that in informations, &c. the offence supposed to be against the penall law, and to be committed in one county, was at the pleasure of the informer, &c. alledged in any country where he would, where neither party nor witnesse was known, against the right institution of the law, that the jury (for their better notice) should come *de vicineto* of the place where the fact was committed").

[10] The term, which describes a species of lawless men who disrupt the normal peace and order of society, can be alternatively translated as, "a wild or disorderly class of men," see Beck, *The False Claims Act and the English Eradication of* Qui Tam *Legislation*, 78 NORTH CAROLINA LAW REVIEW 539, 578 n. 201 (2000).

[11] COKE, THE THIRD PART OF THE INSTITUTES OF THE LAWS OF ENGLAND 191, 194 (1628).

[12] *Protecting Informers*, 8 ELIZABETH I, PROCLAMATION OF NOVEMBER 10, 1566, reprinted with transliteration in II HUGHES & LARKIN, TUDOR ROYAL PROCLAMATIONS, 1553-1587, 288-89 (1969)("The Queen's majesty, understanding the great disorder that of late hath been and yet is daily used in and about the cities of London and Westminster, and especially in and about Westminster Hall and the palace of Westminster, by divers light and evil-disposed persons who in great routs and companies have assembled themselves together against such as be informers upon penal laws and statutes, commonly called promoters; and so being assembled, have not only beaten and very evil treated divers of the same informers but also have made great outcries against the same persons, where the courts and places of justice in Westminster Hall and other places thereabouts have been much disquieted and troubled, and the Queen's majesty's peas broken. . .. Wherefore her majesty doth straightly charge and command all persons that they nor any of them do hereafter commit ... any such disorder or misbehavior ... against any such informers ... upon pain to suffer imprisonment of their bodies by the space of three months ... "). The Proclamation is available without transliteration in GREAT BRITAIN SOVEREIGNS, 1558-1603: PROCLAMATIONS, 373 (1971)(DeCapo Press).

[13] III BLACKSTONE, COMMENTARIES ON THE LAWS OF ENGLAND 160 (1768)(transliteration supplied)("But, more usually, these forfeitures created by statute are given at large, to any common informer; or, in other words, to any such person or persons as will sue for the same: and hence such actions are called *popular* actions, because they are given to the people in general. Sometimes one part is given to the king, to the poor, or to some public use, and the other part to the informer or prosecutor and then the suit is called a *qui tam* action, because it is brought by a person '*qui tam pro domino rege, &c, quam pro seipso in hac parte sequitur.*' If the king therefore himself commences this suit, he shall have the whole forfeiture. But if any one hath begun a *qui tam*, or *popular*, action, no other person can pursue it; and the verdict passed upon the defendant in the first suit is a bar to all others, and conclusive even to the king himself. This has frequently occasioned offenders to procure their own friends to begin a suit, in order to forestall and prevent other actions: which practice is in some measure prevented by a statute made in the reign of a very sharp-sighted prince in penal laws ... ").

[14] *E.g.*, COLONIAL LAWS OF MASSACHUSETTS 8 (1686)(penalties for fraud in the sale of bread to be distributed one-third to inspector who discovered the fraud and remainder for the benefit of the town where the offense occurred); ID. at 54 (penalties for catching mackerel out of season to be distributed one half to the informer and one half to the town where the offense occurred); 1 STATUTES OF CONNECTICUT 531 (1672)(penalties of 10 shillings for permitting a night-time disorderly assembly under one's roof to be distributed half to the town and half to the individual who filed the complaint); 1 COLONIAL LAWS OF NEW YORK, 1664-17 19, 279, 281 (1692)(penalty of £50 for an officer's failure to perform duties for the prevention of piracy to be distributed one moiety to the informer and one to the province); ID. at 845 (1715)(20 shilling penalties for taking oysters

out of season to be distributed half to the informer and half to the benefit of the poor of the town where the offense occurred); 2 COLONIAL LAWS OF NEW YORK, 1720-1737, 988, 989-90 (1737)(penalties of £30 for peddling without a license to be distributed one moiety to the informer and one for the benefit of the town where the offense occurred); 7 VIRGINIA STATUTES (HENNING) 282, 285 (1759)(penalties for peddling without a license to be distributed one moiety to the king for the support of the College of William & Mary and one to informer who brings the action on the debt for its recovery); IV STATUTES OF SOUTH CAROLINA, 1752-1786, 460 (1778)(penalties of £1,000 for acting as a magistrate without authorization to be distributed one half to the public treasury and one half to those who sued for their recover).

[15] *E.g.*, *Churchill v. Blackburn,* 1 Va. Colonial Dec. R26 (Va. Gen. Ct. 1730); *Musgrove, qui tam v. Gibbs*, 1 U.S. 216 (Pa. 1787).

[16] *E.g.*, *Britton, qui tam v. Ridgely*, 4 H. & McH. 503 (Md. Prov. 1768)(3 & 4 GEORGE II, ch. 12); *Anderson, qui tam v. Winston*, 2 Va. Colonial Dec. B201 (Va. Gen. Ct. 1735)(32 HENRY VIII, ch. 9).

[17] *E.g.*, section 3, Act of March 1, 1790, 1 Stat. 101, 102 (1790); section 4, Act of July 20, 1790, 1 Stat. 131, 133 (1790); section 3, Act of July 22, 1790, 1 Stat. 137, 138 (1970); section 44, Act of March 2, 1791, 1 Stat. 198, 209 (1791).

[18] *E.g.*, *United States v. Simms*, 5 U.S. (1 Cranch) 252 (1803); *Adams v. Woods*, 6 U.S. (2 Cranch) 336 (1805); *The Emulous*, 1 F.Cas. 697 (D. Mass. 1 813)(No. 4,479), *rev 'd sub nom., Brown v. United States*, 12 U.S. (8 Cranch) 110 (1814).

[19] *Vermont Agency of Natural Resources v. United States ex rel. Stevens*, 529 U.S. 765, 768-69 n. 1 (2000), referring to 31 U.S.C. 3729-3733; 35 U.S.C. 292; 25 U.S.C. 81; and 25 U.S.C. 201, respectively. A fifth, not identified, 26 U.S.C. 7341 (sale of untaxed, taxable property), appears to have been rarely used.

[20] *United States ex rel. Marcus v. Hess*, 317 U.S. 537, 541 n.4. (1943).

[21] *Bass Anglers Sportsman's Soc. v. U.S. Plywood-Champion Papers, Inc.*, 324 F.Supp. 302, 306 (S.D.Tex. 1971) ("Justice Black's dictum [from *Hess* and quoted above] would appear to state the law too broadly. The *qui tam* action depends entirely upon statutory authorization, as it has never found its way into the common law. The action arises only upon a statutory grant. The fact that someone is entitled by statute to share in some penalty or forfeiture does not necessarily also give such person the right to bring an original action to recover such penalty or forfeiture. There must be statutory authority, either express or implied, for the informer to bring the qui tam action").

[22] *Jacklovich v. Interlake, Inc.*, 458 F.2d 923, 924 (7th Cir. 1972) (no qui tam authority may be drawn from the informer reward provision of the Rivers and Harbors Act); *Connecticut Action Now, Inc. v. Roberts Plating Co.*, 457 F.2d 81, 84-8 (2d Cir. 1972); *Gerbingh ex rel. United States v. I.T.T. Rayoinier Inc.*, 332 F.Supp. 309, 310 (M.D.Fla. 1971); *Bass Anglers Sportsman's Soc. v. Scholze Tannery, Inc.*, 329 F.Supp. 339, 344-45 (E.D.Tenn. 1971); *Bass Anglers Sportsman's Soc. v. U.S. Plywood-Champion Papers, Inc.*, 324 F. Supp. at 306-3 07.

[23] *Vermont Agency of Natural Resources v. United States ex rel. Stevens,* 529 U.S. 765, 777 n.7 (2000), quoting *United States ex rel. Marcus v. Hess*, 317 U.S. 537, 541 n.4. (1943).

[24] *Vermont Agency of Natural Resources v. United States ex rel. Stevens,* 529 U.S. at 768-69 n. 1, citing 18 U.S.C. 962 (vessels armed against nations with whom the U.S. is at peace); 46 U.S.C. 723 (now 46 U.S.C. 801030) (salvage of ship wrecks off the Florida coast). Other statutes of this sort include: 15 U.S.C. 1177 (confiscation of gambling devices pursuant to customs procedures); 16 U.S.C. 422d (theft or malicious mischief involving property on Moores Creek National Battlefield); 16 U.S.C. 425g (theft or malicious mischief involving property on Fredericksburg and Spotsylvania County Battle Field Memorials); 16 U.S.C. 430i (theft or malicious mischief involving property in Guilford Courthouse National Military Park); 18 U.S.C. 512 (confiscation of motor vehicles with altered identification numbers pursuant to customs procedures); 18 U.S.C. 1955 (confiscation of illegal gambling business property pursuant to customs procedures); 18 U.S.C. 1963 (confiscation of racketeering enterprise-related property pursuant to customs procedures); 18 U.S.C. 2513 (confiscation of communications interception devices pursuant customs procedures); 19 U.S.C. 1619 (confiscation under the customs laws); 26 U.S.C. 7214 (unlawful acts by revenue officers or agents); 50 U.S.C. 215 (confiscation of property used in aid of an insurrection).

[25] *Stalley v. Methodist Healthcare*, 517 F.3d 911, 920 (6th Cir. 2008); see also *United Seniors Ass 'n, Inc. v. Philip Morris USA*, 500 F.3d 18, 23 (1st Cir. 2007).

[26] 33 *Cong. Globe* 952-960 (1863).

[27] *Id.* at 955-56 (remarks of Sen. Howard).

[28] Section 1, Act of March 2, 1863, 12 Stat. at 696-97 (1863).

[29] Sections 1 and 3, Act of March 2, 1863, 12 Stat. at 696-97, 698.

[30] Section 3, Act of March 2, 1863, 12 Stat. at 698.

[31] *Id.*

[32] Section 4, Act of March 2, 1863, 12 Stat. at 698.

[33] The term "relator" derives from the style used in qui tam suits. For example, the case that figures prominently in the 1943 amendments was styled *United States ex rel. Marcus v. Hess*. "Ex rel." stands for "ex rationale,"

which in this context means "in relation to." Thus, "United States ex rel. Marcus" means the "United States in relation to the allegations brought by Marcus."

[34] Section 6, Act of March 2, 1863, 12 Stat. at 698.

[35] The qui tam provisions appeared in REV. STAT. §§3490-3494; the criminal provisions in REV. STAT. §5438 (1876). The criminal provisions have remained separate and are now found in 18 U.S.C. 286-287. Their evolution is beyond the scope of this report.

[36] 31 U.S.C. 23 1-235 (1940 ed.).

[37] Printed in S. Rept. No. 77-1708, at 1-2 (1942); H. Rept. No. 78-263 at 1-2 (1943).

[38] S. Rept. No. 77-1708, at 2; H. Rept. No. 78-263 at 2.

[39] *Id.* ("In a recent informer's action, *United States ex rel. Marcus v. Hess*, 127 F. (2d) 233, the Circuit Court of Appeals for the Third Circuit, in reversing a judgment in the sum of $315,100.91 in favor of the informer made the following observations (p. 235): 'Qui tam actions have always been regarded with disfavor: It is wrong for a free country to allow an informer to seek redress for his own pecuniary advantage in respect of a public wrong in which he has no direct personal interest or concern. A wrong to the State should surely be atoned for by a penalty payable to the State alone. * * * Hurst, The Common Informer, 147 Contemporary Review 189, 190'").

[40] 88 *Cong. Rec.* 9138 (1942)(S. 2707).

[41] 89 *Cong. Rec.* 2801 (1943)(H.R. 1203).

[42] *United States ex rel. Marcus v. Hess*, 317 U.S. 537, 541 (1943)("We cannot accept either the interpretive approach or the actual decision of the court below. Qui tam suits have been frequently permitted by legislative action, and have not been without defense by the courts"). In support of this latter point, the Supreme Court cited a nineteenth century opinion which lauded qui tam suits, *Id.* at 541 n. 5, quoting *United States v. Griswold*, 24 F. 361, 366 (D. Ore. 1885) ("The statute is a remedial one. It is intended to protect the treasury against the hungry and unscrupulous host that encompasses it on every side, and should be construed accordingly. It was passed upon the theory, based on experience as old as modern civilization, that one of the least expensive and most effective means of preventing frauds on the treasury is to make the perpetrators of them liable to actions by private persons acting, if you please, under the strong stimulus of personal ill will or the hope of gain. Prosecutions conducted by such means compare with the ordinary methods as the enterprising privateer does to the slow-going public vessel").

[43] S. Rept. No. 78-291, Pt.2 (1943)(minority views of Sen. Langer).

[44] S. Rept. No. 78-291 (1943).

[45] 57 Stat. at 608, 31 U.S.C. 232(C)(1946 ed.).

[46] 57 Stat. at 609, 31 U.S.C. 232(C)(1946 ed.).

[47] 57 Stat. at 609; compare, 31 U.S.C. 234 (1940 ed.), with 31 U.S.C. 232(E)(1946 ed.).

[48] S. Rept. No. 99-345, at 2-3 (1986)("In 1985 ... 45 of the 100 largest defense contractors, including 9 of the top 10, were under investigation for multiple fraud offenses. Additionally, the Justice Department has reported that in the last year, four of the largest defense contractors ... have been convicted of criminal offenses while another ... has been indicted and awaits trial.... The Department of Justice has estimated fraud as draining 1 to 10 percent of the entire Federal budget. Taking into account the spending level in 1985 of nearly $1 trillion, fraud against the Government could be costing taxpayers anywhere from $10 to $100 billion annually"); see also H. Rept. No. 99-660, at 18 (1986).

[49] 31 U.S.C. 3729(a)(7)(1988 ed.). Although some believed the False Claims Act already covered such misconduct, the Justice Department urged adoption of an explicit provision to avoid any ambiguity suggested by the case law, S. Rept. No. 99-345, at 15 (1986); H. Rept. No. 99-660, at 20 (1986).

[50] 31 U.S.C. 3730(h)(1988 ed.). H. Rept. No. 99-660, at 23 ("Under current law, there is no federal whistle blower protection statute for persons who are fired or otherwise discriminated against by their employer because of their lawful participation in a False Claims Act case. Often, the employee within the company may be the only person who can bring the information forward. If the person stands to lose his job, he may be unwilling to expose company fraud"); S. Rept. No. 99-345, at 4-5.

[51] Compare, 31 U.S.C. 3729 (1982 ed.), with 31 U.S.C. 3729(a)(1988 ed.). Recall that the statutory penalty had been set at $2,000 since 1863.

[52] Compare, 31 U.S.C. 3730(c)(2)(1982 ed.), with 31 U.S.C. 3730(d)(2)(1988 ed.).

[53] 31 U.S.C. 3729(b)(1988 ed.). The Committee expressed concerned that absent a specific provision the courts would require actual knowledge of a statement's false character and specific intent, S. Rept. No. 99-345, at 7, citing, *United States v. Aerodex, Inc.* 469 F.2d 1003 (5th Cir. 1972); H. Rept. No. 99-660, at 20-1.

[54] 31 U.S.C. 3731(c). Without a statutory provision, some courts had imposed a more demanding standard, S. Rept. No. 99-345, at 31("Some courts have required that the United States prove its case by clear and convincing, or even by clear, unequivocal, and convincing evidence"), citing *United States. v. Ueber*, 299 F. 12d 310 (6th Cir. 1962); H. Rept. No. 99-660 at 25-6.

[55] 31 U.S.C. 3732(b)(1988 ed.). At least one court had held in a Medicaid fraud action that they could not, *United States ex rel. Wisconsin v. Dean*, 729 F.2d 1100 (7th Cir. 1984).

[56] 31 U.S.C. 3730(e)(1988 ed.).

[57] 31 U.S.C. 373 1(b)(1988 ed.).
[58] 31 U.S.C. 3733. Civil investigative demands are a form of administrative subpoena.
[59] Section 4, P.L. 111-21, 123 Stat. 1617, 1621 (2009).
[60] 31 U.S.C. 3729(a)(1)(A).
[61] 31 U.S.C. 3729(a)(1)(B), (G), (b)(4).
[62] 31 U.S.C. 3729(a)(1)(C).
[63] 31 U.S.C. 3729(a)(1)(G).
[64] *Cook County v. United States ex rel. Chandler*, 538 U.S. 119, 122 (2003).
[65] *Vermont Agency of Natural Resources v. United States ex rel. Stevens*, 529 U.S. 765, 787-8 8 (2000).
[66] *United States v. Menominee Tribal Enterprises*, 601 F.Supp.2d 1061, 1068 (E.D.Wis. 2009).
[67] 31 U.S.C. 3730(e)(1) and (2) provide:

"(1) No court shall have jurisdiction over an action brought by a former or present member of the armed forces under subsection (b) of this section against a member of the armed forces arising out of such person's service in the armed forces.

"(2)(A) No court shall have jurisdiction over an action brought under subsection (b) against a Member of Congress, a member of the judiciary, or a senior executive branch official if the action is based on evidence or information known to the Government when the action was brought.

"(B) For purposes of this paragraph, 'senior executive branch official' means any officer or employee listed in paragraphs (1) through (8) of section 101(f) of the Ethics in Government Act of 1978 (5 U.S.C. App.)."

[68] 31 U.S.C. 3730(c)(2)(C) ("Upon a showing by the Government that unrestricted participation during the course of the litigation by the person initiating the action would interfere with or unduly delay the Government's prosecution of the case, or would be repetitious, irrelevant, or for purposes of harassment, the court may, in its discretion, impose limitations on the person's participation, such as—(i) limiting the number of witnesses the person may call; (ii) limiting the length of the testimony of such witnesses; (iii) limiting the person's cross-examination of witnesses; or (iv) otherwise limiting the participation by the person in the litigation").

The court may also limit the relator's participation in the interest of avoiding undue harassment of the defendant, 31 U.S.C. 3730(c)(2)(D)("Upon a showing by the defendant that unrestricted participation during the course of the litigation by the person initiating the action would be for purposes of harassment or would cause the defendant undue burden or unnecessary expense, the court may limit the participation by the person in the litigation").

[69] 31 U.S.C. 373 0(e)(4)("(A) No court shall have jurisdiction over an action under this section based upon the public disclosure of allegations or transactions in a criminal, civil, or administrative hearing, in a congressional, administrative, or Government Accounting Office report, hearing, audit, or investigation, or from the news media, unless the action is brought by the Attorney General or the person bringing the action is an original source of the information. (B) For purposes of this paragraph, "original source" means an individual who has direct and independent knowledge of the information on which the allegations are based and has voluntarily provided the information to the Government before filing an action under this section which is based on the information"); see also *Rockwell International Corp. v. United States*, 549 U.S. 457, 467-75 (2007).

[70] 31 U.S.C. 3730(b)(5)("When a person brings an action under this subsection, no person other than the Government may intervene or bring a related action based on the facts underlying the pending action"). "The first-to-file bar thus functions both to eliminate parasitic plaintiffs who piggy back off the claims of a prior relator, and to encourage legitimate relators to file quickly by protecting the spoils of the first to bring a claim," *In re Natural Gas Royalties Qui Tam Litigation (CO2 Appeals)*, 566 F.3d 956, 961 (10th Cir. 2009).

A similar bar applies with respect to actions based on civil litigation or administrative penalty enforcement proceedings to which the United States is a party, 31 U.S.C. 3730(e)(3)("In no event may a person bring an action under subsection (b) which is based upon allegations or transactions which are the subject of a civil suit or an administrative civil money penalty proceeding in which the Government is already a party").

[71] *In re Natural Gas Royalties Qui Tam Litigation (CO2 Appeals)*, 566 F.3d at 962; *United States ex rel. Branch Consultants v. Allstate Insurance Co.*, 560 F.3d 371, 377 (5th Cir. 2009); *United States ex rel. Poteet v. Medtronic, Inc.*, 552 F.3d 503, 516 (6th Cir. 2009); *United States ex rel. Hampton v. Columbia/HCA Healthcare Corp.*, 318 F.3d 214, 217-18 (D.C.Cir. 2003); *United States ex rel. Lujan v. Hughes Aircraft Co.*, 243 F.3d 1181, 1189 (9th Cir. 2001); *United States ex rel. LaCorte v. SmithKline Beecham Clinical Labs.*, 149 F.3d 227, 232-3 3 (3d Cir. 1998).

[72] 31 U.S.C. 3730(e)(1).

[73] *United States ex rel. Holmes v. Consumer Insurance Group*, 318 F.3d 1199, 1212 (10th Cir. 2003)(en banc), citing *United States ex rel. Marcus v. Hess*, 317 U.S. 537, 546 (1943)("Thus, we believe that *Marcus*, to the extent it construed the qui tam provision as allowing a government official to file suit as a relator based upon information obtained in the course of his or her official duties, remains valid"); *United States ex rel. Hagood v. Sonoma County Water Agency*, 929 F.2d 1416, 1419-420 (9th Cir. 1991)("The United States further argues that the 'public disclosure' required by the statute occurred when Hagood as a government employee 'disclosed' to himself as a member of the public information on which he based his suit. To say that the argument of the

United States is tortured is to state the obvious.... we hold that no 'public disclosure' was made"); *United States ex rel. Williams v. NEC Corp.*, 931 F.2d 1493, 1496-1500 (1 1th Cir. 1991); *United States ex rel. LeBlanc v. Raytheon Co., Inc.*, 913 F.2d 17, 20 (1st Cir. 1990); see also *United States ex rel. Burns v. A.D. Roe Co., Inc.*, 186 F.3d 717, 722-23 (6th Cir. 1999)(declining to address the argument that government employees are per se ineligible to file False Claims Act qui tam actions, but noting that the argument has been uniformly rejected by other courts). A federal employee may have difficulty qualifying as an "original source" of publicly available information upon which an action is based if the nature of his duties is that he is obligated to disclose the information to his superiors rather than "voluntarily" disclosing it as the definition of "original source" requires, *United States ex rel. Fine v. Chevron, U.S.A., Inc.*, 72 F.3d 740, 742-44 (9th Cir. 1995)("[T]he fact Fine was employed specifically to disclose fraud is sufficient to render his disclosures nonvoluntary").

74 P.L. 111-21, 123 Stat. 1617 (2009).

75 31 U.S.C. 3279 (2006 ed. & Supp. II).

76 S. Rept. No. 111-10, at 10 (2009), quoting, *United States ex rel. Totten v. Bombardier Corp.*, 380 F.3d 488, 490 (D.C. Cir. 2004).

77 S. Rept. No. 111-10, at 11.

78 31 U.S.C. 3729(b)(2)("the term 'claim'—(A) means any request or demand, whether under a contract or otherwise, for money or property and whether or not the United States has title to the money or property, that—(i) is presented to an officer, employee, or agent of the United States; or (ii) is made to a contractor, grantee, or other recipient, if the money or property is to be spent or used on the Government's behalf or to advance a Government program or interest, and if the United States Government—(I) provides or has provided any portion of the money or property requested or demanded; or (II) will reimburse such contractor, grantee, or other recipient for any portion of the money or property which is requested or demanded; and (B) does not include requests or demands for money or property that the Government has paid to an individual as compensation for Federal employment or as an income subsidy with no restrictions on that individual's use of the money or property").

79 *United States ex rel. Burlbaw v. Orenduff*, 548 F.3d 931, 949 (10th Cir. 2008); *United States ex rel. Farmer v. City of Houston*, 523 F.3d 333, 338 (5th Cir. 2008).

80 31 U.S.C. 3729(b)(1)((1) the terms 'knowing' and 'knowingly'—(A) mean that a person, with respect to information—(i) has actual knowledge of the information; (ii) acts in deliberate ignorance of the truth or falsity of the information; or (iii) acts in reckless disregard of the truth or falsity of the information; and (B) require no proof of specific intent to defraud"); *United States ex rel. K & R Ltd. v. Massachusetts Housing Finance Agency*, 530 F.3d 980, 983 (D.C.Cir. 2008); *United States ex rel. Farmer v. City of Houston*, 523 F.3d at 338; *United States ex rel. Taylor-Vick v. Smith*, 513 F.3d 228, 230 (5th Cir. 2008).

81 31 U.S.C. 3720(a)(2)(2006 ed. & 2008 Supp.)(language removed by the 2009 Act in italics).

82 *Allison Engine Co. v. United States ex rel. Sanders*, 128 S.Ct. 2123 (2008).

83 S. Rept. No. 111-10, at 10 (2009), quoting, *Allison Engine Co. v. United States ex rel. Sanders*, 128 S.Ct. at 2128.

84 31 U.S.C. 3729(b)(4). The definition tracks the generally understand materiality standard, *see e.g., United States v. Bourseau,* 531 F.3d 1159, 1171 (9th Cir. 2008), citing *Neder v. United* States, 527 U.S. 1, 16 (1999); *United States ex rel. Sanders v. North American Bus Industries, Inc.*, 546 F.3d 288, 297 (4th Cir. 2008); *but see, Costner v. URS Consultants, Inc.*, 153 F.3d 667, 677 (8th Cir. 1998)(adopting a materiality standard under which the misconduct must have "the purpose and effect of causing the United States to pay out money it is not obligated to pay, or those actions which intentionally deprive the United States of money it is lawfully due").

85 *United States v. Bourseau*, 531 F.3d at 1170-171, noting the agreement of the First, Fourth, Fifth, Sixth, and Eighth Circuits, but pointing out that in *United States ex rel. Cantekin v. University of Pittsburgh*, 192 F.3d 402, 415 (3d Cir. 1999), the Third Circuit had "cast[] doubt on whether materiality is an element under the FCA, but [had] declin[ed] to resolve the issue").

86 31 U.S.C. 3729(a)(3)(2006 ed. & Supp. II).

87 *United State ex rel. Huangyan Import v. Nature's Farm Products*, 370 F.Supp.2d 993, 1102-1003 (N.D.Cal. 2005) ("Admittedly, this creates an unusual lack of symmetry in the FCA's structure: Normal and reverse false claims are equally punishable as a substantive matter, but only conspiracies directed at the former, not the latter, are punishable.... The requirement that the conspiracy be directed at 'getting a false or fraudulent claim allowed or paid,' §3729(a)(3), is unambiguous: Its plain meaning requires that the conspirators seek to be 'paid' or to have a claim on the treasury 'allowed.' This is not what allegedly happened here; the alleged conspirators in this case wanted to avoid paying money to the United States").

88 31 U.S.C. 3729(a)(1)(C)("any person who ... (C) conspires to commit a violation of subparagraph (A), (B), (D), (E), (F), or (G)" incurs liability).

89 31 U.S.C. 3729(a)(1)(E)("Any person who ... (E) is authorized to make or deliver a document certifying receipt of property used, or to be used, by the Government and, intending to defraud the Government, makes or delivers the receipt without completely knowing that the information on the receipt is true ... is liable ... ").

[90] 31 U.S.C. 3729(a)(1)(F)("Any person who ... (F) knowingly buys, or receives as a pledge of an obligation or debt, public property from an officer or employee of the Government, or a member of the Armed Forces, who lawfully may not sell or pledge property ... is liable ... ").

[91] *United States ex rel. Ramadoss v. Caremark, Inc.*, 586 F. Supp.2d 668, 692 (W.D.Tex. 2008), quoting, *United States ex rel. Bahrani v. Conagra*, 465 F.3d 1189, 1195 (10th Cir. 2006).

[92] "Any person who ... (7) knowingly makes, uses, or causes to be made or used, a false record or statement to conceal, avoid, or decrease an obligation to pay or transmit money or property to the Government is liable.... " 31 U.S.C. 3729(a)(7)(2006 ed. & Supp. II).

[93] S. Rept. No. 111-10 at 13-4 ("Section 3729(a)(7) ... is commonly referred to as creating 'reverse' false claims liability because it is designed to cover Government money or property that is knowingly retained by a person even though they have no right to it. This provision is similar to the liability established under 3729(a)(2).... However, the provision does not capture conduct described in 3729(a)(1), which imposes liability for actions to conceal, avoid, or decrease an obligation directly to the Government. This legislation closes this loophole and incorporates an analogous provision to 3729(a)(1) for 'reverse' false claims liability").

[94] *Id.* at 14 ("The Committee also notes that the reverse false claims provision and amendments to that provision do not include any new language that would incorporate or should otherwise be construed to include a presentment requirement. This is consistent with various court decisions that have held that the current reverse false claims provision does not contain a presentment requirement"), citing, *United States ex rel. Bahrani v. Conagra, Inc.*, 465 F.3d 1189, 1208 (10th Cir. 2006) and *United States ex rel. Koch v. Koch Industries*, 57 F.Supp.2d 1122, 1144 (N.D. Okla. 1999).

[95] Recall that section 3729(b)(1) defines "knowingly" to mean actual knowledge, deliberate ignorance, or reckless disregard.

[96] 31 U.S.C. 3729(b)(3)("the term 'obligation' means an established duty, whether or not fixed, arising from an express or implied contractual, grantor-grantee, or licensor-licensee relationship, from a fee-based or similar relationship, from statute or regulation, or from the retention of any overpayment").

[97] *United States ex rel. Marcy v. Rowan Companies, Inc.*, 520 F.3d at 391, quoting, *United States ex rel. Bain v. Georgia Gulf Corp.*, 386 F.3d 648, 657 (5th Cir. 2004); see also *United States v. Pemco Aeroplex, Inc.*, 195 F.3d 1234, 1237 (1 1th Cir. 1999)(the section does cover obligations created by a contract between the government and the defendant).

[98] *United States ex rel. Bahrani v. Conagra*, 465 F.3d 1189, 1202 (10th Cir. 2006)("We agree that there are instances in which a party is required to pay money to the government, but, at the time the obligation arises, the sum has not been precisely determined").

[99] *United States ex rel. Marcy v. Rowan Companies, Inc.*, 520 F.3d 384, 390 (5th Cir. 2008), citing, *American Textile Manufacturers Institute, Inc. v. The Limited, Inc.*, 190 F.3d 729, 735 (6th Cir. 1999) and *United States v. Q Inter'l Courier, Inc.*, 131 F.3d 770, 774 (8th Cir. 1997); see also, *United States v. Bourseau*, 531 F.3d 1159, 1169-170 (9th Cir. 2008).

[100] S Rept. No. 111-10, at 14 (2009).

[101] *Vessell v. DPS Associates*, 148 F.3d 407, 413 (4th Cir. 1998)(the section does not cover independent contractors); *United States ex rel. Siewick v. Jamison Science and Engineering, Inc.*, 322 F.3d 738, 740 (D.C.Cir. 2003) (corporation's President and CEO was not an employer and consequently beyond the section's reach); *Yesudian ex rel. United States v. Howard* University, 270 F.3d 969, 972 (D.C. Cir. 2001)(the section does not apply to an employee's supervisors); *United States ex rel. Morgan v. Science Applications International Co.*, 604 F. Supp.2d 245, 250-51 (D.D.C. 2009)(the section does not apply to the employees of a subcontractor); *United States ex rel. Saragoglou v. Weill Medical College*, 451 F.Supp.2d 613, 625 (S.D.N.Y. 2006)(the section does not apply to an employee's supervisors); *Orell v. UMass Memorial Medical Center, Inc.*, 203 F.Supp.2d 52, 65-7 (D.Mass. 2002)(same).

[102] 31 U.S.C. 3729(a)(1), (3); 3730(d). The 2009 Act amended section 3729(a)(1) to provide for inflationary adjustments of the $5,000-$ 10,000 statutory penalty.

[103] 31 U.S.C. 3729(a)(2)("If the court finds that—(A) the person committing the violation of this subsection furnished officials of the United States responsible for investigating false claims violations with all information known to such person about the violation within 30 days after the date on which the defendant first obtained the information; (B) such person fully cooperated with any Government investigation of such violation; and (C) at the time such person furnished the United States with the information about the violation, no criminal prosecution, civil action, or administrative action had commenced under this title with respect to such violation, and the person did not have actual knowledge of the existence of an investigation into such violation, [–] the court may assess not less than 2 times the amount of damages which the Government sustains because of the act of that person").

[104] 31 U.S.C. 3730(d)(2)("If the Government does not proceed with an action under this section, the person bringing the action or settling the claim shall receive an amount which the court decides is reasonable for collecting the civil penalty and damages. The amount shall be not less than 25 percent and not more than 30 percent of the proceeds of the action or settlement and shall be paid out of such proceeds. Such person shall also receive an

amount for reasonable expenses which the court finds to have been necessarily incurred, plus reasonable attorneys' fees and costs. All such expenses, fees, and costs shall be awarded against the defendant").

[105] 31 U.S.C. 3703(d)(1)("If the Government proceeds with an action brought by a person under subsection (b), such person shall, subject to the second sentence of this paragraph, receive at least 15 percent but not more than 25 percent of the proceeds of the action or settlement of the claim, depending upon the extent to which the person substantially contributed to the prosecution of the action ... Any payment to a person under the first or second sentence of this paragraph shall be made from the proceeds. Any such person shall also receive an amount for reasonable expenses which the court finds to have been necessarily incurred, plus reasonable attorneys' fees and costs. All such expenses, fees, and costs shall be awarded against the defendant").

[106] Id. (" ... Where the action is one which the court finds to be based primarily on disclosures of specific information (other than information provided by the person bringing the action) relating to allegations or transactions in a criminal, civil, or administrative hearing, in a congressional, administrative, or Government Accounting Office report, hearing, audit, or investigation, or from the news media, the court may award such sums as it considers appropriate, but in no case more than 10 percent of the proceeds, taking into account the significance of the information and the role of the person bringing the action in advancing the case to litigation ... ").

[107] 31 U.S.C. 3730(d)(1), (2); 31 U.S.C. 3730(d)(3)("Whether or not the Government proceeds with the action, if the court finds that the action was brought by a person who planned and initiated the violation of section 3729 upon which the action was brought, then the court may, to the extent the court considers appropriate, reduce the share of the proceeds of the action which the person would otherwise receive under paragraph (1) or (2) of this subsection, taking into account the role of that person in advancing the case to litigation and any relevant circumstances pertaining to the violation. If the person bringing the action is convicted of criminal conduct arising from his or her role in the violation of section 3729 that person shall be dismissed from the civil action and shall not receive any share of the proceeds of the action. Such dismissal shall not prejudice the right of the United States to continue the action, represented by the Department of Justice").

[108] 31 U.S.C. 3730(d)(4)("If the Government does not proceed with the action and the person bringing the action conducts the action, the court may award to the defendant its reasonable attorneys' fees and expenses if the defendant prevails in the action and the court finds that the claim of the person bringing the action was clearly frivolous, clearly vexatious, or brought primarily for purposes of harassment"). The term "expenses" does not include "costs" which covers things like court fees and witness fees and may be awarded under the less demanding standards of Rule 54 of the Federal Rules of Civil Procedure, *United States ex rel. Ritchie v. Lockheed Martin Corp.*, 558 F.3d 1161, 1171-172 (10th Cir. 2009); *United States ex rel. Costner v. United States*, 317 F.3d 889, 891 (8th Cir. 2003); *United States ex rel. Lindenthal v. General Dynamics Corp.*, 61 F.3d 1402, 1412-413 (9th Cir. 1995).

[109] *Pfingston v. Ronan Engineering Co.*, 284 F.3d 999, 1005-1006 (9th Cir. 2002); *United States ex rel. Mikes v. Straus*, 274 F.3d 687, 705 (2d Cir. 2001), each citing, S. Rept. No. 99-345, at 29 (1986).

[110] *United States ex rel. Rafizadeh v. Continental Common, Inc.*, 553 F.3d 869, 875 (5th Cir. 2008); *Pfingston v. Ronan Engineering Co.* 284 F.3d at 1006-1007.

[111] *United States ex rel. Grynberg v. Praxair, Inc.*, 389 F.3d 1038, 1058 (10th Cir. 2004). "An action is not frivolous if existing law or a reasonable suggestion for its extension, modification, or reversal supports the action," *United States ex rel. Rafizadeh v. Continental Common, Inc.*, 553 F.3d at 875.

[112] *United States ex rel. Mikes v. Straus*, 274 F.3d at 705; *United States ex rel. Vuyyuru v. Jadhav*, 555 F.3d 337, 356 (4th Cir. 2009).

[113] *Pfingston v. Ronan Engineering Co.,* 284 F.3d at 1006.

[114] 31 U.S.C. 373 1(b)("A civil action under section 3730 may not be brought—(1) more than 6 years after the date on which the violation of section 3729 committed, or (2) more than 3 years after the date when facts material to the right of action are known or reasonably should have been known by the official of the United States charged with responsibility to act in the circumstances, but in no event more than 10 years after the date on which the violation is committed, [–]whichever occurs last").

[115] *United States ex rel. Sanders v. North American Bus Industries, Inc.*, 546 F.3d 288, 294 (4th Cir. 2008)(the extension is only available to the government); *United States ex rel. Sikkenga v. Regence Blue Cross Blue Shield*, 472 F.3d 702, 722-25 (10th Cir. 2006)(same); *United States ex rel. Hyatt v. Northrop Corp.*, 91 F.3d 1211, 1214-216 (9th Cir. 1996)(the extension is available to both the government and to a relator); see also *United States ex rel. Snapp v. Ford Motor Co.*, 532 F.3d 496, 509-10 (6th Cir. 2008)(recognizing the split of authority, but finding it unnecessary to decide the issue).

[116] *Graham Country Soil & Water Conservation District v. United States ex rel. Wilson*, 545 U.S. 409, 421 (2005).

[117] *United States v. The Baylor University Medical Center*, 469 F.3d 263, 267-70 (2d Cir. 2006).

[118] 31 U.S.C. 373 1(c)("If the Government elects to intervene and proceed with an action brought under 373 0(b), the Government may file its own complaint or amend the complaint of a person who has brought an action under section 373 0(b) to clarify or add detail to the claims in which the Government is intervening and to add any additional claims with respect to which the Government contends it is entitled to relief. For statute of limitations purposes, any such Government pleading shall relate back to the filing date of the complaint of the

person who originally brought the action, to the extent that the claim of the Government arises out of the conduct, transactions, or occurrences set forth, or attempted to be set forth, in the prior complaint of that person").

[119] 31 U.S.C. 3731(d); *United States ex rel. Sikkenga v. Regence Blue Cross Blue Shield*, 472 F.3d 702, 724 (10th Cir. 2006).

[120] 31 U.S.C. 373 1(e)("Notwithstanding any other provision of law, the Federal Rules of Criminal Procedure, or the Federal Rules of Evidence, a final judgment rendered in favor of the United States in any criminal proceeding charging fraud or false statements, whether upon a verdict after trial or upon a plea of guilty or nolo contendere, shall estop the defendant from denying the essential elements of the offense in any action which involves the same transaction as in the criminal proceeding and which is brought under subsection (a) or (b) of section 3730").

[121] *United States ex rel. Eisenstein v. New York*, 129 S.Ct. 2230, 2236-237 (2009).

[122] *Vermont Agency of Natural Resources v. United States ex rel. Stevens*, 529 U.S. 765, 769 n. 1 (2000); *Boyd v. Schildkraut Giftware Corp.*, 936 F.2d 76, 79 (2d Cir. 1991); *Third Party Verification, Inc. v. Signaturelink, Inc.*, 492 F.Supp.2d 1314, 1326 (M.D.Fla. 2007).

[123] *Lang v. Pacific Marine and Supply Co., Ltd.*, 895 F.2d 761, 765 (Fed.Cir. 1990). Standing requirements are discussed below under Constitutional Concerns.

[124] *Third Party Verification, Inc. v. Signaturelink, Inc.*, 492 F. Supp.2d 1314, 1326 (M.D.Fla. 2007); *United States Gypsum Co. v. Pacific Award Metals, Inc.*, 438 F.Supp.2d 1101, 1105 (N.D.Cal. 2006); *DP Wagner Manufacturing, Inc., v. Pro Patch Systems, Inc.*, 434 F.Supp.2d 445, 451 (S.D. Tex. 2006); each citing *Clontech Labs., Inc. v. Invitrogen Corp.*, 406 F.3d 1347, 1352 (Fed.Cir. 2005).

[125] *Pequignot v. Solo Cup Co.*, 540 F.Supp.2d 649, 655 (E.D.Va. 2008).

[126] *Clontech Labs., Inc. v. Invitrogen Corp.*, 406 F.3d at 1352; *United States Gypsum Co. v. Pacific Award Metals, Inc.*, 438 F.Supp.2d at 1106.

[127] *Keystone Manufacturing Co., Inc. v. Jaccard Corp.*, 394 F.Supp.2d 543, 565 (W.D.N.Y. 2005)(mistake or inadvertence); *Bibow v. American Saw and Manufacturing Co.*, 490 F.Supp.2d 128, 129 (D.Mass. 2007), citing *Arcadia Machine & Tool, Inc. v. Sturm, Ruger & Co., Inc.*, 786 F.2d 1124, 1125 (Fed.Cir. 1986)(innocent oversight); *DP Wagner Manufacturing, Inc. v.Pro Patch Systems, Inc.*, 434 F. Supp.2d at 457 (honest mistake); *Clontech Labs., Inc. v. Invitrogen Corp.*, 406 F.3d at 1352 (same).

[128] *Keystone Manufacturing Co., Inc. v. Jaccard Corp.*, 394 F.Supp.2d at 566 ("§292 does not distinguish between foreign and domestic patents"); *Pequignot v. Solo Cup Co.*, 540 F.Supp.2d at 653("[T]he term 'unpatented article' in 35 U.S.C. §292(a) is an article unprotected by a patent, and includes an article for which a once valid patent has expired"); *Clontech Labs., Inc. v. Invitrogen Corp.*, 406 F.3d at 1352("When the statute refers to an 'unpatented article' the statute means that the article in question is not covered by at least one claim of each patent with which the article is marked").

[129] *Arcadia Machine & Tool, Inc. v. Sturm, Ruger & Co., Inc.*, 786 F.2d 1124, 1125 (Fed.Cir. 1986).

[130] *Stauffer v. Brooks Brothers, Inc.*, 615 F.Supp.2d 248, 256 (S.D.N.Y. 2009); *Deyerle v. Wright Manufacturing Co.*, 496 F.2sd 45, 54-55 (6th Cir. 1974).

[131] The section applies where Congress established monetary penalties for various prohibitions enacted for the protection of the Indians; it does not create a qui tam cause of action with respect criminal statutes which come replete with terms of imprisonment such as the embezzlement provisions of 25 U.S.C. 450d, *United States ex rel. Burn ette v. Driving Hawk*, 587 F.2d 23, 23-5 (8th Cir. 1978).

[132] *United States ex rel. Hall v. Tribal Development Corp.*, 49 F.3d 1208, 1216 (7th Cir. 1995).

[133] *United States ex rel. Hall v. Tribal Development Corp.*, 100 F.3d 476, 478 (7th Cir. 1996).

[134] *United States ex rel. Keith v. Sioux Nation Shopping Center*, 634 F.2d 401, 403 (8th Cir. 1980).

[135] *United States ex rel. Hornell v. One 1976 Chevrolet Station Wagon*, 585 F.2d 978, 980-8 1 (10th Cir. 1978).

[136] *United States ex rel. Whitehorse v. Briggs*, 555 F.2d 283, 288 (10th Cir. 1977)(to "permit a cow to trespass and graze on Indian land for a day, a month, a year, or forever, upon the payment of a statutory penalty in the amount of $1 ... would completely defeat the intent of, and purpose behind, the statute"); *United States ex rel. Chase v. Wald*, 557 F.2d 157, 161 (8th Cir. 1977)(the Secretary has no authority to increase the statutory penalty).

[137] *United States v. Plainbull*, 957 F.2d 724, 726-28 (9th Cir. 1992).

[138] *United States ex rel. Harlan v. Bacon*, 21 F.3d 209, 212 (1994)(emphasis added).

[139] *James v. Watt*, 716 F.2d 71, 72 (1st Cir. 1983)(emphasis in the original)("this court has held that the INA [Indian Nonintercourse Act, 25 U.S.C. 177] was designed to protect the land rights only of *tribes*; that the INA therefore granted a cause of action to tribes; and that individual Indians could not assert INA rights on their own behalf").

[140] U.S. Const. Amend. VI ("In all criminal proceedings, the accused shall enjoy the right ... ").

[141] *E.g.*, 31 U.S.C. 3730(a)(" ... The Attorney General finds that a person has violated or is violating section 3729, the Attorney General may bring a civil action ...); 31 U.S.C. 3730(b)(1)("A person may bring a civil action for a violation of section 3729 for the person and for the United States Government ... "); 35 U.S.C. 292(b)("Any person may sue for the penalty ... ").

[142] Yet the Court observed in a footnote, "We express no opinion as to whether a *qui tam* action, such as the one in *Hess*, is properly characterized as a suit between private parties for the purpose of this rule," *Id.* at 451 n. 10.

[143] 522 U.S. at 96 ("We hold that the Double Jeopardy Clause of the Fifth Amendment is not a bar to the later criminal prosecution because the administrative proceedings were civil, not criminal. Our reasons for so holding in large part disavow the method of analysis used in *United States v. Halper*. 490 U.S. 435, 448 (1989), and reaffirm the previously established rule exemplified in *United States v. Ward*, 448 U.S. 242, 248-249 (1980)").

[144] *United States v. Ward*, 448 U.S. at 248-49 (internal citations and quotation marks omitted).

[145] *United States v. Hudson*, 522 U.S. at 99 (internal citations and quotations omitted)("Even in those cases where the legislature has indicated an intention to establish a civil penalty, we have inquired further whether the statutory scheme was so punitive either in purpose or effect as to transform what was clearly intended as a civil remedy into a criminal penalty. In making this latter determination, the factors listed in *Kennedy v. Mendoza-Martinez* provide useful guideposts, including: (1) whether the sanction involves an affirmative disability or restraint; (2) whether it has historically been regarded as a punishment; (3) whether it comes into play only on a finding of *scienter*; (4) whether its operation will promote the traditional aims of punishment—retribution and deterrence; (5) whether the behavior to which it applies is already a crime; (6) whether an alternative purpose to which it may rationally be connected is assignable for it; and (7) whether it appears excessive in relation to the alternative purpose assigned"); see also *United States v. Ward*, 448 U.S. at 249.

[146] *United States v. Rogan*, 517 F.3d 449, (7th Cir. 2008)("We know from *Hudson v. United States* ... that penalties under the False Claims Act are not criminal punishment for the purposes of the Double Jeopardy Clause in the Fifth Amendment"); see also *United States v. Lumanna*, 114 F. Supp.2d 193, 197 (W.D.N.Y. 2000).

[147] 522 U.S. at 102-103.

[148] *Browning-Ferris Industries v. Kelco Disposal*, 492 U.S. 257, 264 (1989)(holding that the excessive fines clause did not apply to a treble damage antitrust award). The Court "left open the question whether a *qui tam* action, in which a private party brings suit in the name of the United States and shares in any award of damages, would implicate ... the Eighth Amendment's Excessive Fines Clause," *Id.* at 275-76 n. 21.

[149] *Austin v. United States*, 509 U. S.602, 609-10 (1993).

[150] *Id.* at 610. Once again, however, the Court declined to resolve the question of the clause's application to qui tam penalties, "In *Browning-Ferris*, we left open the question whether the Excessive Fines Clause applies to *qui tam* actions in which a private party brings suit in the name of the United States and shares in the proceeds ... Because the instant suit was prosecuted by the United States and because Austin's property was forfeited to the United States, we have no occasion to address that question here," *Id.* at 607 n.3.

[151] *United States v. Bajakajian*, 524 U.S. 321, 334 (1998).

[152] *United States v. Bourseau*, 531 F.3d 1159, 1173-174 (9th Cir. 2008); *United States v. Mackby*, 339 F.3d 1013, 1016 (9th Cir. 2003); *United States ex rel. Tyson v. Amerigroup Illinois, Inc.*, 488 F. Supp.2d 719, 743-45 (N.D.Ill. 2007); *United States v. Eghbal*, 475 F.Supp.2d 1008, 1016-19 (C.D.Cal. 2007); *United States v. Byrd*, 100 F.Supp.2d 342, 344-45 (E.D.N.C. 2000); but see *United States v. Rogan*, 517 F.3d 449, 453-54 (7th Cir. 2007)(finding it unnecessary to resolve the issue and indicating that the results of double jeopardy and excessive fines analysis should be the same, but noting that it considers the law in the area is "unsettled").

[153] *United States v. Bourseau*, 531 F.3d at 1173-174 ($15.6 million Medicare False Claim Act penalty was not excessive in light of the harm to the U.S. Treasury and to the integrity of the Medicare program); *United States v. Mackby*, 339 F.3d at 1019 ($729,454.92 Medicare False Claims Act judgment was not excessive in light of the defendant's culpability and the harm caused by the offense); *United States ex rel. Tyson v. Amerigroup Illinois, Inc.*, 488 F.Supp.2d 719, 743-45 (N.D.Ill. 2007)($334 million Medicaid False Claims Act penalty was not excessive in light of the fact that the statute permitted a penalty of $524 million); *United States v. Eghbal*, 475 F. Supp.2d at 10 16-19 ($5.85 1 million in mortgage fraud False Claims Act damages and penalties was not excessive in light of the defendant's culpability, the seriousness of the offense, and the harm caused); *United States v. Byrd*, 100 F. Supp.2d at 344-55 ($ 1.575 million food stamp False Claims Act penalty was not excessive in light of the fact that a penalty of $2.895 million was authorized under the statute).

[154] *Marshall v. Jerrico, Inc.*, 446 U.S. 238, 252 (1980).

[155] *Id.* at 250 n. 12 and accompanying text.

[156] *Young v. United States ex rel. Vuitton et Fils S.A.*, 481 U.S. 787, 790-91 (1987).

[157] *Id.* at 791-92.

[158] *Id.* at 809.

[159] *Id.* at 810.

[160] *Id.* at 814-15 (Blackmun, J., concurring).

[161] *Id.* at 815 (Scalia, J., concurring in the judgment).

[162] *United States ex rel. Kelly v. Boeing Co.*, 9 F.3d 743, 760 (9th Cir. 1993); accord *United States ex rel. Phillips v. Pediatric Services of America, Inc.*, 123 F. Supp.2d 990, 994-95 (W.D.N.C. 2000); *United States ex rel. Fallon v. Accundyne Corp.*, 921 F.Supp. 611, 623-24 (W.D.Wis 1995); *United States ex rel. Stillwell v. Hughes Helicopters, Inc.*, 714 F.Supp. 1084, 1088 n.4 (C.D.Cal. 1989); but see *Friedman v. Rite Aid Corp.*, 152

F.Supp.2d 766, 771 (E.D.Pa. 200 1)(finding due process inapplicable because relators merely receive "an appropriate incentive and reward for aiding the Government").

[163] U.S. Const. Art. I, §1; Art. II, §1; and Art. III, respectively.

[164] U.S. Const. Art. I, §8, cl. 18.

[165] U.S. Const. Art. II, §4.

[166] U.S. Const. Art. II, §2, cl. 2. During a recess of the Senate, the President may fill a vacancy in office with a commission which expires at the end of the next session, U.S. Const. Art. II, §2, cl. 3.

[167] U.S. Const,. Art. II, §3.

[168] *Id.*

[169] U.S. Const. Art. I, §7, cl. 2.

[170] U.S. Const. Art. II, §2, cl. 1.

[171] U.S. Const. Art. II, §2, cl. 2. During a recess of the Senate, the President may fill vacancies in office by commissions which expire at the end of the next session, U.S. Const. Art. II, §2, cl. 3.

[172] U.S. Const. Art. II, §2, cl. 1.

[173] U.S. Const. Art. II, §3.

[174] U.S. Const. Art. III, §2.

[175] *Metropolitan Washington Airport Authority v. Citizens for the Abatement of Aircraft Noise, Inc.*, 501 U.S. 252, 273, quoting *Buckley v. Valeo*, 424 U.S. 1, 122 (1976).

[176] *United States v. Mistretta*, 488 U.S. 361, 381 (1989), quoting *Youngstown Sheet & Tube Co. v. Sawyer*, 343 U.S. 579, 635 (Jackson, J., concurring); see also, *Morrison v. Olson*, 487 U.S. 654, 693-94 (1988)("Time and again we have reaffirmed the importance in our constitutional scheme of the separation of governmental powers into the three coordinate branches ... We have not hesitated to invalidate provisions of law which violate this principle. On the other hand, we have never held that the Constitution requires that the three branches of government operate with absolute independence").

[177] Caminker, *The Constitutionality of Qui Tam Actions*, 99 YALE LAW JOURNAL 341 (1989); *The Constitutionality of the False Claims Act's Qui Tam Provisions*, 16 HARVARD JOURNAL OF LAW & PUBLIC POLICY 701 (1993); Edgar, *"Missing the Analytical Boat": The Unconstitutionality of the Qui Tam Provisions of the False Claims Act*, 27 IDAHO LAW REVIEW 319 (1990); *1001 Attorneys General: Executive-Employee* Qui Tam *Suits and the Constitution*, 62 GEORGE WASHINGTON LAW REVIEW 609 (1993); but see Bales, *A Constitutional Defense of* Qui Tam, 2001 WISCONSIN LAW REVIEW 381.

[178] "The constitutional cornerstone of the modern doctrine of standing is injury in fact, and without this a party cannot invoke the power of the federal courts. Since by definition a *qui tam* plaintiff has no injury in fact in a False Claims suit, then the *qui tam* provisions of the Act are unconstitutional under Article III's requirements of 'cases' and 'controversies,'" *Missing the Analytical Boat": The Unconstitutionality of the* Qui Tam *Provisions of the False Claims Act*, 27 IDAHO LAW REVIEW 319, 345 (1990).

[179] "Article II gives the President—and only the President—the power and duty to 'take Care that the Laws be faithfully executed.' Although *Morrison* [*Morrison v. Olson*, 487 U.S. 654 (1988)] held that Congress can place certain executive functions in the hands of persons who are not members of the Executive Branch, the Court has never held that Congress may divest the Executive of the power *to initiate* a lawsuit to vindicate the United States' interest. In fact, a line of cases suggests that this power to initiate lawsuits is a special and inherently executive function.... The FCA's qui tam provision interest with the Executive's 'initiation power.' Once a relator files an action under Section 3730(b), that action will proceed regardless of whether the government chooses to intervene," *Fight for Your Right to Litigate: Qui Tam, Article II, and the President*, 49 STANFORD LAW REVIEW 853, 868, 872 (1997).

[180] "When one combines *Buckley*'s [*Buckley v. Valeo*, 424 U.S. 1 (1976)] holding that only properly appointed officers can litigate on behalf of the United States with *Fretag*'s [*Fretag v. Commission*, 501 U.S. 868 (1991)] holding that Congressional diffusion of the appointment power—and not only aggrandizement—can violate the Appointments Clause, the conclusion is simple: It is unconstitutional for *qui tam* relators to enforce the FCA on behalf of the United States government because they have not been properly appointed to do so," *The Constitutionality of the False Claims Act's* Qui Tam *Provision*, 16 HARVARD JOURNAL OF LAW & PUBLIC POLICY 701, 743 (1993).

[181] Recall that the First Congress passed the Judiciary Act of 1789, section 13 of which unconstitutionally endeavored to enlarge the original jurisdiction of the Supreme Court, *Marbury v. Madison*, 5 U.S. (1 Cranch) 137, 172-80 (1803).

[182] *Bowsher v. Synar*, 478 U.S. 714, 723 (1986), citing *Marsh v. Chambers*, 463 U.S. 783, 790 (1983).

[183] *Friends of Earth, Inc. v. Laidlaw Environmental Services (TOC), Inc.*, 528 U.S. 167, 180-81 (2000), citing *Lujan v. Defenders of Wildlife*, 504 U.S. 555, 560-61 (1992)("to satisfy Article III's standing requirements, a plaintiff must show (1) it has suffered an injury in fact that is (a) concrete and particularized and (b) actual or imminent, not conjectural or hypothetical; (2) the injury is fairly traceable to the challenged action of the defendant; and (3) it is likely, as opposed to merely speculative, that the injury will be redressed by a favorable decision").

[184] *Vermont Agency of Natural Resources v. United States ex rel. Stevens*, 529 U.S. 765, 774 (2000), quoting *Steel Co. v. Citizens for a Better Environment*, 523 U.S. 83, 102 (1998).

[185] *Id.* at 77 1-72 ("It is beyond doubt that the complaint asserts any injury to the United States.... It would perhaps suffice to say that the relator here is simply the statutorily designated agent of the United States, in *whose name* ... the suit is brought—and that the relator's bounty is simply the fee he receives *out of the United States' recovery*.... This analysis is precluded, however, by the fact that the statute gives the relator himself an interest *in the lawsuit* ... For the portion of the recovery retained by the relator, therefore, some explanation of standing other than agency for the Government must be identified").

[186] *Id.* at 773 ("We believe, however, that adequate basis for the relator's suit for his bounty is to be found in the doctrine that the assignee of a claim has standing to assert the injury in fact suffered by the assignor. The FCA can reasonably be regarded as effecting a partial assignment of the Government's damages claim").

[187] *Stauffer v. Brooks Brothers, Inc.*, 615 F. Supp.2d 248, 255 (S.D.N.Y. 2009).

[188] *Buckley v. Valeo*, 424 U.S. 1, 140 (1976).

[189] *United States v. Hartwell*, 73 (6 Wall.) 385, 393-4 (1867).

[190] *United States v. Germaine*, 99 U.S. 508 (1878).

[191] *Id.* at 511-12.

[192] *Auffmordt v. Hedden*, 137 U.S. 310, 327 (1890)(His position is without tenure, duration, continuing emolument, or continuous duties, and he acts only occasionally and temporarily).

[193] *Buckley v. Valeo*, 424 U.S. at 126 n. 162 (parallel citations omitted).

[194] *Freytag v. Commissioner*, 501 U.S. 868, 881 (1991), quoting *Buckley v. Valeo*, 424 U.S. at 126.

[195] *Vermont Agency of Natural Resources v. United States ex rel. Stevens*, 529 U.S. 765, 778 n.8 (2000).

[196] *United States ex rel. Stone v. Rockwell International Corp.*, 282 F.3d 787, 805 (10th Cir. 2002)(parallel citations omitted); *Riley v. St. Luke's Episcopal Hospital*, 252 F.3d 749, 757-58 (5th Cir. 2001)(en banc)("Supreme Court precedent has established that the constitutional definition of an 'officer' encompasses, at a minimum, a continuing and formalized relationship of employment with the United States Government.... There is no such relationship with regard to qui tam relators"); *United States ex rel. Taxpayers Against Fraud v. General Electric Co.*, 41 F.3d 1032, 1041 (6th Cir. 1995); see also *United States ex rel. Kelly v. Boeing Co.*, 9 F.3d 743, 758 (9th Cir. 1993)("The appropriate questions in this case, therefore, are whether qui tam relators exercise 'significant authority' under the FCA, and whether the FCA vests in relators 'primary responsibility' for enforcing the Act by litigating in the federal courts. Our answers to these questions follow logically from our determination ... that the qui tam provisions do not violate the separation of powers principle. We have concluded that the Executive Branch retains 'sufficient control' of relators such that their exercise of authority to sue on behalf of the Untied States does not 'impermissibly undermine' executive functions. In keeping with that conclusion, we find it impossible to characterize the authority exercised by relators as so 'significant' that it must only be exercised by officers appointed in the manner which Article II, §2, cl.2 prescribes").

[197] *Morrison v. Olson*, 487 U.S. 654, 695-96 (1988); cf., *Commodity Futures Trading Commission v. Schor*, 478 U.S. 833, 856-57 (1986).

[198] *Morrison v. Olson*, 487 U.S. at 659-60.

[199] *Id.*, citing 28 U.S.C. 591-599 (1982 ed., Supp. V).

[200] *Morrison v. Olson*, 487 U.S. at 685.

[201] *Id.* at 693, quoting *Buckley v. Valeo*, 424 U.S. 1, 123 (1976).

[202] *Morrison v. Olson*, 487 U.S. at 694-95.

[203] *Id.* at 695-96.

[204] *Id.* at 696.

[205] *United States ex rel. Stone v. Rockwell International Corp.*, 282 F.3d 787, 805-807 (10th Cir. 2002); *Riley v. St. Luke's Episcopal Hospital*, 252 F.3d 749, 757 (5th Cir. 2001)(en banc)("Any intrusion by the qui tam relator in the Executive's Article II power is comparatively modest, especially given the control mechanisms inherent in the FCA to mitigate such an intrusion and the civil context in which qui tam suits are pursued. Hence, the qui tam portions of the FCA do not violate the constitutional doctrine of separation of powers by impinging upon the Executive's constitutional duty to take care that the laws are faithfully executed under Article II of the Constitution"); *United States ex rel. Taxpayers Against Fraud v. General Electric Co.*, 41 F.3d 1032, 1041 (6th Cir. 1995); *United States ex rel. Kelly v. Boeing Co.*, 9 F.3d 743, 757 (9th Cir. 1993)("Taken as a whole, and considering the removal issue in particular, the FCA affords the Executive Branch a degree of control over qui tam relators that is not distinguishable from the degree of control the *Morrison* Court found the Executive Branch exercises over independent counsels"); *United States ex rel. K & R Limited Partnership v. Massachusetts Housing Finance Agency*, 154 F.Supp.2d 19, 26 (D.D.C. 2001); *United States ex rel. Phillips v. Pediatric Services of American, Inc.*, 123 F.Supp.2d 990, 992-93 (W.D.N.C. 2000)("However, the Supreme Court did not intend the analysis in *Morrison* to serve as an unalterable list of the minimum control elements necessary for sustaining all acts implicating the Take Care Clause. On the contrary, by twice stating that the proper inquiry was to take the act as a whole, *Morrison* instructs us to compare the *qui tam* provisions as a whole to the independent counsel provisions as a whole"); *United States ex rel. Chandler v. Hektoen Institute*, 35 F. Supp.2d 1078, 1081-82 (N.D.Ill. 1999); *United States ex rel. Givler v. Smith*, 775 F.Supp. 172, 178

(E.D.Pa. 199 1)("FCA amendments provide far greater executive authority over the conduct of false claims litigation than that provided for in the law validated in *Morrison*"); but see *Riley v. St. Luke's Episcopal Hospital*, 252 F.3d at 766 (Smith & DeMoss, JJ., dissenting)("[T]he most crucial ways in which the FCA fails to provide the executive with sufficient control are that the FCA does not allow the Executive to initiate litigation, terminate litigation (without court approval), control the scope and pace of the litigation, or control the procedures used by the lawyer prosecuting the case. The FCA's most severe violations of the separation of powers principles embedded in the Take Care Clause include the fact that unaccountable, self-interested relators are put in charge of vindicating government rights, and that the transparency and controls of the constitutional system are not in place to influence the outcome of such litigation").

CHAPTER SOURCES

The following chapters have been previously published:

Chapter 1 – This is an edited, excerpted and augmented edition of a United States Government Accountability Office (GAO), Briefing for Congressional Committees. Publication GAO-06-320R, dated January 31, 2006.

Chapter 2 – These remarks were delivered as Statement of Senator Patrick Leahy, before the Committee on the Judiciary of the United States Senate, dated February 27, 2008.

Chapter 3 – These remarks were delivered as Statement of Michael Hertz, before the Committee on the Judiciary of the United States Senate, dated February 27, 2008.

Chapter 4 - These remarks were delivered as Statement of Tina Marie Gonter, before the Committee on the Judiciary of the United States Senate, dated February 27, 2008.

Chapter 5 - These remarks were delivered as Written Statement of John T. Boese, U.S. Chamber of Commerce and the U.S. Chamber Institute for Legal Reform, before the Committee on the Judiciary of the United States Senate, dated February 27, 2008.

Chapter 6 - These remarks were delivered as Statement of John E. Clarke, before the Committee on the Judiciary of the United States Senate, dated February 27, 2008.

Chapter 7 - These remarks were delivered as Written Statement of Pamela H. Bucy, Bainbridge Professor of Law University of Alabama School of Law, before the Committee on the Judiciary of the United States Senate, dated February 27, 2008.

Chapter 8 – This is an edited, excerpted and augmented edition of a United States Congressional Research Service publication, Report Order Code RS22982, dated April 16, 2009.

Chapter 9 – This is an edited, excerpted and augmented edition of a United States Congressional Research Service publication, Report Order Code R40785, dated August 16, 2009.

INDEX

D

E

F

G

H

I

J

O

P

Q

R

S

T

U

V

W